POLITICS OF CONGRESS FACTIONALISM IN KERALA SINCE 1982

POLITICS OF CONGRESS FACTIONALISM IN KERALA SINCE 1982

G. Radhakrishna Kurup

PUBLICATIONS

KALPAZ PUBLICATIONS

DELHI - 110052

POLITICS OF CONGRESS FACTIONALISM IN KERALA SINCE 1982
[*politics*]

Rs. 790

ISBN: 81-7835-284-2

Published in 2004 in India by
Kalpaz Publications
C-30, Satyawati Nagar
Delhi-110052
e-mail: kalpaz@hotmail.com

Laser Typeset at: Alphabet, Delhi
Printed at: Mehra Offset Press, Delhi

Dedicated to the memory
of my Father
N. Gopalakurup

Contents

List of Tables

List of Diagrams

Foreword

The contemporary party system in India developed originally in the context of the struggle for freedom and since 1950 within the framework of Parliamentary Government, both these environments have exerted their influence on the present character and structure of the political parties.

The Congress retained the character of the nationalist movement in seeking to balance and accommodate social and ideological diversity within an all-embracing representative structure — claiming sole legitimacy as the nationalist party. It sought to achieve a national consensus through the accommodation and absorption of dominant social elements that had kept aloof from the nationalist movement. The Congress which functioned as broad-based nationalist movement before independence transformed itself into the dominant political party of the nation with corruption and scramble for power making inroads into the organisation.

In 'Mahatma Gandhi — the last phase' Pyarelal, the Mahatma's secretary says Candhiji was deeply worried over the growing corruption and scramble for loaves in the Congress, discard and personal rivalries among members of the party high command. He was sad that there were pocket boroughs, bogus membership, the deadweight of inert majorities and the electioneering malpractices and hypocrisy of self-seekers. Every body was anxious to get into the Congress bandwagon now that it was in power. The more Gandhiji saw of this, the more his conviction deepened that there was no other way of purging the Congress organisation of corruption except for the party to go out of power politics. At the AICC in November 1947, he mooted the idea that the political goal of the Congress having been achieved with the attainment of independence, it ought voluntarily to liquidate itself. He argued that the dissolution of the Congress as a party would release the energy of all the progressive and patriotic elements in the country and harness it to the great task of nation — building.

Eventually he embodied his wishes in the 'Last Will and Testament' made public a day after his death. In this document, he averred that having attained independence "the Congress in its present shape and form, i.e., as a propaganda vehicle and parliamentary machine has outlived its use." For these and similar reasons, he asked the AICC "to disband the existing Congress organisation and flower into a Lok Seva Sangh". Without even consulting the high command, Nehru decided that the Congress would not disband itself inspite of Gandhiji's testament. Nehru may have good reasons not to go by Gandhiji's advice. But then the Congress of today cannot with any modicum of honesty and legitimacy claim lineage to Gandhiji. Since 1948, the Congress leaders have continued cynically to trade in Gandhiji's name every time they go to the masses to garner votes.

The fact remains that in 1948 the Congress became Nehru's Congress. But it continued to be so only for about two decades that is till 1969, when Indira Gandhi split it asunder. During the Nehru era, characterised by the dominant party system, the Congress enjoyed a virtual monopoly of power both at the centre and in the states, though the Swatantra Party and the CPI ruled in Orissa and Kerala respectively. The general elections held in 1967 when Indira Gandhi was in the saddle, ended the dominant party system. The setback suffered by the Congress in that year gave it a narrow majority in the Fourth Lok Sabha. The Congress (I) lost half the states, where coalition governments were formed.

The Congress split in 1969 because Indira Gandhi nominated V.V. Giri as President against the official candidate Neelam Sanjiva Reddy. This created a serious crisis at the centre, since the Government of Indira Gandhi became a minority. She however managed to continue with the support of DMK, the CPI and the Muslim League. The crisis of 1969 was the outcome of Indira Gandhi's ambition to seize control of the party organisation by dethroning the syndicate with a view to strengthening her position in the government against her rivals.

In 1975, Indira Gandhi finally buried the remains of Nehru's Congress fathoms deep with the imposition of emergency — suspension of Fundamental Rights and press censorship. These were fatal blows to Nehru. Thus the Congress came to snap its links with two of its illustrious ancestors — Gandhi and Nehru. To seal their dismissal from history, the party was Christened Congress (Indira).

Nehru's ghost however continued to haunt the usurpers in the form of a self reliant, socialist pattern of society and the non-aligned movement.

The Janatha party came to power as a consequence of the emergency clamped in India by Indira Gandhi. Janatha was primarily a coalition formed almost overnight by bringing such diverse and disparate elements together for their very survival. Frustrated by its performance, the people rejected Janatha party in the 1980 mid-term polls.

Indira Gandhi who had established an authoritative command over her party after the January 1978 split and had become the undisputed leader and sole arbiter of the party that identified itself with her name. Immediately after she returned to power, it became clear that she was more important than the Congress organization and meant to dominate the political scene personally. But after 1980 elections it led to a politics of manipulation rather than purpose, a quest for power for its own sake. She was confronting disarray in her own party, corruption and inefficiency in State Governments.

Following the assassination of Indira Gandhi in October 1984, many people who might have voted against Indira Gandhi, voted for Rajiv Gandhi for they were in a desperate search for a leader who could stem the rot of declining political and moral standards. Rajiv Gandhi secured the highest ever vote percentage and a number of seats in the Congress history.

Rajiv Gandhi was the first Prime Minister of a generation that had no recollection of the freedom struggle or of the sacrifices and dedication that sustained the movement for independence. Eventually, he also became the first Prime Minister to be accused of countenancing bribery in the Bofors case. Since then the political class as a whole has been dubbed as habitually corrupt, institutionally venal and congenitally amoral, when not outrightly immoral.

The parliamentary elections held in December 1989 brought about a radical transformation of party system. It catapulted to power a coalition government at the centre for the first time and since then there have been six non-congress coalition governments. By 1987 nearly half of the states had come to be ruled by non-Congress parties of various varieties and vintage. The outcome of 1991 elections further strengthened this situation and showed a clear trend of decline of Congress hegemony.

If the history of Indian political parties is suggestive of any pattern, it is a pattern of steady fragmentation and proliferation of political forces reflecting social fragmentation and regional divisions of the country. Neither the Left nor the Right has shown any willingness or capacity to arrest this, there has been steady proliferation on both sides of the political spectrum.

Parties are no more democratic. Not only Congress (I) but other parties also have virtually become fiefs of individual leaders. Their constitutions are presidential and the executive committees are nominated by the President. No party has evolved reliable mechanism and workable procedures for managing internal conflicts. If the congress with long experience in the art of political management and institutional patterns of behaviour has been unable to channel diverse social forces unleashed by the process of modernization then the inescapable conclusion is that proliferation rather than polarisation is likely to be the dominant feature of Indian political scene.

It is one of the contradictions of Indian political parties that a democratic system and a democratic political process are run by political parties which are not only undemocratic but often unabashedly authoritarian. The Congress (I) has conducted its organisational elections in 1992 after a gap of twenty years. Most parties have turned out to be coalitions of elites loosely tied together by personal interests and short-term goals rather than by ideological and programmatic commitment or long range objectives.

It is against this background that one has to examine the relevance of G. Radhakrishna Kurup's work on 'Politics of Congress Factionalism in Kerala since 1982'. The work has grown out of his doctoral dissertation submitted to the University of Kerala.

The study proceeds on the assumption that the Congress in

Kerala is a replica of the national organisation and like other state units of the party, Congress in Kerala is also embedded in factionalism. Factionalism was very acute prior to the formation of the State in 1956. The Congress at present is too fragmented and divided and continues to be a coalition of groups rather than a well-knit party system. It was after the installation of popular Government in power that factions took concrete shape and started fighting for their share.

Radhakrishna Kurup's study is an attempt to analyse the factional dynamics in the Congress party in Kerala and is based on primary data collected from the Congress party offices and activists working at different levels of the organisation. The empirical nature of the study based on original data makes this work distinctly different from other studies in the field. As such it could easily be rated as a pioneering work on Congress politics in Kerala.

The relationship between the party faction and socio-economic structure, the aggressive and integrative functions of factions, changes in factional participation and strategy over the years, the nature of fragmentation, the techniques of accommodation and the assessment of the comparative strength, role and appeals of the different factions — all these with reference to the politics of Congress factionalism in Kerala since 1982 form part of the scope of the study. Divided into seven chapters including the findings and conclusions, the study is descriptive, explanatory, empirical and analytical in nature. After introduction, Kurup undertakes the historical analysis of Congress factionalism in Kerala since 1982 against the national background followed by a discussion on politics of Congress factionalism in Kerala. In the following chapters he discusses the methodology for empirical analysis, the social base of factionalism and the nature of Congress factionalism in the politico-economic context.

The study has validated all the hypotheses formulated by him except the one which suggests that the Congress factionalism has no ideological roots and that it is a product of the desire for personal power and prestige. The large volume of statistical data collected from various primary sources and processed so meticulously adds to the credit worthiness of the study. On the basis of this empirical study painfully undertaken by Kurup, he comes to certain valid and uncontestable findings and conclusions. These findings and conclusions throw a good deal of light on the undercurrents of Congress factionalism in Kerala politics — certainly a valuable contribution on the part of the researcher on the nuts and bolts of Kerala Politics — an enigma to the foreign scholars.

The study reveals that there is no relationship between caste and factional orientation in the politics of Congress factionalism. It denies the existence of a caste support base for Karunakaran. However there is a slight Christian consolidation behind the (Antony) 'A' faction. Though the (Indira) 'I' group at present enjoy a majority among the Hindu, Christian and Muslim communities there are indications pointing to the possibility of a growing preference of the Muslim Community for the 'A' faction. Congressmen consider Karunakaran to be the most effective leader to counter the challenges of the CPI (M) and BJP. He is also rated far ahead of Antony in providing leadership to the Congress party, UDF and the government.

In fact no political leader in Kerala has the reputation that Karunakaran has as the protector of party men. It is the consistency of positions that made him the most respected leader of the Congress party in Kerala. Karunakaran's significance in Kerala politics lies in the fact that he has transformed the Congress party with only mine MLA's in the Assembly in 1967 to the position of the major party in the Assembly having 62 MLA's in 2001.

Kurup has clearly identified five major determinants of Congress factionalism on the basis of his indepth study of factionalism of Congress in Kerala and observes that the Congress party in Kerala has lived through factionalism right from the very beginning by its ability for survival.

Dr. G. Radhakrishna Kurup's study on politics of Congress factionalism in Kerala has come out at a time when the Congress party in Kerala is plagued by factionalism of the worst kind. The study will be very useful not only for students of Kerala politics but also for professional politicians. No one can challenge his findings and conclusions as they are based on solid evidence and statistical support. This pioneering work will definitely be a valuable contribution to the existing literature on Kerala politics. Kerala politics has always been a fascinating subject for scholars from abroad. This study is unique in the sense that it has been carried out by a scholar who is very well aware of the undercurrents of Kerala politics for well over quarter of a century. I have great pleasure in presenting this excellent study to a wider audience.

Prof. (Dr.) K. Raman Pillai
Former Professor and Head
Department of Political Science
and Dean, Faculty of Social Science
University of Kerala

Thiruvananthapuram

Preface

Studies on factionalism cannot be restricted to any one sector since it is omnipresent in all sectors of human activity. Factionalism can be viewed as the mode of ideological renewal and organisational regrouping. Personalities and events influence this. This book subjects the Congress Party in Kerala to the prism of factionalism in the background of Congress politics at the national level. In this process, the Congress party structure, its social bases and ideological orientations are empirically examined to identify the ultimate determinants of factionalism. The relationship between party faction and socio economic structure, the competitive and integrative roles of factions, the changes in techniques and strategies over the years and its appeals are systematically examined. This study is not simply limited to a political analysis of factionalism, rather it highlights the socio-economic scenario brewing in the state since 1982.

Thiruvananthapuram

G. Radhakrishna Kurup

Acknowledgments

I am immensely obliged to my beloved teacher Dr. R.K. Suresh Kumar, Reader and Head, Department of Political Science, Government Arts College, Thiruvananthapuram under whose guidance I have carried out this study. His inordinate and persistent drive for perfection, immaculate style, profundity, enduring commitment to academic values and unparalleled dedication to the spirit of enquiry have constantly motivated me in many ways. In fact he is an *acharya* who shapes and designs the total personality of a student. Without his scholarly guidance, help and encouragement, this endeavour would not have been possible. I also express my heartfelt gratitude to his family members who have helped me in many ways.

I owe a deep sense of gratitude and indebtedness to Dr. K. Raman Pillai, former Professor and Head, Department of Political Science, University of Kerala for his valuable suggestions. I express my gratitude to Dr. V. Gangadharan Pillai, former Reader, Department of Political Science, University of Kerala, for his constant encouragement.

I have benefited much from my friends and colleagues who have read this draft and offered their comments. I sincerely thank all of them. In particular I should mention Dr. B. Mohanan, Professor, Department of Political Science and Development Administration, Gandhigram Rural Institute, Dr. V. Muraleedharan Nair, Reader, Department of Political Science, University College, Thiruvananthapuram and Dr. J. Sreekumar, Reader, Department of Statistics, University College, Thiruvananthapuram.

Thanks are also due to Dr. M. Bhaskaran Nair, Professor and Head, Department of Political Science, University of Kerala, Dr.G.Gopakumar, Professor of Political Science, University of

Kerala, Dr. K. Gopinathan Pillai, Reader, Department of Political Science, Government College, Nedumangadu, Dr. D. Jayaraj, former Professor of Political Science, University College, Thiruvananthapuram and Dr. N. Vikraman Achary, University College, Thiruvananthapuram.

I am also obliged to my friends Oommen P Saj, P.M Ussain, Narayanan Nair and G. Suvarna Kumar for their help in the collection of data.

I also acknowledge the prompt services rendered by the librarian and staff of the Kerala University Library, Library of the Department of Politics, the Legislative Assembly Library, CDS Library, Public Library, Jawaharlal Nehru Memorial Museum and Library Teen Murti Bhavan, New Delhi, ICWA Library New Delhi and the JNU Library, New Delhi. I am also grateful to all the Congress workers who sincerely co-operated with this endeavour particularly to the office staff of the KPCC office, Thiruvananthapuram.

I shall be failing in my duty if I do not mention the co-operation extended to me by my wife Sreelatha and daughters Ravya and Sravya during the period of the research. I also take this opportunity to express my sincere thanks to Kalpaz Publications, Delhi, for executing the work promptly and neatly.

I owe a debt of gratitude to my departed Parents and 'The Almighty' for giving me the blessing at every stage of my career.

G. Radhakrishna Kurup

Abbreviations

A.I C.C.	All-India Congress Committee
AIML	All India Muslim League
AK	A.K Antony
Cong (A)	Congress (A)
Cong (I)	Congress (I]
Cong (R)	Congress (R)
Cong (S)	Congress (S)
Cong (U)	Congress (U)
CPI	Communist Party of India
CPI (M)	Communist Party of India (Marxist)
CEC	Central Election Committee
CWC	Congress Working Committee
CPB	Congress Parliamentary Board
DCC	District Congress Committee
FC	Forward Caste
GK	G. Karthikeyan
INC	Indian National Congress
IUML	Indian Union Muslim League
JD	Janata Dal
KK	K. Karunakaran
KPCC	Kerala Pradesh Congress Committee
KPCSS	Kerala Pradesh Congress Samudharana Samithi
KPYCC	Kerala Pradesh Youth Congress Committee
KC (J)	Kerala Congress (Jacob)
KC (M)	Kerala Congress (Mani)
KC (P)	Kerala Congress (Pillai)
KMPP	Kerala Mazdoor Praja Party
KSU	Kerala Students Union
LDF	Left Democratic Front

MBC	Most Backward Classes
MLA	Member of Legislative Assembly
MP	Member of Parliament
NDP	National Democratic Party
NSS	Nair Service Society
OBC	Other Backward Classes
PSP	Praja Socialist Party
RSP (B)	Revolutionary Socialist Party (Baby John)
SC	Scheduled Caste
SNDP	Sree Narayana Dharma Paripalana Yogam
SRP	Socialist Republican Party
SSLC	Secondary School Leaving Certificate
ST	Scheduled Tribe
TTNC	Travancore Tamil Nadu Congress
UDF	United Democratic Front
VR	Vayalar Ravi

One

Introduction

Politics of factionalism constitutes an important area as well as an empirical theme in contemporary study of political science. Factional tendency is a growing phenomenon which has affected almost all organisations including political parties, social organisations, voluntary associations and other grassroot level associations. Even the family is not free from factional tendencies. The concept of faction and the term factionalism has assumed so much importance and significance that this has drawn the attention of sociologists, anthropologists, political scientists, decision makers, administrators etc. It calls for the involvement of more and more people in the process of decision making. Factions occur in a democratic polity in varying degrees and no country having such a system can be called an exception in this regard. Regional politics is also considered in a democratic system as expressions of factions. All the socio-economic and psychological factors like caste, community, personal considerations, status, lust for power, greed for wealth etc. has directly and indirectly paved the way for the emergence of cleavages and conflicts in society.

Intra and inter party conflicts have eroded the legitimacy and reputation of both parties and leaders. Parties and politicians have been accused of eroding the democratic system by practicing corrupt politics, eschewing a long term stand on national interest, and maximising their personal gains and influence (Zoya Hasan 2002:2). This tendency is found in almost all political parties, pressure groups, trade unions, voluntary associations and even religious and social groupings. Theoretically, factions or factionalism in a political system may develop as a lever of pressure to have access to power (Sajal Basu 1990:2).

The study of parties in India seems to emphasise their deviation from ideology. The ideology seeks to appeal to one section while the organisation is placed in the hands of persons coming from another section of society. This is understandable because an organisation has its own logic through which some educated, rich, resourceful persons find their places on the top. Political parties in India seem to have weak, rather amorphous, base. Their grassroots units are, without exception, weak. Such units are weak both ideologically and organisationally (Kumar 1990:335). All these developments are conducive to the emergence of factional politics. Over the past few years attention has shifted to other parts of the party system. There are two reasons why more and more attention is paid to the different and emerging aspects of factionalism. The first and more general reason is that behavioural cohesion of parliamentary parties has been declining for sometime (Paul Webb 2000:166). The second and more specific reason for the growth of academic interest in intra-party politics has been the growing propensity of the party activists to air their differences in public.

Statement of the Problem

The Congress party has always been an organisation with heterogeneous and indeterminate character. Commenting on the astonishing nature of Congress Robert Crane (1960:181) says: "from the time of the first civil disobedience campaign the internal history of the Congress was the reconciliation of the multitude of special interest and different points of view". This character of the Congress party continued even after independence and it became a party of different factions. Inside the Congress party, various factions interact in a continuous process of pressure, adjustment and accommodation to provide an inbuilt opposition. The factions operating inside the Congress party are "loose coalitions of local, district faction leaders, tied together at the state level partly by personal bonds of friendship, partly by caste loyalties, and most of all by political interests" (Paul Brass 1965:54).

Factionalism is nothing new to the Indian National Congress. Some kind of factionalism always existed in the Congress since its inception. Differences of opinion and attitude associated with ideologies were common in the pre-independence period. Groups and factions formed around personalities were based on principles or ideologies and not on personal rivalry (Lal 1991:253). The ideological differences between Nehru and Patel were known to all. After the death of Patel, Nehru dominated the scene through his charismatic leadership. Indira Gandhi's period was really the period of decline of Congress ideology and its traditional character. She undermined the institutions that Nehru cherished and imposed instead an authoritarian interlude substituting for the elite institutional culture a new 'culture of illegalities' (Dua 1985:407).

The Congress unit in Kerala is a replica of the national organisation. Like other state units of the party, Congress in Kerala is also embedded in factionalism. Factionalism was very acute prior to the formation of the state in 1956, which even led to the emergence of new political parties in Travancore-Cochin and Malabar. The state also witnessed open political conflicts between the warring factions in the fifties and sixties leading to governmental instabilities. The Congress at present is too fragmented and divided and continues to be a coalition of groups rather than a well knit party system.

The seeds of the origin of the Congress in Kerala can be traced back to the *Malayalee* Memorial Movement. In 1891, all the non-Brahmin communities of Travancore, the Nairs, the Christians and the Ezhavas joined together and submitted a memorandum to the Maharaja demanding that responsible government jobs be given to 'sons of the soil'. In 1937 the *Samyukta Rashtriya Congress* became State Congress in which, for the first time all the four communities Nairs, Ezhavas, Christians and Muslims were represented. The Congress in Kerala was not a carbon copy of the Indian National Congress, its parental body at that time. Only in Malabar did it directly take part in the freedom struggle. The Congress in Travancore-Cochin areas concentrated on local issues and problems. The party had in its leadership persons drawn from different communities (Thomas 1985:18-19).

In Kerala there was not much of factionalism in the Congress party during the pre-independence days. All the Congress men worked together to achieve freedom. It was after the installation of popular government in power that factions took concrete shape and started fighting for their share. Hereafter, factionalism began to play a dominant role in the management of Congress party affairs (Sadasivan Nair 1970:217). The three men primarily responsible for factionalism in the Congress party in Kerala in the earlier days were Kumbalathu Sanku Pillai, T.M.Varghese and Panampilly Govinda Menon(Sadasivan 1977:31). Sanku Pillai and Varghese, who were responsible for the fall of the first four Congress ministries made a determined effort to regain their lost prominence. This was defeated by the then Congress leadership with the support of Govinda Menon and his faction. The ministry of R.Sankar also collapsed due to intense factionalism.

In the aftermath of the 1969 split, the state witnessed the resilience of the Congress party mainly through its youth and student wings. This culminated in the selection of A.K. Antony as the Kerala Pradesh Congress Committee (KPCC) President in 1973 at the young age of thirty three. The vision of these younger elements that belonged to the later generation was different from the earlier generation of Congressmen (Balakrishnan Nair 1994:69). The post 1969 period saw Congress adopting cadre party techniques and a new leadership emerged under A.K Antony and the old stalwart K. Karunakaran who headed the organisational wing and the parliamentary party respectively. In the 1978 split, ideology had a secondary role unlike in 1969. The two powerful groups viz; the Antony faction and the Karunakaran faction played their cards well in the new split (Gopakumar 1986:56).

The Congress party of Kerala which was already faction ridden, now openly got divided into two. The faction led by K. Karunakaran remained with Indira Gandhi and that led by A.K Antony was with Reddy at the national level. Later the Antony faction joined hands with the Marxist party to form a government. Alliance of Antony with the Marxists was short lived. With the help of the Antony faction, Congress (I) under Karunakaran returned to power in the 1982 Assembly election. This led to the merger of the Antony faction into the Congress (I) in December 1982. Despite the merger of the 'A' faction into the Congress (I) and the unity declaration, the former two groups continued to exist known as the Antony group and Karunakaran group. The rift in the party centered on issues such as the re-organisation of the student wing of the party, groupism, practice of taking policy decision without discussing it in the party and hostility towards the followers of Antony in organisational matters etc came in for severe criticism. These developments led to the outbreak of a fresh bout of factionalism. At present there are four factions, each associated with leaders representing various interests. However the factional feud centres mainly on the 'A' and 'I' groups.

Kerala offers a classic example of how inspite of intense factionalism within the party, the Congress could still maintain its vote base intact for over a period of four decades. Maintaining the solidarity of the party is essential in Kerala as its main opposition party; namely the CPI(M) is a cadre party with well oiled party machinery and its reaches extends to every aspect of the social life of a *Malayalee*. It is well known that factionalism has not allowed the Congress to express its full potentiality in the state. Despite this the party has continuously proved its relevance in Kerala politics. This study therefore is an attempt to analyse the factional dynamics in the Congress party in Kerala since 1982. The pre-1982 Congress politics was discussed in many academic studies. But the nature and effects of factionalism after 1982 has not formed part of any serious academic study.

The writings on Congress factionalism that has appeared in the form of articles and books remain general in nature. Most of them look at the problem from a particular point of view in which the author's value preferences predominate. There is also a dearth of sufficient empirical data with which one can study and interpret the politics of Congress factionalism in Kerala. This study attempts to bridge the gap and aims at providing an insight into the dynamics of factionalism based on primary data collected from the Congress party offices and activists working at different levels of the organisation.

Review of Literature

Serious academic studies on Indian factions and factionalism focusing on political parties, divisiveness and social conflict, village life, elite politics in rural areas, social structure, society and caste, elections, ideology and groups have been undertaken by scholars foreign as well as Indian. These theoretical writings enable us to formulate a conceptual framework for studying Congress party factionalism in the Kerala context.

So far no serious and scientific investigation has been carried out on the politics of Congress factionalism in Kerala. The available literature on Congress factionalism is very negligible. There are only very few academic studies in this regard but one can find abundant literature of a general nature in the form of books which also includes autobiographies and biographies by political leaders and journalists. The first written work on Congress party was that of Moyyarathu Sankaran's *History of Congress* (1938). The writer was a renowned freedom fighter. It was followed by a large volume of general literature (Maurice Duverger 1957) that traces the history of the party from two broad sources (i) the electoral and parliamentary origin and (ii) extra parliamentary origin.

For analytical convenience the literature relevant to the present study is given under three categories. They are:-

i. Political, Anthropological and Sociological studies on Indian faction and factionalism by foreign and Indian scholars of a theoretical nature.
ii. Academic studies dealing specifically with factionalism in the Congress party at the national and state levels.
iii. Autobiographies, biographies and other books and periodicals of a general nature in Malayalam and English.

Party and Democracy in India by S.N.Sadasivan (1977) is an authentic work on the nature of the party system from a sociological angle. His classification of the party system in to major, medium, minor and sub-minor categories covers every type that is in existence in our country. To him all these types of parties, by and large, are oriented towards democracy and although they have not attained any significant structure, some of them play crucial roles in our political system. The social temperament for dissent and disintegration that universally dominates the radicals and the left is the principal cause for the proliferation of parties every where.

Another work, *Divisiveness and Social Conflict: An Anthropological Approach* by Alan R. Beals and Bernard J. Siegel (1966) focuses on the nature of factional dispute and its relation to other forms of conflict. They studied the varieties of conflict at Taos Pueblo in Mexico and Namhalli in Karnataka as both these settlements had similarities on the pattern of divisive conflict. In both cases the problem solving capabilities of the local organisation declined. An attitude of factionalism identified in the work is the tendency of disputes to come to a head over seemingly trivial incidents.

The pioneer work in the sociological field was associated with Oscar Lewis in his *Village Life in Northern India* (1958). He discovered new dimensions of the social structure namely the existence of small cohesive groups within castes, which contribute to the compartmentalised and segmented nature of village organisation. He very minutely understood even the literal meaning of the term 'dhar' and translated it as 'faction'. Through his distribution of 'faction' by caste in terms of three sets, Jats, Brahmins and Harijans he developed a well built theory of his own after elaborately studying the village life. He distinguished between factions and kinship, factions and panas, and factions and thollas. The factions show significant differences in a number of important economic and social characteristics. The varying degrees of cohesiveness of the factions depends on the size of the group, geographical compactness, closeness of kinship ties, the degree of economic self sufficiency, the past history of factionalism, and the age factor.

Elite Politics in Rural India: Political Stratification and Political Alliances in Western Maharashtra (1975) by Anthony T.Carter is another sociological study attempting a descriptive analysis of political stratification and political alliances existing in Girvi, a large village in rural western Maharashtra. In western rural Maharashtra power was concentrated in the hands of few persons and among them a large majority belonged to a small section of the population. He examined the relations between leaders and followers in their roles as members of castes, as patrons, clients, landlords or tenants and noted the contrast between the relatively stable alliances between leaders and followers within what he called 'factions' and the unstable alliances between faction leaders. Both horizontal and vertical alliances were examined in his analysis.

Factionalism, Politics and Social Structure(1984) is a politico-sociological analysis by B.K Nagla. His analysis is based on themes such as caste and factions, political parties and factions, issues and factions, leadership and factions, and land ownership and factions. In the comparative analysis of five case studies he observed five characteristics of factions (1) Factions are conflict groups (2) Factions are political groups (3) Factions are corporate groups (4) Faction members are recruited by a leader (5) Faction members are recruited on diverse principles. He considered factions in two ways, as tools of structural analysis and as an ideology. In the first case factions have been understood as caste or sub-caste, kinship and lineage divisions. Thus factions are spontaneous divisions and become basic to social structure. Factionalism as an ideology refers to the role of leaders in dividing the people and their followers. According to this view, faction leaders are not necessarily caste, clan or lineage heads, hence factional divisions need not correspond with caste, clans and lineage divisions. In such circumstances, factions are mainly a creation of political parties and their ideologies. There is a reference to 'groups' which tries to extricate the maximum possible benefits and privileges by competing with each other for the available resources. He attempted at the blending of factionalism as a tool of structural analysis and factionalism as an ideology.

In yet another work titled *Political Sociology* (1999) Nagla explains the sociological components of factions and their usage in communities. The micro studies conducted by Lewis, Yogendra Singh, the macro level studies by Yadav, Beals, Mc Comark, Nicholas and the unstructured studies by Weiner and Rastogi illuminated his field of enquiry. Various faction groups seemed to have total disregard for the development of the rural society. Social structural elements continue to find an important place not only in the Indian social organisation but in factions also.

Another notable work in the field of factionalism is Masaaki Fukunaga's *Society, Caste and Factional Politics* (1993). According to him, the political trends resulting from factional activities can be summarised as (1) faction is a group (2) existence of factional fight (3) the period of factional disputes as a period of activity (4) the faction as a small political group (5) recruitment of faction members by the leader (6) formation of the factions vs. the dominant caste.

Ranajit Guha's (ed.) *Subaltern Studies I: Writings on the South Asian History and Society* (1982) contains a contribution by David

Hardiman titled 'The Indian Faction: A Political Theory Examined'. According to Hardiman, factions, it is believed, link the lowest in the low to the highest: the humble share cropper is a member of his land lord's faction; the landlord is a member of one of the district level factions; the district boss is a key member of one of the factions in the provincial legislative assembly; the provincial minister is a member of the all India faction which go by different names. In this manner, the factional networks are supposed to encompass the nation, linking the peasant masses to their rulers. In this study he placed much emphasis on the importance of faction leader (*dalapatis*). The first difficulty with the factional interpretation was that during the early days influential persons acted as agitators rather than as faction leaders. They were supposed to be driven by the desire to win seats for the members of their factions in the legislature so that they could extend their powers of patronage. Factions are seen as a form of traditional politics based on patron-client relationships of a traditional type in contrast to 'modern' class based politics. His concept is that factional conflicts are not ideological conflicts. They compete among themselves for personal power.

Factions, Ideology and Politics: Coalition Politics in West Bengal by Sajal Basu (1990) views at factionalism as a continuous process. Anti-government movements led to the formation of political factions and united front governments in the late 1960's and 1970's in West Bengal (WB). He studied it in the context of ideological transformations and personal human factors that influenced the decision of aligning with particular groups. He also studied the dynamics of factional interests like attachment to local leaders, local sentiments, personal incompatibility of leaders etc. He explains the positive aspect of factionalism, leading to the radicalisation and coalition building in state politics. His argument is that the factions in social life have been responsible for factionalisation of politics and theorisation of splits politics. In the Indian situation or in WB for e.g., factionalism and coalition of factions emerged without any consideration of power. The militant stance imported ideological content into Indian politics and led to the emergence of political groups. Subsequently as these groups got allied to different parties and were exposed to cross currents of differing ideologies, the whole gamut of factional struggles and pattern of coalition changed. A process of ideological transformation in national politics set in.

Factional Politics in Rural India by Padma Charan Misra and K.S Padhy (2000) is a political study and is concerned with various aspects of factionalism, like its definition, meaning and approaches, dimensions, functions and causes. It is a fact that the economy influences to a large extent the politics of a village, community or society. They studied factionalism in Orissa with special reference to a village, Nuapada, in the district of Ganjam, which was located in the southern part of Orissa. It is of interest to those who probes the nature of factionalism in rural India.

Among the second category, *Factional Politics in an Indian State: The Congress Party in Uttar Pradesh* by Paul R. Brass (1965) is the pioneer study. It discusses the political aspects of factionalism in the Congress party in Uttar Pradesh. Brass shows that the problem of maintaining internal unity has been of much more serious concern for the Congress party in Uttar Pradesh than the organisation of popular support. He provides the real picture of the faction ridden Congress party and asserted that the faction is actually the basic unit of the Congress party in Uttar Pradesh. The party has survived because it was adaptive. In fact, the Congress party in UP has become traditionalised and performs its modernising role through traditional social organisation, the faction. The factions perform both the integrative and disintegrative roles. He concludes by saying that the Congress party is surviving due to the social character of its factions. The strength and cohesiveness of a faction depend very heavily upon the ability of the leader to distribute material benefits to his followers. A very important source of strength for the faction leader is control over local institutions of self government. A non economic basis for faction building is community support. Factional conflict in UP was based not merely upon struggle for power but also upon the struggle for personal prestige. Congress factions in UP performs functions for the society as well as for the organisation. A particularly important function in this regard is the politicisation of social and religious groups in secular terms.

Another study of Paul R. Brass on faction and party appeared in the volume *Caste, Faction and Party in Indian Politics (Vol.I)* (1984). In it he explains the growth of personal and factional politics in UP. He pointed out three aspects for the growth of factional politics in UP (i) the absence of external threat (ii) the presence of an internal consensus upon ideological issues and (iii) the absence of authoritarian leadership. He analysed the characteristics of factions and factional conflict, the composition of factions and groups, the state and district level factions and the functions of factions. Factional loyalty is intermediate and susceptible to changes. It is more than parochial politics, a politics based on language, caste, tribe or religion and something less than party politics in the European and American sense.

The book by Rajni Kothari and others titled *Party System and Election Studies* (1967) consists of two articles dealing with party factionalism. They are 'Intra-party Conflict in Bihar' by Ramshary Roy and 'Caste Orientation of Political Factions: Modasa Constituency - A case study' by Rajni Kothari and Ghanshyam Shah. Roy examines the tendency towards fragmentation of the sub coalitional structure in a dominant party such as the Congress party of India functioning in the state of Bihar. The growing heterogeneity in the party's social composition and the incompatibility of interests pursued by these socio-economic groups result in the emergence of factions in the party each of which competes for capturing the party organisation as a means to gain control of government offices. He observed that the lure for power is enough of a stimulant to political activists for organising their own support structure and this encourage the tendency of proliferation of factions. Kothari and Shah analyse caste orientation of political factions.

The Congress Party in Rajasthan: Political Integration and Nation Building in an Indian State by Richard Sisson (1972) is a political study of Congress affairs in Rajasthan. Sisson analyses three interrelated aspects in his study. They are (i) the social and political antecedents governing the emergence of the Congress party after independence (ii) the structure and process of organisational adaptability and (iii) the process of conflict management and organisation integration. Conflicts between parties and also between competing factions within parties have tended to mobilise new political resources and has been conducive to increased demands for political entry and mobility within party organisations. He analyses the formation and representation of interest groups or faction within the organisation and their bases of support, goal orientations, and the conditions of their continuity. The factional system and the patterns of interest accommodation that developed in Rajasthan from the elections of 1967 are clearly depicted.

Cohesion in a Predominant Party: The Pradesh Congress and Party Politics in Bihar by Mahendra P. Singh (1975) discusses in detail the conceptual and theoretical aspects pertaining to party cohesion. Intra party conflicts make their appearance in almost all parties with varying degrees of intensity, and one frequently finds identifiable sub groups of party members with variable extent of interaction and formal organisation. He clearly defined his concept about factions. To him, "The sub-groups within political parties are most continuously referred to as party factions". He points out the reasons for intra-party conflicts and faction formation; such as differences among party leaders on overall ideology, differences over strategy and tactics to be used to achieve the ideological objectives of the party, differences on specific issues such as elections, passage of legislation and even due to personality conflicts among leaders. He also examines the reasons for the emergence of multi factionalism, in place of bi-factionalism during the pre-independence period.

Factional Politics in India by J.K. Mahapatra (1985) studied the nature and intensity of factionalism in the Congress party in Orissa during 1967-77 period. In his indepth analysis, he depicted the various dimensions of factionalism in Orissa and concluded that factions in the Congress owes its origin mainly to the policy of 'delay and procrastination' pursued by the central leadership of the party. His analysis of personalised power centre and caste hegemony sheds light on the composition and nature of leadership patterns in Orissa politics.

Surya Narayan Misra also looks at Orissa politics in his work entitled *Party Politics and Electoral Choice in an Indian State* (1989). He asserts that Orissa politics hither to experienced two spells of competitive regionalism and acute factional politics. The political regrouping could not provide a stable majority to either of the warring factions. The longer stay in power by a political party often resulted in the growth of factions. He pointed out the most important issues which paved the way for factionalism and also studied the attitude of prominent leaders deserting the party during critical periods. The role of the Congress high command in settling the issues were also examined.

Coming to the politics of the Congress party in Kerala the pioneering work is that of K.S Nair's *Congress Party and Kerala Politics* (1984). The book gives information about the formation and functioning of the Congress party in Kerala since its origin. He points out that the role of Congress in Kerala is different from its role in other states. Since its very formation radical forces in the party were in a position to pressurise the leadership of the party. The Congress party is a thoroughly integrated and hierarchical organisation. He discusses factionalism in the Congress party during the pre-independent and post independent periods. The ideological and personal issues which resulted in the collapse of the ministries are also examined. Certain hints are also given about the kind of factionalism found in Communist parties. He points out that factionalism is a common phenomenon in the party system.

The Congress Party and State Politics: Emergence of New Style Politics by G.Gopakumar (1984) examines the origin and development of the party, covers the major splits of 1969 and 1978 and evaluates the performance of the party during the various elections up to 1982. The influence of its mass organisations radicalised the entire programme and policies of the Congress party. The Congress party in Kerala could successfully adapt the communist technique of organising united front. The book also examines the different sources of the party's strength and attempts to find out the reason for the longetivity and relevance of the party in Kerala.

The third category consisting of biographies, autobiographies and other books of a general nature also deserves attention. These books enable us to understand the origin, causes and nature of Congress party factionalism in Kerala in a general way. Among these, *Thiruvithamkoorile Swathantriya Samara Charitram* (1972) by C. Narayana Pillai, *How the Communists Came to Power* (1964) by R.

Ramakrishnan Nair, *Keralathile Congress Prasthanam* (1967) by Perunna K.N Nair, *Congressum Keralavum* (1986) by A.K Pillai, *Keralam Malayalikalude Mathrubhumi* (1969) and *Communist Party in Kerala: Six Decades of Struggle and Advance* (1994) by EMS Namboodiripad, *The Melting Pot* (1975), *Kerala Rashtreeyam Oru Asambandha Natakom* (1999)and *Beyond the Dead line* (2001), by K.C John, *Kaal Noottandu* (1995) by Cherian Philip, *K. Karunakaran* (1994) by K. Govindan Kutty, *A Concise History of Kerala: 1885-1957* (1987) by A. Sreedhara Menon, *Communism in Kerala* (1982) by T.J Nossiter, *The Government and Politics of Kerala* (1994) by A.Balakrishnan Nair, *Ente Kazhinja Kaalam* (1997) by M.K Hemachandran and *P.Balan:Thalaratha Porali* (2000) by S. Ramachandran, are worth mentioning.

In general, all the above mentioned studies are helpful in understanding the nature and depth of the Politics of Congress factionalism. However there is great scope for a serious investigation into the factional politics of the Congress party in an empirical framework. This is particularly so in the case of the Congress party in Kerala. This study undertakes a historical, analytical and empirical study of the politics of Congress factionalism in Kerala since 1982. The empirical nature of the study based on original data makes this work different from other studies in the field. In the light of the above discussion, the following specific objectives will be pursued in the present study.

Objectives of the Study

1) To examine the events, issues and causes leading to the formation of 'faction' and the resultant 'politics of factionalism' in the Congress party in Kerala since 1982.
2) To empirically analyse the nature of factional alignment in the Congress party in Kerala based on factional support bases and goal orientation.
3) Aims to unravel the relationship between party faction and socio-economic structure, if any.
4) Aims at examining how the competing factions in the party ensure continuous support through recruitment of followers and successfully mobilise new political resources.
5) Aims at understanding the organisational capability and

effectiveness of the Congress party and its top leadership in dealing with the challenges of factionalism.

6) To find out the comparative strength, role and appeals of different factions in the party.

Hypotheses

1. Factions actually constitute the basic unit of the Congress party in Kerala that provides momentum to Congress politics in the state.
2. Groupism in Congress is permanent but group loyalty is fluctuating
3. In spirit Congress groupism is bi- factional even today inspite of the presence of four groups
4. Different classes and various economic interest groups find adequate representation in all factions.
5. Congress factionalism is not ideological, caste-communal based or issue oriented; it tends to be a product of the desire for personal power and prestige.
6. Congressmen are not favourably inclined to the practice of nominations to party posts.

Conceptualisation of Factionalism

The term faction has existed since Roman days when it used to signify divisions into which Roman chariots were separated. A faction seems to subordinate the public good to private gain and the term has been so adopted in the dialectics of political struggle especially as a means of defence and counter defence by those in power. The transition from faction to party was indeed slow and tortuous both in the domain of ideas and in fact. That the name faction was loathsome, from the Roman times until the nineteenth century is a statement in want of proof (Giovanni Sartori 1976:3). The term party thus seems applicable to the factions that are not seditious.

During the seventeenth Century the term 'sect' became associated with religion and especially with protestant sectarianism. There is little doubt that no eighteenth century author aside Burke, really disentangled the two concepts – faction and party. Whenever the two terms are not used interchangeably, the difference is that the term 'faction' applies to a concrete group, where as 'party' is far more than an analytic partition. To Hume factions subvert government, render them impotent and beget the fiercest animosities among men of the same nation.

Etymologically and semantically speaking, 'faction' and 'party' do not convey the same meaning. Faction which is by far the older and more established term derives from the Latin verb Facere (to do, to act) and faction soon came to indicate, for the authors writing in Latin, a political group bent on disruptive and harmful facere, or 'dire doings'. Thus the primary meaning conveyed by the Latin root is an idea of hubris, of excessive, ruthless, and thereby harmful behaviour (Sartori 1976:4).

In a general sense, factionalism can be defined as a competition for power between organised groups within a political party (Thomas Blom Hausen & Christophe Jaffrelot 1998: 267). The term 'faction' refers to "groups or sections of society in relation of opposition to one another, interested in promoting their objects rather than those of the society as a whole and often turbulent in their operations" (Raymond Firth 1957).

R. Zariski proposes an unrestricted definition of 'faction', which he took to mean, "any intra party combination, clique , or grouping whose members share a sense of common identity and common purpose and are organised to act collectively so as a distinct bloc within the party-to achieve their goals" (Zariski quoted in Moshemaor 1997:147). Focusing on the invisible level of politics, Nicolson suggests that "faction system is a political system (or subsystem) characterised by the informal competition of plurality of amorphous segments (factions) operating within a cultural context which places a high value on diffuse and unrestricted personal power and led by an elite whose orientations are self centered and instrumental" (Nicholson as referred in Moshe Maor 1997:147).

V.O Key regarded single party dominance, and consequently factionally structured politics, as healthy condition in a democracy. He felt that personalisation of leadership fractionalises the electorate. Most of the contemporary students of politics, in other words view faction as an integral component of political parties. Harold Laswell defines a faction as "any constituent group of a larger unit which works for the advancement of a particular person or policies" (Harold A. Gould 1994:152).

Factionalism as a form of conflict organisation reflects the tendency of party sub groups to engage in collective action inorder to advance factions goals. Factionalism amounts to a breakdown of co-operation between party members. Factions are essentially internally structured counterparts of the spectrum of the constituencies in the wider society whose interests a given political party has decided to champion (for whatever reason) in the course of pursuing power.

A political faction can be defined as "a group of individuals based on representation in parliament who seek to further a broad range of policies through consciously organised political activity" (Richard Rose 1974:320). Factions may be distinguished from pressure groups. Factions may also be distinguished from opponents of a political tendency because factions are self consciously organised as a body with a measure of discipline and cohesion. Conflict between ideologists and electoralists is perhaps the major constant of the intra-party factionalism (Marcus F. Franda 1971:214). In the intra party factionalism of the Congress party in Kerala this has taken the form of conflict between the parliamentary wing and the organisational wing.

Here it will be worthwhile to have a look at some of the theories of factionalism. It may be stated that factions can play both associative and conflictual roles. Most sociologists and political scientists however view it only in conflictual roles. Accordingly, most of the empirical studies focus on faction as they contest with the socio-political system for political power or influence with a view to furthering the interests of their respective members. Thus factions emerge to achieve power positions.

Oscar Lewis observed that factionalism is a basic characteristic of the traditional social organisation. He pointed out the insufficient attention given in the past to the existence of small cohesive groups within castes which are the locus of power and decision making and contribute to the compartmentalised and segmented nature of village social organisation. After intensive study of Rampur he found twelve small groups locally known as *dhar* (Oscar Lewis 1958:113-14). The factions are generally referred to by the names of their leaders or in some instances by the nickname of a lineage, that is, when the factions and the lineage are synonymous. Factions follow caste lines.

To Lewis for a faction to operate successfully over an extended period of time it must meet certain essential conditions (ibid:115). Perhaps the most dramatic evidence for the socio economic basis of the faction emerges from the study of the renting and mortgaging of the land. However in principle no faction will rent out the land outside of its own faction. The varying degrees of cohesiveness of the factions appears to depend on factors like the size of the group, geographical compactness, closeness of kinship ties, the degree of economic self sufficiency, the past history of factionalism and the age of the group (ibid:123). When all factors are considered together he found that the factions fell into three groups. (i) the most cohesive (ii) less so and (iii) the least cohesive. Based on the relationship between factions he distinguishes three broad types: positive or friendly, negative or hostile and neutral. Viewed broadly, one of the fundamental causes of factionalism is limited resources. More specifically Lewis pointed out that new factions developed as a result of quarrels over inheritance of land, adoption of sons, and quarrels between the castes.

To Nagla, the term factions denote certain objective condition or state of affairs, without implying a value judgment. The components of faction are (a) definite personnel (b) enough organisation to provide sub–group with the rudiments of structure and cohesion (c) common interest which brings them together (d) common objectives to keep them together for sometime (e) an awareness by themselves and by others outside that they are identified having these relationships; and (f) an opponent or opponents (e.g. a rival faction) regarded as competitors (Nagla 1999:170). Structurally, a faction is viewed as an arrangement of individuals bound together by some common interest for securing power with a view to safeguarding the interest of the constituent membership. He adds that, factions refer to a segment of alignments with in a political system vis-à-vis other segments of alignments within the same political system (ibid:172).

Even members belonging to different castes, classes and occupational groups were found in the same faction. Eventhough a faction included the rich and poor, members drawn from high castes and those who were well off economically wielded a significant influence on the course of action chosen. Though a faction group may ally itself with one political party or another from time to time this need not have any impact on its nature and internal composition (Nagla 1984:23). Factions are found at different levels of the society, such as village, block and regional levels, and in ethnic, linguistic, caste and religious groups. Factions may emerge in a wide variety of conflicting situations.

Factions may emerge not only on account of certain issues which are internal to a local community that create cleavage within its social organisation, rather these may take their birth also on account of the problems of the party to bring about adjustment with the broader social milieu. The emergence of (a) government faction (b) anti- government faction and (c) neutral faction is a case in point. All the three factions are related to the way the community in question tries to define its relationship with the outside power structure corresponding to the social and political hierarchy of factions.

Masaaki Fukunaga has analysed the characteristics of Indian village factions in his study on 'Society Caste and Factional Politics'. The term faction has been used inconsistently by sociologists, mainly due to the lack of a proper definition. The characteristics of the Indian village factions are (i) permanence (ii) composition of membership (iii) openness of membership, and (iv) political role of factions (Masaaki Fukunaga 1993:7).

Pocock says that "factions are not permanent but are expedient groupings temporarily created through a coincidence of the conflict of interest, the resolution which automatically terminates the faction's raison and therefore its existence" (David F Pocock 1957:296). Membership composition of a faction changes whenever different issues occur. But the core element in the faction remains relatively steady. Moreover as far as membership is concerned, factions cut across kinship and caste lines. However factions also tend to provide a common platform of action to the members of different castes. It provokes individuals to enter into inter personal relations that cut across the boundaries of established groups. Pocock too reported that even brothers were potential members of opposite factions.

Factional behaviour is one of the most important indications of political process existing in the village. As political activity results in conflict over power and prestige, factional behaviour becomes political. Pocock noted that it attempts to bend the power and potentiality of the whole of which it is a part to its own particular interest and dominate the other faction or factions which are similarly motivated (Oscar Lewis 1958).

To Myron Weiner an essential characteristic of an Indian faction is not only the strength of its members allegiance to it, but the amount of time devoted to its activities (Myron Weiner 1957:238). In fact social life of a party member is built within the party and consequently within its faction. The factions are like the traditional organisations. The party members will talk to the faction head about the personal problems as much the same way that he might, in olden days, have gone to the father or elder brothers. A faction within a party may have high status in its local community because the factional leader is some one of local importance.

It is well known that political parties in India have a large number of factions. Weiner examined the factors that keep the factions working together in the same party. There is first of all the unique role of party leader as a unifier. What makes the party leader, a unifying force is his detachment from various factions. The leader has three functions:—

(i) He is the compromiser of all factional disputes
(ii) He is the source of prestige to the members of the party
(iii) He is the absolute source for the articulation of values held by the group, and he may, as Gandhi did articulate, a new set of values (Weiner:242).

How important the leader is as a unifying factor and symbol for the party factions is indicated by what has happened after the death of various leaders. While the loss of the leader was not the only factor involved, in at least three case studies described in the book it was a major element in subsequent splits. Another unifying factor is the level of tolerance which one faction has for the other. The tolerance was at its greatest with in the Congress party during the pre-Independence era, when a wide variety of groups, socialists, communists, Marxist and the Hindu communalists – worked together inside it (Ibid).

Weiner in his study of Congress Party pointed out that the urban middle class Indian who joins a political party is in search of belonging to a group, a role within the group, a status in the society, and a set of values by which he can judge. The party recruits joins, not just a party, but one of the many factions which most of the political parties contain. These party factions are held together, by a common leader, a tolerance within the party for the existence of various factions, and a general agreement on the basic ideology of the party. A threat may come from loss of status of the members of the faction from the parent organisation which wants the faction to disband or in the form of a challenge to the faction's values (Myron Weiner 1957:246).

Brass maintains that factions and factional conflicts in India are a part and parcel of the indigenous social and political order. In the absence of external party competition, internal factional conflicts scale to new heights. Evidences suggested that factional conflicts decline in intensity as external competition increases.

The leader-follower relationship is a characteristic form of social and political organisation in India. Loyalty to a faction is one form of loyalty which is politically important in the traditional order. One of the important characteristic of the Indian faction lies in the primacy of factional interest over the party loyalty (Scalapino and Masoomi 1971:19). There were varieties of factions like a single faction, multi-factional system, and bi- factional system. Brass points out the bases of faction building. He analyses both the integrative and disintegrative functions of the factions. For the new political leaders, politics is avocation; the contemporary faction leader does not bring status and prestige to office but rather seeks status and prestige through office (Paul R. Brass 1984: 143).

Another interpretation of faction was given by James Walch. He defines the term faction as a group working within the party but not created by the party or with its consent. The faction is usually organised around the person of the factional leader, but it also reflects socio-economic group interest (James Walch 1976:16). Two kinds of definitions are offered. In the first, "the faction is a tightly knit group of leaders who are out to win power and patronage". This type of faction has multi-interest and is multi caste. In the second, a faction "is a part of a political party and can often be related to some specific interests". (ibid). The concept of factionalism has been used in a number of ways to cover several types of intra (and inter) party behaviour at various levels of the system. Thus the usage of the term has become somewhat unclear. The polarised disintegration has been interpreted as the outcome of the unbridled factionalism. James Walch in his interpretation of factionalism also distinguishes between micro factionalism and macro factionalism. Micro factionalism refers to the leader follower arrangement (ibid:349). Macro factionalism refers to the type of faction which can be related to certain group interests often reflecting some basic division.

To Richard Sisson the ultimate focus of conflict with in the Congress system was over the control of the chief ministership, representation in the ministry and the favourable allocation of important ministerial portfolios (Richard Sisson 1972: 205).

The above discussions show that the term faction and its derivatives has been inconsistently and interchangeably used by anthropologists, sociologists and political scientists, mainly due to the lack of a uniformly accepted theory and definition. However as a grand theory the above discourse answers how it emerged, what exactly is its nature, why factions prevail and how certain people take over the leadership of the factions.

It is also clear that defining and understanding 'faction' or 'factionalism' has to be context specific. No macro theory of faction can encompass the entire gamut of factional dynamics taking place at different levels of social and political activity. When the discourse on 'faction' takes place in the context of a political party this is more so. The real nature and causes of its origin often lies hidden beneath the apparently visible features and to comprehend its real nature is a complex task.

In the case of the present study, the contextual specificities of the factional dynamics of the Congress party unit in Kerala demand a careful micro level analysis so that certain generalisations can be attempted. Identifying such specificities will enable us to understand the nature of Congress factionalism in Kerala objectively. However this does not mean that we should conduct our study without a theoretical framework. Since the grand-theories on 'faction' takes into consideration the basic issues involved in that tendency, by integrating such theories with our understanding of the context of this work, it is possible for us to probe effectively the politics of Congress factionalism in the state since 1982. Such an effort would suggest that in the context of politics of Congress factionalism in Kerala, factionalism is basically understood as 'power politics' in which different ideological positions, personal interests, group interests and different styles of leadership matter. As a political activity it is a never ending process in all political parties with difference only in the degree of factional assertion.

Based on the intrinsic peculiarities of the factional dynamics of the Congress party in Kerala as understood by its leading practitioners in the state unit, the concept and the factional tendency has been defined variously as 'the way to acquire power through selfish means' (K. Karunakaran 26-1-2002), 'the fallout of the personal ambitions of the leaders' (P.Balan 18-1-2002), 'differences in the styles of functioning of leaders' (K. Muraleedharan 29-11-2001), 'an activity of a group of politicians to project a leader for the sake of realising their own selfish motives' (A.C Jose 27-11-2001) and as 'a group created by the leaders for their existence' (Rosakutty Teacher). The faction leaders identify their group with the party and contemptuously refer to the other groups as indulging in factional politics. However, in an academic discourse faction or factional tendency is taken as a neutral concept without any inherent positive or negative aspects.

Scope of the Study

From the above survey it is clear that most of the studies in the field draw sustenance from case studies. But at the ultimate theoretical level of the factional phenomena, the contextual distinctions vanish and they can be organised under a theoretical framework. Studies on factionalism can not be restricted to any one sector since it is omnipresent in all sectors of human activity. The insights from all these sectors are important since their findings and conclusions often coincide. In short the sociological and anthropological insights on factionalism provide us with an angle of vision to understand and interpret the politics of factionalism.

Inspite of the above complementary aspects an indepth understanding of factionalism as a 'political tendency' assumes significance and this certainly falls within the scope of the study. Political behaviour is the product of historical evolution and factional tendency is also conditioned by history and culture. This is what we mean by contextual specificities. It is within the scope of the study to empirically examine the nature of factionalism as a political tendency found in the Congress party in Kerala. It also includes an enquiry in to its causes, the major issues involved and the important events connected to it. In a case study like this, the intrinsic peculiarities of the Congress factional phenomena in Kerala assume importance. Naturally, a micro analysis of the above falls within the scope of the study. It is also proposed to revalidate or restate atleast some of the generalisations. The relationship between the party faction and socio-economic structure, the aggressive and integrative functions of factions, changes in factional participation and strategy over the years, the nature of fragmentation, the techniques of accommodation, and the assessment of the comparative strength, role and appeals of the different factions - all these with reference to the politics of Congress factionalism in Kerala since 1982 - forms part of the scope of the study.

Limitations of the Study

There are certain limitations in conducting a study like this. The most important limitation is the non-availability of proper data in the Congress party offices. Naturally, primary investigation becomes a laborious process. The records in the KPCC office had to be supplemented and cross checked with the records available in the District committee offices to prepare tables. Since this study is the first of its kind that empirically analyses party factionalism in Kerala, it could not be undertaken on set patterns. It necessitated extensive collection of original data from various sources including sample data from Congress party activists all over the state.

Inspite of the limitations mentioned an attempt has been made in this work to evaluate the nature and effect of factionalism in the Congress party in Kerala objectively.

Methodology

The present study is descriptive, explanatory, empirical and analytical in nature. As such it required both qualitative and quantitative data for properly comprehending the dynamics of factionalism in the Congress party in Kerala. Primary and secondary sources where used for the study. Published research documents, news paper articles, press clippings and books constituted the main source material for generating secondary data. The data thus generated have been processed and analysed in accordance with the enumerated objectives of the study.

The nature and methodology of the empirical study is given in chapter IV.

Chapter Design

This study is structured into seven chapters. The first chapter is introduction which deals with the research design and the conceptual framework of the study. The historical analysis of Congress factionalism in Kerala till 1982 in the All India background constitutes the subject matter of the second chapter. The third chapter examines the politics of Congress factionalism in Kerala since 1982. The fourth chapter deals with the methodology for empirical analysis. The social base of factionalism is discussed in the next chapter. Nature of Congress factionalism in the politico-economic context is the theme of the sixth chapter. The seventh chapter consists of the findings and conclusions of the study.

References

Balakrishnan Nair A (1994): *The Government and Politics of Kerala*, Thiruvananthapuram: Indira Publication.

Balakrishnan Nair. A (1996): *Landmarks in the Administration of Kerala*, Thiruvananthapuram: IIPA Regional Branch.

Beals R. Alan and Bernard J. Siegel (1966): *Divisiveness and Social Conflict: An Anthropological Approach*, Bombay: Oxford University Press.

Bipan Chandra and others (1999): *India Since Independence*, New Delhi, Viking.

Brass R. Paul (1965): *Factional Politics in an Indian State*, London: Cambridge University Press.

Brass R. Paul (1975): *Language, Religion and Politics in North India*, New Delhi, Vikas.

Brass R. Paul (1984): *Caste, Faction and Party in Indian Politics* Vol.I, Faction and Party, New Delhi, Chanakya.

Brass R. Paul (1994): *Politics of India Since Independence*, Cambridge, Cambridge University Press.

Brennen Geoffrey and Alan Hamlin (2000): *Democratic Devices and Desires*, Cambridge: Cambridge University Press.

Carter T. Anthony (1975): *Elite Politics in Rural India: Political Stratification and Political Alliances in Western Maharashtra*, New Delhi, Vikas.

Cherian Philip (1995): *Kaal Noottandu* (M), Kottayam, DCB.

Dua B D (1985): *Presidential Rule in India: 1950-1984: A study in Crisis Politics*, New Delhi, rev. ed. S.Chand.

Duverger Maurice (1959): *Political Parties*, London, Methun & Co.

Firth Raymond (1957): "Introduction to factions in Indian and Overseas Indian Societies", *The British Journal of Sociology* Vol.8, No.4.

Franda M. Marcus (1971): *Political Development and Political Decay in West Bengal*, Calcutta: Firma KLM.

Fukunaga Masaaki (1993): *Society Caste and Factional Politics: Conflict and Continuity in Rural India*, New Delhi, Manohar.

Gopakumar. G (1984): *The Congress Party and State Politics: Emergence of New Style Politics.*, New Delhi, Deep & Deep.

Gopakumar. G (1986): "Party System" In Jose Chander's (ed) *Dynamics of State Politics in Kerala*, New Delhi Sterling .

Gorman O' Frank (1973): *Edmund Burke: His Political Philosophy*, London: George Allen and Unwin.

Govindan Kutty.K (1994): *K. Karunakaran: A Political Biography*, New Delhi, Har Anand.

Gould A. Harold (1994): *Grass Roots Politics in India: A Century of Political Evolution in Faizabad District*, New Delhi: Oxford University Press.

Hausen Thomas Blom and Christophe Jalfrelot (1998): (Ed), *The BJP and the Compulsions of Politics in India*, New Delhi, Oxford University Press.

Hemachandran M.K (1997), *Ente Kazhinja Kaalam* , (M),Kottayam, DCB.

John K.C (1975): *The Melting Pot: Kerala 1950's-1970's*, Trivandrum, Prasanthi Printers.

John K. C (1999): *Kerala Rashtreeyam Oru Asambandha Natakom*, Aluva, Penn Books.

John K C (2001): *Beyond the Dead Line*, Thiruvananthapuram,. Kesari Memorial Trust

Jones Morris. W H (1978): *Politics Mainly Indian*, New Delhi, Orient Longman.

Kumar K.N (1990): *Political Parties in India: Their Ideology and Organisation*, New Delhi, Mittal.

Lal J.N (1991): "Factionalism in the Congress party: causes and consequences", In N S Ghelot (ed) *Congress Party in India: Politics culture and Performance*, New Delhi, Deep & Deep.

Laswell D Harold and Abraham Kaplan (1957): *Power and Society: A Framework for Political Enquiry*, USA, University of Yale.

Lewis Oscar (1958): *Village Life in Northern India*, USA, University of Illinois.

Mahapatra J K (1985): *Factional Politics in India*, Allahabad, Chugh Publication.

Mahendra P. Singh (1975): *Cohesion in a Predominant Party: The Pradesh Congress and Party Politics in Bihar*, New Delhi, S. Chand.

Maor Moshe (1997): *Political parties and Party Systems: Comparative approaches and the British experience*, London, Routledge.

Merriam E.Charles & Harold Foote Gosnell (1949): *The American Party System: An Introduction to the Study of Political Parties in the US*, USA, Macmillan.

Nagla B.K (1984): *Factionalism, Politics and Social Structure*, Jaipur, Rawat.

Nagla B.K (1999): *Political Sociology*, New Delhi: Rawat.

Namboodiripad E M S(1968): *Kerala- Yesterday, Today and Tomorrow*, Calcutta, National Book Agency.

Namboodiripad E M S (1969): *Keralam Malayalikalude Mathrubhumi*, Trichur.

Namboodiripad E M S (1984): *Kerala Society and Politics: An Historical Survey*, New Delhi, National Book Agency .

Namboodiripad E M S (1994): *The Communist party in Kerala: Six Decades of Struggle and Advance*, New Delhi, National Book Centre.

Nair K.S (1984): *Congress Party and Kerala Politics*, Trivandrum, College Book House.

Narayana Pillai. C(1976): *Pattom Muthal Panampally Vare* (M),Kottayam, DCB.

Narayana Pillai. C (1972): *Thiruvithamkoorile Swathanthiya Samara Charitram*, (M), Trivandrum.

Nossiter T.J (1982): *Communism in Kerala*, London, Oxford.

Padma Charan Misra and K.S Padhy (2000): *Factional Politics in Rural India*, New Delhi, Discovery Publishing.

Pattom G. Ramachandran Nair (2000): *Pattom Muthal Nayanar Vare* (M), Sindhu, Palkulangara, Trivandrum.

Perunna K.N Nair (1967): *Keralathile Congress Prasthanam* (M), Trichur, Current Books.

Pillai A.K (1986): *Congrassum Keralavum* (M), Thiruvananthapuram, Prabhath Book House.

Pocock F. David (1957): "The Bases of Congress Factions in Gujarat" *The British Journal of Sociology* Vol.VIII.

Rajni Kothari, Gopalakrishna, Ramshray Roy and Ghanshyam Shah (1967): *Party System and Election Studies*, New Delhi, Allied.

Rajni Kothari (2001):The Crisis of the Moderate State and Decline of Democracy" In Niraja Gopal Jain (ed) *Democracy in India*, New Delhi, Oxford.

Ramachandran S (2000): *P. Balan Thalaratha Porali* (M), Kottayam, DCB.

Ramakrishnan Nair R (1964): *How the Communist Came to Power*, Thiruvananthapuram, Kerala Academy of Political Science.

Ranajit Guha (1982): *Subaltern Studies: Writings on South Indian History and Society*, New York, Oxford.

Rose Richard (1974): *The Problem of Party Government*, London, Macmillan.

Robert I. Crane (1960): "Leadership of the Congress party" In Richard L Park and I. Tinker (ed) *Leadership and Political Institutions in India*, Princeton. N.J Princeton University Press.

Sadasivan S. N (1977): *Party and Democracy in India*, New Delhi, Tata Mc Graw Hill.

Sadasivan Nair. K (1970): *The Congress Party in Kerala 1947-63* (PhD Thesis), Trivandrum, Department of Politics, University of Kerala.

Sajal Basu (1990): *Factions, Ideology and Politics: Coalition Politics in West Bengal*, Calcutta: Minerva Associates.

Sartori Giovanni (1976): *Parties and Party system: A Frame Work for Analysis*, Vol.I, Cambridge, Cambridge University Press.

Scalapino A. Robert & Junnosuke Masumi (1971): *Parties and Politics in Contemporary Japan*, USA, University of California Press.

Sisson Richard (1972): *The Congress party in Rajasthan Political Integration and Nation Building in an Indian State*, London University of California.

Sreedhara Menon A (1987): *A Concise History of Kerala*, Madras, S. Viswanadhan Publishing Company.

Subrata Mukherjee & Sushila Ramaswamy (1974): *Niccola Machiavelli*, New Delhi, Deep & deep.

Suryanarayana Misra (1989): *Party Politics and Electoral Choice in an Indian State*, New Delhi, Ajanta.

Thomas E.J (1985): *Coalition Game Politics in Kerala*, New Delhi, Intellectual Publishing House.

Walch James (1976): *Faction and Front: Party Systems in South India*, New Delhi, Young Asia Publications.

Webb Paul (2000): *The Modern British Party system*, New Delhi, Sage.

Weiner Myron (1957): *Party Politics in India: The Development of Multiparty system*, Princeton, University of Princeton.

Weiner Myron (1967): *Party Building in a New Nation: The Indian National Congress*, Chicago, University of Chicago.

Zoya Hasan (2002): *Parties and Party politics in India*, New Delhi: Oxford University Press.

Interview with

Ajay Tharayil, KPCC General Secretary at MLA Hostel, Thiruvananthapuram.

Aryadan Muhammad MLA, at MLA Hostel, Thiruvananthapuram.

Balan P, Former KPCC General Secretary at his Palakkad residence.

Jose A.C, MP at his New Delhi residence.

Joseph Vazhackkan, KPCC General Secretary at KPCC Office, Thiruvananthapuram.

Karunakaran. K., at his residence in Thiruvananthapuram.

Muraleedharan K. KPCC President, at KPCC office, Thiruvananthapuram

Rosakkutty Teacher. KPCC General Secretary, MLA Hostel, Thiruvananthapuram.

Two

Factionalism in the Congress Party: A Historical Perspective

Conflicts between groups started in the Congress almost within a year of its establishment. It is interesting to note how groups functioned all-through the earlier stages of the party's history without degenerating into groupism (Alexander 1995:59). It is pointed out that signs of conflict and discord in the Indian National Congress (INC) were visible even before the organisation had taken shape as the premier national organisation. This is evident from the fact that a national conference of Indian Association under the stewardship of Surendranath Banerjee was hurriedly convened at Calcutta almost at the same time when the Conference of the Indian Union, the precursor of the INC, was scheduled to meet and discuss almost the same issues on the agenda (Zaidi 1984:19). Some regard the INC as the creation of an individual, others seek to give it an impersonal origin, a birth of circumstances. Its spontaneous character can be discovered in the several political associations that sprang up in various parts of the country. There are few others who regard it as a child of 'Russo-Phobia' (Chopra, Ram Gopal, Bhargava 1986:1). The birth of INC was a response to the total situation prevalent in India, especially since the 1880s. The Indian Association led by Surendranath Banerjee held its conferences in 1883 and 1885. It was an act as much of supreme wisdom as of magnanimity when he decided to merge the Conference in the Congress, which in Surendranath's own words, was conceived on the same lines and had the same programme as National Conference (Pande 1985:28).

The evolution of the Congress elite can be divided into different periods, each of which produced a slightly different complex of social strata. There was a period of moderates from

1885 to 1900 (Stanley A. Kochanek 1968:319). The members of the Indian National Congress pursued different interests and ideologies. There were moderates, with their liberal ideology and commitment to social reform and there were radicals, less committed to constitutionalism but often socially conservative on matters of Hindu social customs (Myron Weiner & Ashuthosh Varshney 1989:185). Paradoxically, the struggles within the Congress party often strengthened the party as each faction vigorously mobilised the people. Local village factions and castes that wanted greater access to the government were encouraged by dissident groups within the Congress to join intra party struggles. As a result new social groups and new local elites joined the party (ibid:196).

Moderates and Extremists

The first major clash was between the moderates and extremists. The words 'moderates' and 'extremists' had according to Tilak a specific relation to time. The extremists of today will be the moderates of tomorrow just as the moderates of today were the extremists of yesterday" (Shankar Ghose 1975: 30). Leading stalwarts of the party's earlier years were themselves leading the rival groups – Dadabhai Naoroji, Gokhale and Pherozshah Metha leading the moderate group and Balagangadhara Tilak, Bipan Chandra Pal, and Lala Lajpat Rai, the extremist group. In all its actions the Indian National Congress projected the image of a norm oriented movement working under a collective leadership. For three decades this approach remained the stock-in-trade of the moderate leadership of the national Congress (John L. Hill 1991:58). The split at Surat in the Annual Session of the INC between the moderates and the extremists or the militant nationalists was not for any material gains. The issues at the Surat were fundamental, basic and not negotiable (ibid:68). The two widely different views of society were in conflict. More over, this basic conflict arose from a context that contributed powerfully to the division over strategy and tactics. The normative Congress of the moderates was under assault by the rising forces of the new value oriented extremists. The Congress which was till then confined to a few elites now became a dynamic national movement capable of enlisting a large number of followers (Harihara Das 1998:310).

There was considerable unrest particularly among unemployed youth who constituted the backbone of the strong militant nationalist movement which resulted in the rift between 'militants' and 'moderates' (Verinder Grover 1997:92). In the earlier days along with the annual sessions of the Congress, the annual sessions of the Social Reform Conference were also held (Tope 1986:16). The moderates believed in self help and considered the swaraj and swadeshi programmes as the first step in this direction. The moderates regained control in 1908 through constitutional manoeuvres. Instead of 'swaraj' it declared the attainment of 'dominion status' to be the goal of the Congress, a goal to be achieved through constitutional means. However, because of war return of extremism was not possible. The association of political radicalism with social sectarianism on the one hand, and political and social liberalism on the other, best indicated by a comparison between the activities of the Poona Sarvajanik Sabha and the Deccan Educational Society or between the ideas of Gokhale and Tilak was the characteristic of the pre Gandhian politics in India (Om P. Gautam 1985:66).

Kerala remained isolated from the national mainstream till 1920. Political campaigns and issues were based on local issues. Though in 1903 the first meeting of the INC was held in Calicut, it could not arouse much interest. The District Congress Committee founded in 1910 also failed to become active until 1914. In Travancore and Cochin there was no Congress organisation at all until 1920. The first All Kerala Congress Conference was held at Ottappalam near Palghat in 1921 (George Woodcock 1967:233).

The foregoing discussion of the emergence of cultural and political nationalism in India indicates that the group identity initially produced by the process of social mobilization, though broader than the primordial identities of village, locality or caste, was not a national identity, but regional and religious identities. The national identity was primarily the result of the change, from regional to national. The 32nd Annual Session of the Congress met in Calcutta in December 1917. Annie Beasant was elected as the President. The Calcutta Congress although largely dominated by extremists passed a resolution favouring the British Indian administration (Girija K. Mookerjee 1947:143). The language as well as the ideology of the militants served to spread its appeal broadly. Whereas the reformists or moderates neither sought nor secured mass support, the extremists did (John H. Hill:69).

Pro Changers and No Changers

Group conflicts broke out again in the Congress in the early years of nineteen twenties between the no-changers and pro-changers on the issue of Council entry and this led to the formation of the Swaraj party headed by C.R. Das and Motilal Nehru (Alexander 1995:59). The cleavage between the two groups became more pronounced. C.R Das's resignation in connection with this was not accepted in the AICC meeting held on 27 Feb.1923 at Allahabad. It was postponed for consideration at the next meeting. Meanwhile the two parties, the Pro-changers and No-changers were advised to call a truce and cease carrying on propaganda for their respective views (Zaidi 1984:73). The Congress workers adhered to this position as they were the disciplined soldiers of their organisation (Sarat Chandra Mallick 1986:37). On 27 May 1923 the working committee and the AICC which met at Bombay decided that no propaganda in furtherance of the resolution passed at Gaya disapproving the council entry should be carried on.

The emergence of Gandhi and his non cooperation movement involved the common man in the national movement and this brought about a change in mass psychology in terms of the courage and confidence that it injected. Kamalapathi Chathopadhyaya felt that the emergence of the Congress Socialist Party (CSP) "was at least partly due to the mass base Gandhi had given to the national movement" (Mahendru 1948:4). Thus the establishment of the Congress socialist forums in 1934 under the leadership of Narendra Dev and Jaya Prakash Narain was another landmark in the history of the formation of groups within the Congress (Alexander 1995:59). Indian Politics then witnessed a new wave of radicalism, the most important feature of which was the influx of socialist ideas. As a result, a strong youth movement emerged and a number of organisations such as All India Youth League, the Swadeshi Bharat Sangh and the All India Youth Congress were formed. Before this, in 1928 Nehru along with Subhash Chandra Bose and S. Iyengar founded the Independence of India League aimed at propagating socialism (Mahendru 1984:6). This was the first organisation with an express preference for socialism within the Indian National Congress. Gandhiji admitted that he was not moving as fast as the younger generation. The Congress socialists realised that there was a need to radicalise or to rationalise the whole base of the national movement both ideologically and organisationally. Again socialists believed that Gandhism has become a cloak for promoting the vested economic interests of some groups who had nothing in common with Congress ideology and the struggles launched by it.

A unit of the Indian National Congress was working in Cochin as early as 1919. When the non-co-operation movement was launched in 1921 under the leadership of Mahatma Gandhi, Cochin Congress participated in it and many courted arrest. In the Nagpur session of the Congress under the leadership of Gandhiji it was decided to organise district committees in all the princely states. A Pradesh Congress Committee was organised in 1921 for the activities covering Malabar, Cochin and Travancore (Perunna K.N. Nair 1967:24). As a result the members of different communal groups too joined the Congress party. Gandhi's insistence on non-violence as a creed was not acceptable to the Congress Socialists. However nobody could accuse the Congress Socialists of groupism because they were guided by ideological convictions and not by consideration of personal advancement. Congress Socialists dominated the Congress affairs in Kerala.

Leftists and Rightists

By the mid-thirties two distinct groups emerged in the Congress; namely, the leftists and the rightists. This grouping was otherwise known as Militants and Gandhians. In the beginning Subhash and Jawahar jointly led the revolt against Gandhi (Kaushik 1986:53). Nehru's overgrowing loyalty to Gandhi sealed the fate of their friendship. To Nehru, Gandhiji was the biggest guru but to Bose, "as a political leader Gandhiji has failed" (ibid). Nehru became the political heir apparent of Gandhi, and Bose, the standard bearer of revolt against Gandhian leadership. Subhash Chandra Bose energised the youth of the country. It was this youth force that instilled the Congress with the spirit of revolution and made it a heroic rebel (Sadasivan 1977:150).

Nehru was indeed dissatisfied with the behaviour of the big zamindars and industrialists under whom the peasantry and the labor were living in perpetual poverty. His deep involvement in the civil disobedience movement and the quit India movement along with the millions of satyagrahis picked up from various levels of our society strengthened his commitment to socialist ideas (Bakshi 1985:59).

The difference between the left and right in the Congress leadership in the years 1929-39 hinged not so much on differences in the formal programmes advocated, or on factional pressures. They were due to basic differences in the right and left attitudes and approaches to key socio-economic and political problems of the day (Reba Som 1995:264). The formal programmes adopted by the Congress leadership, were generally accepted by both the right and left groups who operated within a broad consensus framework. Though the small coterie of the right wing leadership did not have a clearly articulated ideology, they had similarity in outlook. Patel, Prasad and Rajagopalachari were all from well to do rural landed backgrounds and grew up with traditional values. Exposure to western education did not shake their belief in such values.

They subscribed to the non-violent Gandhian political creed not merely because it helped to consolidate their respective provincial positions but basically because they had belief in the principles, relevance and practicability of Gandhism. They believed with Gandhi in a gradualistic approach while dealing with the British. The left inclined Congress leaders thought of restructuring Indian society along the lines of imported socialist models. Their socio-economic perspective was larger and leaders like Nehru and Bose constantly related developments in India with current world events. To them difference with Gandhism was infact the difference between modernism and conservatism (ibid:265).

The Congress session held at Nagpur in December, 1920 decided to reorganise Congress provinces on the basis of language. The Kerala Pradesh Congress Committee was formed in 1921 in pursuance of the decision of the Nagpur Congress. When the new

Kerala Pradesh Congress Committee (KPCC) was formed K. Madhavan Nair was elected as the secretary (Sadasivan Nair 1970:20). Under the chairmanship of T. Prakasom the first KPCC conference was held on 23 April 1921 at Ottappalam (Keraleeyan 1969:219). This was a conference of Congressmen who believed in secularism and religious toleration. The Congress gave support for the formation of Khilafat committees in Malabar (Perunna K.N. Nair 1967: 29). The first conference in which the Muslims participated in large numbers soon after the rebellion was the Tellichery Khilafat Conference held on 1 May 1923. Inspite of the success of the conference it soon became clear that there was a general withdrawal of Muslims from active political life in Malabar. The second KPCC meeting was held at Palakkad. In the annual session of the Congress held at Kakinada T.K Madhavan submitted a representation about the untouchables in India. On the basis of the decision of the Kakinada Congress of 1923, the KPCC setup a special committee to take up the issue (Perunna K.N. Nair 1967: 206). In 1924 the KPCC met at Vaikkom and took decisions in connection with the Vaikom Satyagraha aimed at eliminating the social evils prevalent in the traditional Kerala society.

During the first half of the nineteen thirties there were some members in the Pradesh Congress who had a left orientation. These men simply represented the radical and progressive wing of the Congress to which Nehru belonged. This left wing demanded more representation in the party. They organised workers and peasants and functioned as a powerful group within the Congress. During this time the leadership of the Congress was in the hands of a few eminent lawyers. They could devote only Sundays for the work of the Congress. So it was nicknamed as 'Sunday Congress' (Namboodiripad 1984:381). Differences began to develop between the younger generation and senior leaders of the party. The younger generation favoured a revolutionary movement capable of capturing political power. They were not ready to accept the Gandhian concept of non-violence. The sudden withdrawal of satyagraha by Gandhiji further widened the rift.

The rift between the right and left wings in the provincial committee became serious when a resolution was passed at its meeting held at Shornur in 1934. This resolution expressed lack of faith in the efficiency of the Gandhian principles. Gradually ideological differences developed between the leftists who leaned more to socialism and the rightists who were stout-champions of Gandhism (Sadasivan Nair 1970:32). The differences in the Congress became very acute and it led to the formation of the Congress Socialist Party in 1934. Young leaders like E.M Sankaran Namboodiripad and P. Krishna Pillai who subscribed to the communist ideology along with the socialists like P. Kunjiraman Nambiar organised a unit of the CSP in Kerala in 1934 (ibid:33). In the 1934-35 elections the leftists secured a majority in the KPCC and all other subordinate committees. The rightists regained their majority in the KPCC by the end of 1935. In the 1937 election to the KPCC, the leftists again secured majority and this leftist control continued without interruption until the KPCC was disbanded by the Congress Working Committee (CWC) on disciplinary grounds in 1940. A working committee was constituted with Janab Abdur Rahman as president and E.M.S Namboodiripad as secretary (Ibid:37).

In 1940 a further shift in the left took place, whereby the most radically minded chose a different course and formed the Communist Party (Victor M Fic:9). Immediately after the Wardha session of the AICC, ninety Congress Socialist Party (CSP) members from Kerala met secretly at Tellichery to formalise the transformation of the Kerala CSP into the Communist Party (CPI). In line with the party's national policy, the Kerala unit continued to work through the Congress as well as independently (Nossiter 1982:84). Indiscipline in the KPCC provided CWC with an excuse to purge the Kerala unit of its communist elements. The Communist group began to grow very powerful during that period. On 26 January 1941, a new political organisation called the Cochin Praja Mandal took shape at the initiative of a few young politicians under the leadership of V.R. Krishnan Ezhuthachan. The Praja Mandal actively participated in the quit India movement of 1942. In Cochin, a political conference under the auspices of the Cochin Congress was held under the presidentship of Pattabhi Sitaramayya. KPCC was formed again in 1946. It elected K. Kelappan as president and C.K Govindan Nair as secretary. The leftist elements widened their base by organising the working class. The All Kerala Malabar Karshaka Sangham came into existence in 1937 with P. Narayan Nair as President and K.A Keraleeyan as Secretary inorder to do organisational work among the peasants (Sreedhara Menon 1987:61).

The communists wielded considerable influence in the Congress organisation and this helped them get many recruits to their party. Muhammed Abdur Rahman, the President of the KPCC joined the new party founded by Bose (Ibid:62). The developments at the national level led to a serious split in the Kerala Provincial Congress which was being controlled by the communists. The Congress high command took serious note of the developments in Kerala and on the basis of the Subbarayan enquiry report nominated R.K Nanda Kolyar, a Bihar Congressman, as President and C.K. Govindan Nair as Secretary of the KPCC in 1940 (ibid:64).

Nehruvian Era

In the post independence period, the left faction led by Nehru sought redistribution of economic resources through state socialism while the right led by Sardar Patel, was more inclined towards an economy based upon free enterprise. It was Gandhi's wish that a socialist, preferably Jaya Prakash Narayan, or Acharya Narendra Dev should lead the Congress but Patel foreclosed all possibilities of its fulfillment (Sadasivan 1977:154). In 1948, at the insistence of Sardar Vallabhai Patel, the CWC passed a resolution banning all the factions that had been allowed to operate within the INC. This action led to the exit of various factions, which then converted themselves into new political parties. While Congress became the ruling party of India, for many dissidents the only other course left open was to form opposition parties.

It can be seen that after independence 'Congress' got transformed from a movement to a party. As a party, it had to have a certain organisational cohesion, that it secured by introducing at Sardar Patel's initiative a provision that no person having faith in other ideologies have a room in Congress. But it retained its ideological and programmatic diversity and openness as also a certain organisational looseness (Bipan Chandra 1999:186). Rejection of the socialist programme widened the gulf between the socialists and the Patel loyalists.

After Patel's death Nehru's control over the party became virtually unchallenged. In fact the socialist parties were the direct descendants of the CSP which was formally founded in 1934 by certain younger elements who were influenced by Marxism (Kamal, Ralph 1977:91-92). After winning the general election in 1952 Nehru made his most serious effort to work together with the socialists hoping to build a broad political front to promote economic development and strengthen the left trend in the Congress. He also hoped to bring Jayaprakash into his cabinet. In response, Jayaprakash wanted the Congress Party to adopt the radical programme framed by him before he and the socialists joined it. Nehru was in agreement with many of Jayapraksh's fourteen points but he refused to enter into prior commitment. Nehru was prepared to strengthen the radical forces inside the Congress and not to split the party inorder to accommodate the socialists (Bipan Chandra 1999:195).

With his failure in seeking the help of the socialists to rejuvenate the Congress and shake it out of its staleness, Nehru decided to act on his own by radicalising party policies, especially with regard to the limited steps taken so far. It led to the adoption of the socialist pattern of society as the objective of the Congress at its Avadi session in January 1955. The indirect result of this left turn was the adverse impact that it generated on the political fortunes of the parties of the left and right which tended to get marginalised. In particular, by stealing the thunder of the socialists and communists it also tended to promote discussions and divisions among them (ibid:196).

The Congress further moved to the left, programmatically when at its Nagpur session in January 1959 it passed resolutions declaring that the future agrarian pattern should be that of co-operative joint farming. The Nagpur decisions faced opposition both within and outside the party and were quietly jettisoned.

In 1963 the Congress suffered three prestigious electoral defeats. The victors were Kripalani, Lohia and Minoo Masani who were known critics of the party. An introspection of the state of affairs forced the Congress high command to take steps for revamping the party set up. K. Kamaraj Nadar, the chief minister of Madras declared that some senior Congressmen in government were to resign to takeup full time organisational work inorder to revitalise the party. This came to be known as the 'Kamaraj plan'. Nehru took the lead the following day by seeking permission to resign; but as in 1954, and 1958 his colleagues proclaimed his indispensability as the head of the government (Michael Brecher 1966:9). The rationale of the Kamaraj Plan was that the party wanted Congressmen not to go after power or positions. In short, it was the acknowledgement of the need to balance two considerations i.e. strengthening the party and minimising the harm to the government (ibid:11). An indirect effect of the plan was to weaken Morarji Desai's position in the party. Another outcome of it was that, it increased the power of the state party bosses in central politics till Indira Gandhi cut them to size (Bipan Chandra 1999:198).

The period following the attainment of independence saw the rapid deterioration of the Congress party in Kerala and in 1957 it was voted out of power. This was due to two major reasons. In the first place, it can be attributed to the rivalries within its leadership. The second factor responsible for the deterioration of the Congress was the political polarisation that took place in the state (Victor M. Fic 1970:31). The organisational affairs of the Congress party in 1948 were in such a mess that the fall of the Thanu Pillai ministry was inevitable. The Congress party became a coalition of communal organisations consisting of various groups such as NSS, SNDP and the Catholics (John John 1983:52). Pattom Thanu Pillai the foremost leader of the Congress had to leave the party inorder to form the Praja Socialist Party (PSP) unit in the state. The different factions and groups in the party and the various communities fought for their own interests. Even Pattom Thanu Pillai, the Congress President in the ultimate analysis had a communal support base. If A.J John was the protector of Catholic interests, C. Kesavan was of the Ezhava interest, T.M Varghese and E.John Philipose were spokesmen of the Marthoma and Jacobite interests (ibid:53).

As a result of the split in the Congress party Acharya Kripalani founded Kisan Mazdoor Praja Party (KMPP). It had repercussions in Kerala Politics. Two of the Congress leaders K. Kelappan and K.A Damodara Menon left the party and founded the KMPP in Kerala. This incident considerably weakened the Congress party in Kerala (ibid:55). The first popular ministry in Travancore-Cochin was headed by T.K. Narayana Pillai, the chief minister of Travancore at the time of the integration. He continued in office with occasional changes in personnel till February 1951 when he was forced to resign in the wake of internal dissensions in the Congress party (Sreedhara Menon 1967:356).

C. Kesavan, as the leader of the Congress party became the next chief minister. C. Kesavan thought that by limiting the size of the cabinet he could eliminate the factional strife which had become so deadly affecting the stability of the government (Victor M Fic 1970:36). The operation of the 'Cochin group' in the party was directed against the Kesavan Ministry. The Cochin Congressmen worked as a regional group to secure due representation and legitimate rights for their area. The government however, managed to rule till the general elections (Sadasivan Nair 1970:231). In the general election Congress secured the highest number of seats for any single party, but did not get an absolute majority. A. J John, the leader of the victorious Congress party formed the ministry, but within six months his ministry resigned as the no confidence motion moved by the Travancore Tamil Nadu Congress (T.T.N.C) was carried (Bhagat 1962:6). The mutual rivalry and jealousy within the Congress party was the main reason for its failure to secure an absolute majority during the elections.

The 1954 election results once again made it clear that the Congress was unable to substantially increase its seats in the Assembly. Pattom Thanu Pillai now as the leader of the PSP formed the government with the support of the Congress party. The PSP ministry would have been a success had not the Congress, on whose behalf it ruled, withdrawn its support in the Assembly. Several factors were responsible for the collapse of the Congress-PSP alliance. When Panampally Govinda Menon was elected as the KPCC President the old personal rivalry between him and the Chief Minister, Pattom Thanu Pillai got revived (Victor M Fic 1970: 45). When TTNC, led an agitation for the merger of Tamil speaking areas of South Travancore to Madras state, Pattom ordered the police to fire on the agitators. This firing infuriated the TTNC group in the assembly and it was looking for an opportunity to discredit the Pattom Ministry. To add to it, Panampally Govinda Menon, the leader of the Congress in the Assembly through clever manovuering brought two PSP legislators and one nominated member to the Congress side. At this time the TTNC moved a no confidence motion against the Pattom ministry (Bhagat 1962:10). Panampally Govinda Menon was an ambitious man. He could not realise that the fall of Pattom was infact the fall of Congress as it was the Congress party which helped him to form the ministry.

Panampally Govinda Menon, the veteran Congress leader from Cochin, was elected as the chief minister with the backing of a manipulated precarious majority (Ramakrishnan Nair 1967:41). Other ambitious politicians followed his suit. Shanku Pillai, a rebel within the Congress group in the Assembly now staked his claim with the support of A.R Menon, T.M Varghese and C. Kesavan (Bhagat 1962:10). A new crisis within the Congress erupted soon which resulted in the defection of six Congress members of the assembly, who formed a group and then withdrew their support to Panampally's cabinet. The crisis was precipitated by the intervention of the Congress high command in the affairs of Kerala in an effort to end the suicidal factional struggle which slowly but surely was killing it (Victor M Fic 1970: 48). At the time of the election of the KPCC President, the high command threw its weight behind Udaya Bhanu, who was the nominee of the ruling Panampally-Madhavan Nair group. The rebels demanded the resignation of Panampilly's cabinet. He had no choice but to resign, because the strength of the Congress was reduced to fifty four (Bhagat 1962:10). When Panampally fell from office in 1956 Nehru remarked in disgust that Travancore-Cochin had proved so ungovernable by democratic means (George Woodcock 1967:261). Because of internal divisions Congress could not form the government. Not only were there conflicts between Congress and the Travancore Tamilnadu Congress but conflicts were developing inside the Congress leadership also. The outgoing chief minister exclaimed that "It is not the opposition that defeated my government, but my own party people" (EMS 1984:187). In the absence of unity among Congress leaders, Presidents rule was imposed. It is an accepted fact that factionalism in the Congress party contributed to instability in administration and inefficiency in organisational activities. The disparity between the three regions may be reckoned as one of the factors that has thwarted the emergence of one party government in Kerala. In the erstwhile State of Travancore-Cochin the Congress party and its government succumbed to communal pressures. The dominance of the Christian community compelled the Nairs and Ezhavas to leave the Congress and form the Hindu Mandalam (Balakrishnan Nair 1996:184).

On the basis of the linguistic reorganisation of states, the first Assembly election was held along with the Lok Sabha elections in March 1957. In the house of 127 members, CPI emerged as the largest single party with 60 members. They also enjoyed the support of five independents. A few days after the general election the legislature wing of the Communist party met at Cochin and elected EMS Namboodiripad as its leader. For the formation of the ministry, the CPI needed the support of A.R. Menon. He had defeated a Congress candidate at Trichur which had for long been a safe Congress constituency. And in neighbouring Chalakudy, he saw to it that his political opponent, Panampilly Govinda Menon, was defeated by the Samyuktha Socialist Party (SSP) candidate C.H. Gangadharan. This forced Govinda Menon out of Kerala politics permanently (John 1975:35).

The conflict inside the camp led to the fall of the Congress ministry. Another reason for the communist victory was the reorganization of the state. The inclusion of Malabar where the communists had decisive influence in the state of Kerala and the exclusion of South Travancore where they had practically no influence had doubly strengthened their position in the new state (Ramakrishnan Nair 1965:25). The Congress lost its credibility due to factionalism within its ranks. "People lost faith in Congress's ability to provide a stable government (ibid:27). The Congress organisation was also weak and inefficient. Some of the important Congress leaders had also become discredited. Allegations of corruption against some leaders adversely affected the party. The communist victory in 1957 was, attributed also to the tilting of the balance in its favour by the Nair community. (ibid:30). The powerful Catholic church apprehended that the continuance of Panampally as chief minister might necessarily lead to the revival of the former education scheme (Private Secondary School Scheme), part of which was once kept in cold storage owing to the opposition of the church (ibid:68).

A historic landmark was reached in the advancement of the communist movement in India, in the 1957 election when the CPI won an absolute majority in Kerala and formed a government (Narang 1985:238). The opposition to the communist regime steadily grew in volume and strength and developed itself into an irresistible mass upsurge. In the last week of July 1959 the liberation struggle reached the final stage. The members of the Christian church, the NSS, the Muslim League, the Congress party, the PSP and the RSP actively participated in the liberation struggle (Bhagat 1962:29). Explaining the main object of the *Vimochana samaram*, Mannath Padmanabhan declared that the aim was not limited to redressal of specific issues but extended to the 'removal of the communist ministry'. On the basis of the governor's report the communist ministry was dismissed in July 1959.

The KPCC leadership entered into an informal understanding with the major communities in order to face the mid term poll. It forged a new united front with PSP and IUML to fight the Communist Party. The INC led alliance got a thumbing majority. The PSP leader Pattom Thanupillai was elected as the chief minister and the Congress party leader R. Sankar as deputy chief minister. Speakership was given to Muslim League. The only way to avoid further troubles was to bring about an honourable exit for Pattom Thanu Pillai (Sankara Pillai 1969:56). Lal Bahadur Sastri, the then Union home minister was closely in touch with the developments in Kerala. Very soon an understanding evolved between Shastri, Giri and Chacko. Pattom tendered his resignation and was appointed as Governor of Punjab. P.T Chacko was the leader of the Congress party while the party was in opposition. But he was dropped in favour of R. Sankar who enjoyed the support of the Congress high command (Sadasivan Nair 1970:231).

It should be noted that R. Shankar was elevated to the position of the chief minister just because of the intervention of the high command. This policy had the undeclared purpose of placating the Ezhava community even by overlooking the claims of P.T Chacko for leadership (Varghese 1982). Groupism started again with the traditional conflict between the organisational and the parliamentary wings. The opposition brought forward a few corruption charges against R. Sankar and K.A Damodara Menon. In the joint KPCC executive meeting, the President C.K. Govindan Nair announced that he was using his discretionary power to refer the corruption charges to Nehru for his personal enquiry (John 1978:76). The charges were sent to Nehru and he found that they were not serious enough and did not enquire further. When the time for election of a new KPCC chief came, the parliamentary and organisational wings prepared for another showdown. Both Kamaraj and Lal Bahadur Shastri visited Kerala to see if the two groups could be reconciled. They failed to avoid a contest. K.P Madhavan Nair, of the organisation wing was elected as KPCC chief by defeating M.C Chacko, the candidate of the legislature wing. Both Shankar and Chacko came out of the election hall with grim faces and grimmer determination (ibid:77).

It was during this period that the Peechi episode took place. In the morning of 8 December, 1963, home minister P.T Chacko's car collided with a hand cart. The minister's car sped away after this incident. A sex scandal was woven around this incident which caused wide spread sensation and criticism (Joseph Vadakkan 1974:167). PT Chacko was accused of violating traffic rules, and refusing to stop the car when asked to do so by the policeman, speeding and knocking down pedestrians (Link 1963:20). Instead of coming to the rescue of his colleague the chief minister threw his weight behind the organisation wing. Commenting on this development, U.N. Dhebar observed that, the late P.T Chacko built up R. Shankar to fight Pattom Thanu Pillai and got him ousted, when R.Shankar-Chacko combination succeeded in that objective, the two fell out. Chacko wanted to become the chief minister by replacing Shankar (Mankekar 1965:30). The KPCC leadership therefore decided to use the incident for demanding P.T Chacko's resignation. Congress MLA P. Gopalan started an indefinite hunger strike in front of the Assembly to oust Chacko from the cabinet. A memorandum was submitted to the Congress high command demanding the expulsion of P.T Chacko from the cabinet (Kerala Kaumudi:1-2-64). Kerala leaders were called to attend the Congress parliamentary board meeting in Delhi. On their return from Delhi R. Shankar and P.T Chacko made diametrically opposite statements regarding the decision of the Congress parliamentary board. Chacko felt that the chief minister had acted as a double dealer and had cheated him (*Malayala Manorama*: 16-2-1964). At last P.T Chacko resigned from the cabinet on 20 Feb, 1964, seventy five days after the Peechi episode.

After the resignation of P.T. Chacko from the ministry, the attitude of his group to the government underwent a total change. The Churuli-Keerithode developments and the arrest of Kottayam District Congress Committee (DCC) President Mathachan Kuruvinakunnel, who was a Chacko loyalist, worsened the situation further. K.M George, one of the MLA's loyal to P.T Chacko, demanded a judicial probe. The pro-Chacko group in the assembly had twentythree MLAs. When Congress President K. Kamaraj visited Kerala two memorandums were submitted to him for a change of leadership. The Congress President advised P.T Chacko to show his strength in the forthcoming organisational elections. In the PCC election P.T Chacko lost to K.C Abraham. The Chacko group decided to launch an attack against R.Shankar, the chief minister. The sudden death of P.T Chacko was a heavy lose to the Chacko group in the Congress. The no-confidence motion introduced by them was one of the factors that made the followers of P.T Chacko to organise themselves into a separate group. The Congress high command suspended fifteen MLA's from the party for six years. The Chacko group in the Congress and the NSS found this as a good opportunity to knock down the R. Shankar ministry. In a meeting held at Kottayam the Chacko loyalists formed a separate political party called the Kerala Pradesh Congress *Samudharana Samiti*. The KPCSS soon adopted a new name – the 'Kerala Congress' (*Indian Express*:10-10-1964). K.M. George became the Chairman of the new party. Along with casteism and communalism, now regionalism also engulfed the Congress party in Kerala (Mankekar 1965:73).

Shastri's Period

Different interest groups in the party played a role in the struggle for finding a successor to Nehru. Along with this the institutional interest groups were also at work, such as the Working Committee, the CPP executive and the PCC leaderships. In the aftermath of Nehru's demise the importance of the organisational wing increased (Rajni Kothari 1989:17). Nehru's position as the chief decision maker in the party was now shared by the Congress President and the Prime Minister in that order of importance. The innate simplicity and humility of Lal Bahadur Shastri stood him in good stead at the critical moment of transition (Asok Metha 1979:24). Now free from the charismatic leader, the Congress decision making centres became bodies for free discussions and decisions (Michael Brecher 1966:124). The Congress president Kamaraj wanted to put the stamp of authority on the new relationship through his call for 'collective leadership'. But events dictated otherwise. Shastri knew that he was the genuine choice of Congress and the country regardless of the managerial skills of Kamaraj and the caucus.

In the 1950's and 1960's the state party bosses who ran party machines based on control over patronage wielded much power (Myron Weiner & Ashuthosh Varshney 1984:219-20). Party factions, sometimes a single caste but more often a multi caste group, fought for power within the party. During the period of Shastri the pre eminence of the party over government became evident. Within the Congress, "factions interacted in a continuous process of pressure, adjustments and accommodation to provide a built-in opposition" (Robert L.Hardgrave 1975:142). The enormous power, prestige and patronage inherent in the Prime Ministership gave Shastri a marked advantage. Kamaraj had neither the pretentions nor ambition to occupy the centre stage. The Prime Minister strongly favoured a second term for Kamaraj- as the party President which required an amendment to party constitution. It is an accepted fact that after Nehru's death factionalism appeared more forcefully within the party and government. Lal Bahadur Shastri survived it through his politics of conciliation and consensus (Ramesh Kumar1994:131).

While Kamaraj was earnestly trying to set things right in the State Congress, Gulzarilal Nanda, short-circuiting his efforts, conferred on Mannathu Padmanabhan official honours as the advance portion of the prize for the return of the Kerala Congress to the parent body (Sadasivan 1977:34). Although Mannath Padmanabhan and the Christian bishops favoured the merger,

K.M George was prepared only for an electoral alliance. The 1965 elections to the state assembly added a new chapter to the political history of Kerala. No party or coalition of parties secured adequate majority to form a government. On that ground the legislature was dissolved even without convening it. President's rule continued till the next election in 1967.

Indira Gandhi's Period

Lal Bahadur Shastri died at the height of his power and prestige on 11 January, 1966. Thus India faced once more the task of selecting a new Prime Minister in a period of travail. A multitude of pressures clashed and coalesced in public view culminating in the election of Indira Gandhi as the leader of the CPP. It was a contest between the unbending Morarji and the graceful Indira (Pande 1989:133). Although both belonged to the same party, they represented two ideologies, two ways of life, and two social view points. On 24 January, 1966 Indira Gandhi entered upon a long innings of power. Her eleven years of Prime Ministership can be broadly divided into three segments, conveniently labeled as pragmatic, populist, and authoritarian (Asok Metha 1979:30). If one looks for a crucial year in the post independence experience of the Congress, it is hard to ignore 1967, the year of a critical general election.

By 1967, the momentum gained from the struggle for independence was spent, Nehru was dead and the opposition electorally organised. The electoral reverses and the emergence of non Congress coalition governments in the states, first of all precipitated the crisis in the party leading to the split and the demise of the Congress party which won independence (Mayer 1987:187). Indira Gandhi was trying to release herself from the shackles of the 'Syndicate' consisting of the party bosses who had been discredited by the electorate but who were nevertheless trying to control the party in the name of collective leadership. The Congress split into two groups after the defeat of the official Congress candidate in the race for the office of the President of India. As the 'Indicate group' headed by the Prime Minister was reduced to a minority in Lok Sabha, it started playing over the issue of privy purses and privileges of the former rulers (Sood

1981:57). Those who favoured radical economic policies supported Indira Gandhi (Dhar 2000:134). The party President issued a notice calling a meeting of the AICC. Indira Gandhi became desperate and opted for the extreme step. It was indiscipline that had given her a victory and a sizeable party vote. Indira Gandhi called a meeting of her own group in the AICC and declared itself as the real Congress, dismissed the president, the working committee and made new appointments. The great divide that occurred in November 1969, when Indira Gandhi caused large scale defections among Congressmen and set up parallel organisation came as a rude shock to all those who believed in the righteousness and ethical values of life. The so called split was the outcome of a conflict between 'Reactionaries' and 'Progressives' as it was projected by her (Subhash C. Kashyap 1971:20).

The factional makeup of the parties tends to make them closed organisations or exclusive clubs. On Indira Gandhi's side were Kamalapati Tripathi, D.P Misra, Jagjivan Ram and Fakrudin Ali Ahmed and against her, were K.Kamaraj, Athulya Ghosh, S.K Patil and Morarji Desai. Whether accidental or not polarisation took place along familiar lines. While it has been widely and perhaps rightly assumed that Indira Gandhi, unlike her father, was not ideological and a real pragmatist, it is also a fact that faced with a challenge she moved to the left of the centre than Nehru ever did (Meenakshi Jain1991:90). A small minority felt that the Congress was drifting from the Gandhian path. Even during pre-independence days, groupism in the party arose mainly on the basis of conflict of personalities (Rao 1971:8). Paul Brass viewed that in the 1969 split language and religion also played an important role. But it was the political parties and their leaders who played decisive roles in determining the outcome (Paul R. Brass 1975:41). The Congress system of power now consisted not only of the consensual accommodation of various groups and the factional interactions with them, it also provided a single framework of power, a degree of policy, commitment and a certain measure of internal consistency and discipline, which at the same time provided a system of politics for the whole country (Rajni Kothari 1989:169).

The emergence of a vibrant and young leadership in the

Congress party ardently advocating modernisation, socialisation and democratisation, - known as 'Young Turks' – constituted a very important event of the period. They discovered in Indira Gandhi, a potential leader capable of carrying the revolutionary upsurge of the left wing supporters to the point of fighting (Johari 1997:60-61). The reproductive process of Indian politics is very similar to that of an amoeba. The original amoeba being the Congress party which is more than hundred years old, has split a hundred times and is in danger of splitting another dozen times (Mahendra Prasad Singh 1981:1). But the exit of Indira Gandhi's faction from the Congress in 1969 was not an ordinary split. It was perhaps the most momentous upheaval in the organisation since the split between the extremists and moderates (Rahman 1970:1).

Indira Gandhi dubbed her critics as 'rightists' who obstructed her progressive programmes. This helped her to gain the communist support to maintain majority in the Lok Sabha. She vindicated herself within few months by nationalising fourteen banks to lay the foundation for a new economy. She soon became occupied in East Pakistan's secessionist internal warfare. The war with Pakistan came a few months later and it ended with another splendid victory for India, but the end was the beginning of an upheaval culminating in her disaster (Ram Gopal 1986:16).

The next three years saw serious crises in the economic and political spheres. The simmering discontent arising from the rapidly rising food grains prices further flared up as a result of drought and lean crops of 1973 in many parts of the country. In the political arena the railway strike of 1974 was the biggest manifestation of workers discontentment. Gujarat had been a strong hold of the Congress, and for the first time it lost the Assembly election there. All these made the Prime Minister more arrogant and Jaya Prakash Narayan announced his comeback to politics from his self imposed exile. The Bihar movement apart from securing the co-operation of four political parties became a potent force intensifying political awareness in the country side and organising new sections of population against the Congress. By June 1975 the cracks were plain to see, but it was plainer still that Indira Gandhi had to fight ahead of her times. For those who were grouping against her, she represented the autocratic structure that would have to be dismantled if Congress were to recover the confidence of its own rank and file as well as mass sympathy and backing (Nayantara Sahgal 1978:203). By an Allahabad high court order Indira Gandhi was unseated from parliament. Amidst the mounting opposition to her rule, the Prime minister declared internal emergency on the night of 26 June, 1975.

The decade (1970's) marked the organisational demise of the Congress party which had dominated national politics as well as political life in the states. The decline of party organisation was paralleled by experiments in political coalition (Mahendra Prasad Singh 1990:57). During the emergency period the PM's secretariat became a very important 'power house of influence'. Indira Gandhi had established herself as the leader of the party and government. Naturally she had to use her position as the head of the government to establish her position in the party. A type of decentralised autocracy came into being where 'chief ministers became local satraps'. It was also the heyday of Indira Gandhi's younger son, Sanjay, who wielded much power without any responsibility except to his mother (Arie De Ruijter 1998:21). The Prime Minister feared revolts in the party against her leadership. The stripping of H.N Bahuguna from the chief ministership of Uttar Pradesh (UP) in 1976 is a classic example of Indira Gandhi's treatment of popular leaders. Rival power centres in the states were not permitted to surface (Nayantara Sahgal 1978:192-93). In protest against the declaration of emergency the young Turks – Chandrasekhar, Mohan Dharia, and Krishna Kant - left the party.

Indira Gandhi's main objective was to stay in power some how and in achieving this she had the help of her son who had acted as a bulldozer to clear the path for all her improper acts. Congress became a toy in her stern hands and her colleagues were reduced to ridiculous puppets in the game of politics (R.K.G 2000:87). In 1977 various opposition parties came together to form the Janata Party. A new party by name the Congress For Democracy was formed by Jagjivan Ram and others who left the Congress in protest against Indira Gandhi's behaviour (Arie De Ruijter:28). In January, 1977 the Prime Minister announced her decision to seek a fresh mandate from the people. In the 1977 election the Congress party was routed and a government headed by Morarji Desai assumed office under the banner of the Janata Party. The Janata Party government, India's first national alternative to Congress, emerged from the merger of five parties. There were personal rivalries among the leaders of the five constituents of the Janata Party.

Factionalism within the Congress party accentuated due to the absence of any established norms for resolving conflict or regularising such rudimentary functions such as recruitment of party members, the election of office bearers, enforcement of the rules of party discipline and so forth (Marcus Franda 1979:201). Within eight years after the great rift in 1969, the Indian National Congress was subjected to another major division. The split began over the leadership issue and it virtually divided the Congress party into two, the INC (R) and INC(I). The former was led by the President of the Congress, Brahmananda Reddy and the latter by Indira Gandhi (Gopakumar 1980:150). Even before her defeat, Indira Gandhi had imposed something very close to a personal and dynastic rule on the political system and in the party. Defeat only intensified this tendency. The reconstitution of her version of the Congress party in January 1978 under the label of the INC (Indira) or Congress 'I' was emblematic of this increased personalisation (James Manor 1997:106).

Due to defections, Morarji government resigned and on 26 July, 1979. Charan Singh became Prime Minister leading a coalition government with the support of Cong (I). The bye elections in the country were mostly in favour of the Cong (I). The Cong (I) emerged as the chief beneficiary when President Sanjiva Reddy announced a mid term election. As Indira Gandhi's prospects improved, waves of deserters re-defected to her camp. Each wave tended to create a new faction in an already factionalised Cong (I) due to the inability to apply standards consistently to these returnees. Late comers were sometimes promoted over the old loyalists. This process continued even after Indira Gandhi's return to power in January 1980 and Sanjay's death six months later (Ibid:107). With the death of Sanjay his supporters became aggrieved and they formed what was called the 'Sanjay Vichar Manch'.

After the death of Sanjay Gandhi, Rajiv Gandhi entered

politics. The Congress party during Indira Gandhi's regime lapsed into inactivity between elections in most of the states. At the district and taluk levels there were Congress organisations but their role as animators and channels of popular participation was either non existent or restricted in its benefits to a limited clientele (John Wood 1984:13). A common criticism about Indira Gandhi's style of working was that she did not give much importance to the views expressed by her colleagues either in the party or in the government. But on important matters relating to the party in the states Indira Gandhi often accommodated the views of some of her senior colleagues in the cabinet (Alexander 1991:52).

The period from 1964 to 1967 was a period of unprecedented developments in Kerala politics characterised by splits in the CPI and the Kerala unit of the Congress party, confusion in the socialist camp, a minor split in Muslim League, an abortive election, a food crisis of high magnitude, a state wide agitation by school teachers and non-gazetted officers and an extraordinary long spell of President's rule under three successive governor's (Jayaraj 1977:190).

During these years the Kerala Pradesh Congress Committee was evolving strategies to free Kerala politics from the domineering influence of caste-communal groups and parties. Many Congressmen realised that aligning with the above forces would ultimately ruin the Congress party in the state. As a result the Congress contested on its own in the Assembly election of March 1965 and won 36 seats. The party was in a position to form a ministry with the support of Kerala Congress, a regional party. But the move was thwarted since the KPCC headed by C.K Govindan Nair did not sanction it (Ramachandran 2000:56).

The Congressmen in the state fought the 1965 and 1967 elections unitedly without any serious division in their ranks. Since the party could not win in both it was decided in the KPCC meeting held at Kottayam in1968, to form a 'Peoples Front'. A section of the Congressmen in the state were against this and criticised it as a deviation from the earlier line of going it alone. The youth wing and the KSU became the two powerful wings of the Congress party during this period. In 1969 the Youth Congress under the Presidentship of A.K.Antony passed a resolution for bank nationalisation. The resolution was moved by M.A John (N.P.Moideen:12-1-2002). The KSU was critical of the conservative leadership of the party and wanted to replace it by a dynamic one capable of transforming it into a mass movement. The youth and student wings fielded M.A John, against T.O Bava, the official candidate of the party in the election to the office of the KPCC chief in 1968 (Jayadevan 1999:205).

The 1969 split had its repercussions in Kerala also. In Kerala the crisis developed only after the meeting of the CWC on 1 November, 1969. Immediately after this on 8 November,1969 the KPCC executive met but was not able to take a decision on whether the Congress members should attend the requisite session of the AICC, which was to be held on 23 November, 1969 at New Delhi (*Mathrubhumi*:9-11-69). The committee decided to call a meeting of the general body of the KPCC on 16 November, 1969. In that meeting the emergence of two separate groups were evident. T.O. Bava, the President of the KPCC remained with the organisation. Soon an ad-hoc committee under K.K Viswanathan was nominated by Indira Gandhi. Youth Congress under Antony and KSU led by Kadannappali Ramachandran was with Congress(R). The Congress (ruling) faction led by Indira was known as Congress (R) as against the official Congress (old) which was called as Congress (O). Later Congress (R) reconstituted the KPCC with K.K Viswanathan as President and A.K. Antony as general secretary along with a fifteen member executive committee. There was also a split in the legislature party with K.Karunakaran and George Thomas heading the two groups. Vayalar Ravi and A.K. Antony were the first to come out with a public statement supporting Indira (Jayadevan 1999:206). Immediately after the split three bye-elections took place in Kerala. These by-elections clearly showed that the Cong (O) had no popular support in Kerala.

The 1970 mid term elections provided an opportunity to assess the political strength of each group. The Congress (R) which fielded 56 candidates won 32 seats (Valsarajan 1969:75). The post-1969 period witnessed group rivalry between the Youth Congress and the elder leadership of the Congress(R). This turned out to be a technical conflict between the organisational wing of the party and the parliamentary wing.

In 1970 C. Achutha Menon, the CPI leader resigned from the chief ministership and went for fresh elections to the legislative assembly. An alliance of different parties named as the United Front (UF) came into being. Congress (R) was also in this front. After the election Achutha Menon became the chief minister. Congress (R) with 32 MLA's supported the UF without joining the ministry initially. There were differences regarding the party's participation in the cabinet. The anti-Muslim League attitude of the Congress considerably changed during this period. The Youth Congress opposed the entry of Congress into the ministry. The Congress high command gave green signal for participation in the ministry. On 20 September, 1971, the Congress joined the ministry. K. Karunakaran, K.T. George, Vakkom Purushothaman and Vella Eacharan became ministers. When Congress joined the front ministry, A.K. Antony, the KPCC General Secretary became the Convener of the Liaison Committee to coordinate the UF activities (Abdul Azeez 1992:99).

In June 1975 internal emergency was clamped. Antony and Karunakaran visited Delhi to discuss the issue relating to the reported offer of Kerala Congress which enjoyed considerable support in certain pockets of the state to extend its co-operation to the ministry. The Pradesh Congress believed that the co-operation of the Kerala Congress would add to its strength particularly if an election was to be held soon. Antony and others in the KPCC who at one time were not enthusiastic about seeking the co-operation of Kerala Congress, now took the stand that it would be advantageous in the larger interest of the state to promote greater unity between the two parties (*The Hindu*:10-10-75). Thus Kerala Congress joined the UF. Later in the Delhi talks the organisational disputes were settled in the presence of Congress President D.K. Barooah. It was decided that the organisational and legislative wings of the party would regularly meet so that they have perfect co-ordination and complete harmony (*The Hindu* 14-10-75). The state cabinet was expanded by inducting the new Kerala Congress ministers. In the meantime the KPCC(O) President K.SankaraNarayanan and some of his supporters merged with the dominant Congress faction (*Kerala Kaumudi* :19-4-76).

As most of the internal problems in the KPCC were settled it was hoped that "Congress leadership in Kerala would follow the path of unity and discipline" (A.K Antony quoted in Mathrubhumi:7-6-76). Even in the midst of these declarations there were some souring points between the two groups. The most important was the attitude of the police towards Youth Congress and KSU activists, especially during the emergency period (John 1978:33). The selection of Congress candidates for the general election of 1977 also became a serious issue for dispute between the contending groups.

On 25 March, 1977 a new UF ministry headed by K. Karunakaran, the Congress leader, was sworn in. The Muslim League leader C.H Mohammed Koya, became the deputy chief minister. But the ministry led by K. Karunakaran was forced to resign in the light of the verdict in the Rajan Case. On 25 April 1977 K. Karunakaran submitted his resignation. After the resignation of K. Karunakaran, again a Congress ministry headed by A.K. Antony was sworn in on 25 April, 1977 (*Malayala Manorama*:26-4-77). Thus the parliamentary party leadership passed into the hands of the youth wing of the party soon. Antony resigned from the Presidentship of the KPCC. The convener of the ruling front, S. Varadarajan Nair was elected as President of the KPCC defeating C.M Stephen M P and member, CWC by a margin of thirteen votes (*The Hindu*:13-11-77). Karunakaran group attributed the defeat of its candidate C.M Stephen to interference by ministers belonging to other coalition parties.

During this period the Congress politics at the All India level was going through a tumultuous phase. Congressmen realised that many in the top leadership of the party lacked the courage to fight the Janata government. Consequently, an unofficial plenary session was called on 1 and 2 of January 1978 at the behest of Indira Gandhi to consider the whole issue. In this session, attended by a majority of AICC members and delegates with full voting rights, Indira Gandhi was unanimously requested to take over the Congress Presidentship. The split took place over the leadership question. This irritated the then Congress President Brahmananda Reddy which caused the expulsion of Indira Gandhi from the party. Indira Gandhi retaliated by becoming the President of the Congress (I) which claimed to truly represent the ethos of the

Indian National Congress. Brahmananda Reddy's interference in the organisational affairs of Karnataka, Andhra and Gujarat had already created sharp cleavages between the two camps (Zaidi 1981:334).

During this period, due to internal troubles the Janata Government at the centre collapsed. Indira Gandhi approached the rebel Janata leader Charan Singh and readily agreed to extend support to him to form a government. She played her cards well, she waited for the next election and in January 1980 she again occupied the Prime Ministers chair (Ram Gopal 1986:87).

The KPCC also split into two as a result of the split at the national level. The split divided the strength of the Congress in the parliament. In the state legislature the Congress(I) faction occupied the opposition benches along with other opposition parties. Karunakaran became the leader of the opposition in the Kerala Assembly while Congress (Reddy) under Antony's leadership remained in the government. Antony resigned from the chief ministership in protest when the Congress parliamentary board decided to support Indira Gandhi in the Chikkamaglore by-election in 1978. Thus P.K Vasudevan Nair, the CPI leader became the new chief minister of Kerala.

The pro-Indira supporters formed a parallel KPCC on 18 January, 1978 with K.M Chandy as President (Gopakumar 1984:107). The Pro-Indira supporters organised a parallel Youth Congress and KSU with Mullappally Ramachandran and G. Karthikeyan as Presidents. The Congress (Reddy) elected Devaraj Urs as its President at the national level. Though the Congress (U) wanted a leftist alternative to alienate Congress(I) and to defeat the rightist forces, it made a somersault by joining hands with Congress (I) to support a government headed by C.H.Mohammed Koya of the Muslim League. Meanwhile the Congress (U) was trying to reach an understanding with the CPI(M), CPI, Lok Dal and others at the national level to fight the Congress (I). This made the Congress (U) in Kerala led by Antony to withdraw their support to the Muslim League headed government and the party entered into an alliance with the CPI(M). The Cong (U), CPI(M), CPI, RSP, Muslim League (O) and the KC(M) elected K.M Mani as their leader and staked claims for the formation of a ministry. The governor accepted the advise of the chief minister and dissolved the Assembly. This paved the way for the formation of a new political front in Kerala.

The stage was set for the eventual emergence of two political combines – the United Democratic Front (UDF) consisting of the INC(I), the KC(J), the PSP, the NDP and the SRP, and the Left Democratic Front (LDF), comprising of the CPM, the CPI , INC(U), the KC(M), the KC(PG), the AIML and the RSP. The UDF had worked out seat adjustments with the Janata Party in a number of constituencies (Assembly Election Reportage 1996:11). In the 1980 Assembly and Lok Sabha elections held together in the state, the LDF came to power with a thumbing majority. The UDF got only 46 seats. Congress(I) became the chief opposition party in the Kerala Assembly with K. Karunakaran as its leader. The split of 1978 and the subsequent events at the national level and the state level made Karunakaran the undisputed leader of the Congress(I) in Kerala. The parliament election was in favour of Cong (I) and Indira Gandhi came back as the Prime Minister of India. In Kerala, five out of eleven Congress(I) candidates won and the party secured 26.06 per cent of the votes polled (Lok Sabha Election Reportage 1999:5).

In the 1980 Assembly and Lok Sabha elections, the Congress (U) under Antony which had by now become the Congress (S) joined the LDF in Kerala. The situation now was that the Congress (S) had to support and align with the communists and the communists had to take the support of, or owe their existence to the Congress (Madhavan Kutty 1998:33). The Congress(I) in Kerala became the mainstay of Karunakaran faction. The Congress(I) consistently carried the Muslim League and at least one faction of the Kerala Congress, the two trump cards in Malabar and Travancore with it (Gopakumar 1986:57).

The relationship between the Marxist party and Antony group did not last long. The Antony faction withdrew its support to the government in October 1981. After few days KC(M) also decided to withdraw its support following which the Nayanar ministry resigned on 20 Oct 1981. After the resignation of the Nayanar ministry an eight member ministry was formed by K. Karunakaran on 28 December 1981 (*The Indian Express*: 29-12-81). The UDF ministry was supported by the Congress faction under the leadership of Antony and the KC(M). When Lonappan Nambadan the KC(M) legislator defected from the ruling front, the ministry had to resign on 15 March 1982 (*Kerala Kaumudi*: 16-3-1982). Political events took a full circle with the Congress under Antony coming back to the democratic camp represented by the UDF.

It is by now accepted that factional tendency is a growing phenomenon within the party system. It affects all democratic as well as cadre political parties. While analysing the pre 1982 factionalism in the Congress party, it is evident that factional tendencies had a domineering presence through out its history. Since its formation up to the present, factionalism made its presence in the party in different forms. At the All India level prior to independence factions emerged based on the ideological divide. Balagangadhara Tilak and Gokhale were the champions of the extremist and moderate concepts. In the 1920's the ideological divide brought into existence the Left and the Right factions within the party. Nehru and Subhash Chandra Bose were the champions of the leftist orientation of the Congress. Sardar Patel and others were on the other side. Even Gandhi was helpless in dealing with the factional fights in the party. The birth of the congress socialist party and other political parties can be cited as examples. Personal considerations, lust for power, differences in approach, and ideological differences were the factors that influenced the formation of factions during the pre-independence period.

Nehruvian period also witnessed factional feuds. But the charismatic leadership of Nehru survived everything. The introduction of the Kamaraj Plan was a type of settlement to deal with factional problems. Lal Bahadur Sastri followed the policy of consensus through mutual discussion and consultations and thus overcame such tendencies. Through stern decisions and hierarchical structuring of the party system Indira Gandhi controlled the party machinery and the government in an autocratic way.

Rajiv Gandhi followed the policies of his mother, but challenges were emerging from many quarters to his leadership. During Narasimha Rao's leadership of the party, the position of the central leadership weakened as never before. Now Sonia Gandhi is finding it extremely difficult to put the Congress house in order. Factionalism is at its peak in all the states. The post independence period saw factionalism at its worst since it was totally devoid of any ideological underpinnings as subsequent developments revealed.

The Kerala situation was not different from that of the other states. In the pre-independence period, regional, linguistic and caste oriented factions were in existence. The post independence scene witnessed the emergence of factions craving for power which contributed to ministerial instability and the resignation of prominent leaders from the party. Factionalism in the Congress party in Kerala also resulted in the emergence of new regional and communal parties. During the late 1960's and the 1970's the student and youth wings became a force to be reckoned within the Congress party. Indira Gandhi's pro-socialist programmes in the aftermath of the 1969 split attracted them. The youth and student movement brought to the forefront of Kerala politics a committed group of youngsters like A.C Jose, Vayalar Ravi, A.K Antony, Kadannapally Ramachandran, V.M Sudheeran etc. The party elders led by Karunakaran worked systematically to strengthen the base of the party by forming an alliance with the anti-communist parties and groups since it was the CPI(M) which was the major threat to the party's designs in Kerala. The strenuous work of both these sections laid the foundation for a vigorous and active phase in the Congress party's advance in Kerala in the 1970's. The concept of faction during the 1960's and 1970's centered on the age factor as they were known as elders and youngsters. But it was not generational difference that alone caused the formation of factions at that time. Other factors like lust for power, personal rivalry, differences in the style of functioning, differences in ideological perception etc also characterised this phase of Congress factionalism. How it reached its zenith in the post 1982 period is discussed in the next chapter.

References

Abdul Azeez (1992): *Rise of Muslims in Kerala Politics*, Thiruvananthapuram, CBH.

Abdur Rahiman K.K (1964): *Kerala Congress Directory*, Ernakulam, Crescent Publication

Acharya Kripalani J B (1948): *The Future of the Congress*, Bombay, Hind Kitabs Ltd.

Alexander P.C (1991): *My Days with Indira Gandhi*, New Delhi, Vision Books.

Alexander P.C (1995): *The Perils of Democracy*, Bombay, Somaiyya Publication.

Asok Metha (1979): *A Decade of Indian Politics 1966-77*, New Delhi, S. Chand & Co.

Attar Chand (1991): *Prime Minister P V Narasimha Rao: The Scholar and Statesman* , New Delhi, Gian Publishing House.

Balakrishnan Nair A (1996): *Landmarks in the Administration of Kerala*, Thiruvananthapuram, IIPA Regional Branch.

Baker Christopher John (1976): *The Politics of South India*, New Delhi, Vikas.

Bakshi S.R (1985): *Nehru and Congress: The Emergence of New Ideology*, New Delhi, Criterion.

Bakshi S.R (1994): *EMS Namboothiripad*, New Delhi, Anmol publishers.

Barnett Marguerite Ross and others (1975): *Electoral Politics in the Indian States: Party Systems and Cleavages*, New Delhi, Manohar Book Service.

Basant Chatterjee (Undated): *The Congress Splits*, New Delhi, S. Chand & Com.

Bhagat K.P (1962): *The Kerala Mid Term Election of 1960*, Bomaby, Popular Book Depot.

Bhat Nagar S. & Pradeep Kumar (1988): *Regional Political Parties in India*, New Delhi, Ess Ess Publications.

Bipan Chandra, Auditya Mukherjee & Mridula Mukherjee, (ed) (1999): *India Since Independence*, New Delhi, Viking.

Brass R. Paul (1975): *Language Religion and Politics in North India*, New Delhi, Vikas.

Brecher Michael (1966): *Succession in India: A study in Decision Making*, London, Oxford.

Carras Mary (1972): *The dynamics of Indian Political Factions: A study of District Councils in the State of Maharashtra*, Cambridge, Cambridge University Press.

Chopra P.N, Ramgopal, M L Bhargava (1986): *A Century of Indian National Congress*, New Delhi, Agam Prakasam.

Dhar P.N (2000): *Indira Gandhi, The Emergency and Indian democracy*, New Delhi, Oxford.

Douglas Tom (1979): *Group Processes in Social Work: A Theoretical Analysis*, U.K, John Wiley & Sons.

Fic M Victor (1970): *Kerla: Yenan of India, Rise of Communist Power 1937-1969*, Bombay, Nachiketa Publications.

Franda Marcus M(1979): *Small is Politics: Organisational Alternatives in India's Rural Development*, New Delhi, Wiley Eastern.

Gajarani. S (1998): *Sonia Gandhi: President of AICC*, New Delhi, APH.

Gandhi M.K (1999): *Congress and Its Future*, Ahmedabad, Navajeevan Trust.

Gopakumar. G (1980): *The Congress Party in Kerala Since 1967* (PhD Thesis), Trivandrum, Department of Politics, University of Kerala.

Girija K.Mookerjee (1974), *History of Indian National Congress*, Meerut, Meenakshi Prakasam.

Girija Sankar (1995): *A History of the Congress Socialist Party*, Jodhpur, Twenty First Century Publishers.

Hardgrave L. Robert (1975): *India: Government and Politics in a Developing Nation*, Princeton, Princeton University Press.

Haridwar Rai & Jawaharlal Pandey (1997): "Intra Party Democracy: The Experience of the Indian National Congress" In Verinder Grover (Ed) *Political Parties and Party System*, New Delhi, Deep & Deep.

Harihara Das (1998): *Political System of India*, New Delhi, Anmol Publications.

Hemachandran M.K (1997): *Ente Kazhinjakalam* (M), Kottayam, D C Books.

Hill L. John (1991): (ed) *The Congress and Indian Nationalism*, London, Curzon Press.

Jayachandran T.N (2000): *Kerala 2000*, Thiruvananthapuram, State Institute of Languages

Jayadevan N (1999): *Student Movement and Kerala Politics from 1956-80* (PhD Thesis), Trivandrum, Department of Politics, University of Kerala.

Jayaraj D (1977): *Democratic Governments in Kerala 1957-70* (PhD Thesis), Trivandrum, Department of Politics, University of Kerala.

Johari J.C (1997): "Young Turks and Radicalisation of Politics" In Verinder Grover (ed) *Political Parties and Party Systems*, New Delhi, Deep & Deep.

John K.C (1975): *Melting Pot: Kerala 1950's-1970's*, Trivandrum, Mudralaya Quality Printers, Thycaud.

John P. John (1983): *Coalition Governments in Kerala*, Trivandrum, Institute for the Study of Public Policy and Management.

Joseph Vadakkan Fr. (1974): *Ente Kuthippum Kithappum* (M) Autobiography, Kottayam, New man Publishers.

Kamal K L, Ralph C Meyer (1977): *Democratic Politics in India*, New Delhi, Vikas.

Kaushik P D (1986): *The Congress Ideology and Programme 1920-1985*, New Delhi, Gitanjali Publishers.

Keraleeyan V. S (1969): *Keralathinte Veera Puthran* (M), Kozhikode.

Kochanek A Stanley (1968): *The Congress Party in India: Dynamics Of One Party Dominance*, Princeton: Princeton University Press.

Kovoor E.M (1965): *T.M Varghese* (M), Kottayam NBS

Madhavan Kutty V. K (1998): *The Southern Discomfort*, New Delhi, Har Anand.

Mahendra Prasad Singh (1981): *Split in a Predominant Party: The Indian National Congress in 1969*, New Delhi, Abinav Publication.

Mahendru K.C (1984): *Gandhi and the Congress Socialist Party 1934-38: An Analysis of their Interaction*, Jalandhur: ABS Publication.

Mankekar D.R (1964): *Red Riddle in Kerala*, Bombay, Manakthala and Son.

Manor James (1997): "Parties and Party System", In Partha Chatterjee (ed) *State and Politics in India*, New Delhi, Oxford.

Mayer P.B(1987): "Development and Demise", in Jim Masselos (ed) *Struggling and Ruling: The Indian National Congress 1885-1985*, New Delhi, Sterling

Meenakshi Jain (1991): *The Congress Party (1967-77): Role of Caste in Indian Politics*, New Delhi, Vikas.

Nageswar Prasad (1980): *Ideology and Organisation in Indian Politics: A Study of Political Parties at the Grass Roots*, New Delhi, Allied.

Namboodiripad EMS(1984): *Kerala Society and Politics: An Historical Survey*, New Delhi, National Book Agency.

Narang A.S (1985): *Indian Government and Politics*, New Delhi, Gitanjali Publishing House.

Nayanar E.K (1982): *My Struggles: An Autobiography*, New Delhi, Vikas Publishing House.

Nossiter T.J (1982):*Communism in Kerala:A study in Political Adaptation*, New Delhi, Oxford.

Om P.Gautam (1985): *The Indian National Congress; An Analytical Bibliography*, New Delhi, B.R Publishing Corporation.

Pande B.N (1985): *The Concise History of Indian National Congress (1885-1947)*, New Delhi, Congress Centenary Committee.

Pande B.N (1989): *Indira Gandhi*, New Delhi, Govt. of India Publication Division.

Pattabhi Sitaramayya (1935): *The History of Indian National Congress*, Vol.I (1885-1935), Bombay, Padma Publications.

Pattabhi Sitaramayya (1947): *The History of Indian National Congress*, Vol.II (1935-1947), Bombay, Padma Publications.

Perunna K.N Nair (1967): *Keralathile Congress Prasthanam* (M), Thrissur, Current Books.

Prasannan R. (2000): *Adiyandhravasthayude Alayolikal: Niyama Sabhayil Nisabdanayi* Part II (M), Thrissur, Current Books.

Puthupally Raghavan (1996): *Viplava Smaranakal*: Part V (M), Kottayam, DCB.

Rahman M.M (1970): *The Congress Crisis*, New Delhi, Associated Publishing House.

Rajni Kothari (1989): *Politics and the People: In Search of Humane India* Vol.I, New Delhi, Ajanta Publication.

R.K.G (2000): *India A Nation in Turmoil*, New Delhi, UBSPD.

Ramachandran S. (2000): *P. Balan: Thalaratha Porali*, (M), Kottayam, Current Books.

Ramakrishnan Nair. R (1964): *How the Communist came to Power in Kerala*, Trivandrum, Kerala Academy of Political Science.

Ramesh Kumar (1994): *Congress and Congressism in Indian Politics*, New Delhi, Deep & Deep.

Ram Gopal (1986): *India Under Indira*, New Delhi, Criterion Publication.

Ruijter Arie De (1998): *The Purse and the Power: Aspects of Centre State Relations in India*, New Delhi, B.R Publishing Corporation.

Sahgal Nayantara (1978): *Indira Gandhi's Emergence and Style*, New Delhi, Vikas.

Sanker Ghose (1975): *Indian National Congress: Its History and Heritage*, New Delhi, AICC.

Scalapino A Robert & Junno Suke Masumi (1971): *Parties and Politics in Contemporary Japan*, USA, University of California Press.

Sadasivan S.N (1977): *Party and Democracy in India*, New Delhi, Tata McGraw Hill.

Sankara Pillai T.P (1969): *Democracy in Kerala and Pattom A. ThanuPillai*, Trivandrum, Mahatma Printing, Thycaud.

Sethi J.D (1975): *India in Crisis*, New Delhi, Vikas Publishing House.

Sood P (1981): *Re emergence of Indira Gandhi*, New Delhi, S. Chand & Comp.

Sreedhara Menon A (1987): *A Concise History of Kerala (1885-1957)*, Madras, S.Viswanathan Publishing Com.

Subhash C.Kashyap (1971): *Indian Political Parties: Programmes, Promises and Performance*, New Delhi, Research Publication in Social Sciences.

Suresh K. Tameri (1971): *The Wonder elections 1971: Indira Versus the Right*, New Delhi, Vivek Publishing House.

Tope T.K (1986): *Bombay and the Congress Movement*, Bombay: Maharashtra State Board of Literature and Culture.

Valsarajan V.K (1971): *The Congress Split in Kerala 1969*, (Dissertation), Trivandrum, Department of Politics, University of Kerala.

Verinder Grover (1997): *Political Parties and Party system*, New Delhi, Deep & Deep.

Weiner Myron, & Ashuthosh Varshney (1989): *Indian Paradox: Essays in Indian Politics*, New Delhi, Sage.

Wood Cock George (1967): *Kerala: A Portrait of Malabar*, London, Faber & Faber.

Wood R. John (1984): *State Politics in Contemporary India,* USA, West View Press.

Yamuna Devi. S (1998): *The Nair Service Society and Kerala Politics Since 1970- A Study,* (PhD Thesis), Thiruvananthapuram, Dept. of Politics, Uty. of Kerala.

Yogendra Malik K. & Asok Kapur (1998): *India: Fifty years of Democracy and Development,* New Delhi, APH.

Zaidi A.M (1984): *Aloud and Straight: Frank Talks at Party Meetings,* New Delhi, Indian Institute of Applied Political Research.

Three

Congress Factionalism in Kerala Since 1982: Causes, Issues and Events

This chapter analyses the causes, issues and events providing momentum to the factional dynamics in the state Congress organisation and explores how it has contributed to the continuity and relevance of the party in Kerala. In the assembly elections held on 19 May 1982, the UDF won 77 seats but its effective strength was 76[1]. K. Karunakaran was elected as the leader of the UDF and assumed office as chief minister on 24 May 1982. The UDF coalition comprised of national, regional and communal parties[2]. Soon the remarkable event of reunion of the two Congress factions took place in Kerala (Krishna Kumari 1994:151). This brought together the two major Congress parties in Kerala on a single platform to effectively compete with the LDF. Despite the merger of 'A' Congress into the Cong (I) and the unity declarations, the two groups namely the Karunakaran group and the Antony group continued to exist in the Congress. With the reunion a new type of factionalism emerged in the Congress party.

Events and issues associated with the politics of Congress factionalism are not discussed separately since they take a dual role as the 'cause' and 'effect' of the factional phenomena. So events and issues are dealt with in a chronological order as far as possible under the five major causes identified in this chapter. In other words they lie scattered under the five sub heads dealing with the causes of factionalism. The causes and issues seem to be the two sides of the same coin as far as the Congress party in Kerala is concerned. These are discussed in the following pages centering around five major causes as well as issues connected with Congress factionalism, namely; the nature of the party, the UDF and the leadership role of the Congress, personal factors, indiscipline and public statements and the weakening of the high command.

1. Nature of the Party

As the fifth and sixth chapters empirically examine the nature of Congress factionalism in Kerala in its entirety, here we look only into those essential aspects of the Congress party's organisational structure and the resultant behavioural pattern that by itself promotes factional tendencies.

As a political organisation the Congress is matchless in the contemporary world (Chopra 1988:VII). Kochanek expresses the view that "the Indian National Congress has been one of the most successful of the nationalist movements of Asia and Africa" (Stanley A Kochanek 1968: XIX). In fact the Congress had possessed a mixed character, with a particular trait predominating during a particular period (Om P Gautham 1985:347).

The first cause of factionalism lies in the very nature of the party. Members having divergent views and interests – caste, class, communal, regional and linguistic – constitute the membership of the Congress party in Kerala. Groupism is a reality (*Kalakaumudi* 6.11.1983) that provides dynamism to the party organisation at all levels. It activates the group loyalists. During the 1980's Congress factionalism in Kerala was bi-factional (*Kalakaumudi* 17.11.1983). After the merger the Antony supporters remained dissatisfied under the leadership of Karunakaran. They felt that they were not getting fair treatment from the Congress led coalition government. Naturally the new found unity and co-operation failed to take off. Conflicts between the rival group leaders were mainly personal in nature rather than ideological or organisational (Krishnakumari 1994: 154). The two major groups ensured that they have enough supporters among all castes, communities, class organisations and mass organisations. They made it a point to recruit loyalists from all these sections [3].

The following table reveals that different factions in the party enjoy the support of all the three major communities. A look into the communal composition of the executive Kerala Pradesh Congress Committee (KPCC) from 1982 onwards will reveal this. The KPCC Executive consists of persons recommended by different factions. As such they are in a position to provide adequate representation to all groups.

TABLE NO: 1
THE COMMUNAL COMPOSITION (IN PERCENTAGE) OF THE KPCC EXECUTIVE SINCE 1982

Year and President	*Religion*		
	Hindus %	*Christians* %	*Muslims* %
1982 A L Jacob (Nominated)	52.94	29.41	17.65
1983 C.V Padmarajan (Nominated)	54.84	29.03	16.13
1987 A.K Antony (Nominated)	59.73	25.5	14.77
1992 Vayalar Ravi (Elected) (*)	55.72	25.71	18.57
1998 Thennala BalakrishnaPillai (nominated)	55.17	27.59	17.24
2001 K.Muraleedharan (Nominated)	57.78	22.22	20.00

(*) It was in 1992 that the Congress party conducted its organisational election after a long period. In this election Vayalar Ravi defeated his one time close associate Antony as the nominee of the 'I' group. (See appendix No. I for the details).

The composition of the KPCC executive at different periods reflects some what the demographic structure of Kerala society. The plural pattern of representation characterises the party organisation as a whole. The party had successfully adapted itself to the specific socio-political context of Kerala from the very beginning because of its flexible approach to the emerging realities. The members of the KPCC are not constituted as corporate and cohesive elite. They are divided into distinct factions that have contested for control over strategic positions within the party organisation at all levels. This struggle also characterises the KPCC executive committee, which is the central focus of decision making and power in the party organisation.

(a) Organisational election

As the general secretary of the AICC Rajiv Gandhi realised that non conduct of organisational elections was the real cause of the party's sickness. The only way to revitalise the party was through decentralisation. He asserted that party elections would be the first step towards decentralisation. The only way the party could regain its full strength was through organisational elections (Bhabani Sen Gupta 1989:13). Later in 1984 when he became the Prime Minister and President of the Congress party he boldly declared that 'we are having party elections next year' (ibid:80). Eventually he was also compelled by circumstances to proceed without a strong Congress organisation. He had spurned a clear opportunity to make radical changes in the party (James Manor 1997:124).

Rajiv Gandhi's handling of the Congress (I) party affairs proved to be a chain of political misjudgment and errors. When Rajiv Gandhi purged Pranab Kumar Mukherjee and Gundu Rao, and neutralised Kamalapathi Tripathi, it was reminiscent of Nehru's purge of P.D Tandon and perhaps, Indira Gandhi's purge of Morarji Desai (Lloyd l. Rudolph :98). The tussle for power between the working president Kamalapathi Tripathi and Arjun Singh, meant further enfeebling the party organisation which was now split vertically between two factions. Arjun Singh cleverly and skillfully pushed himself to the forefront as he was the crucial link between the party's inaccessible President and its workers. A.K Antony was nominated as the KPCC President to rejuvenate the organisation in Kerala to face the incoming 1989 parliament elections. The scandal over the kick backs from the purchase of Bofors guns from Sweden and submarines from West Germany greatly contributed to the declining popularity of the Prime Minister. The resignation of V.P Singh from the Central cabinet in 1987 resulted in further erosion of his popularity (Bhabhani Sen Gupta 1989:169).

In the 1989 elections, V.P Singh's image as 'New Mr. Clean' posed a big threat to Rajiv Gandhi. Though he tried his best to paint V.P Singh as a traitor in the Bofors controversy the latter could easily unseat him from power (Subratha Mukherjee 2000:113). The National Front government of V.P Singh was in fact a continuation of the earlier Janata Dal experiment. For Rajiv the transition from Primeminister to leader of opposition was not painful (Minhaz Merchant 1991:265). Rajiv Gandhi admitted that it was one of the greatest failures of his five years in office not to have reformed the party and inculcated his own modernist values into this centenarian organisation (Nicholas Negent 1991:158).

After Rajiv Gandhi's tragic death in 1991 P.V Narasimha

Rao, a Congress stalwart with a long career in politics and government emerged as the leader. Senior leaders of the party reconciled to the choice of Rao as interim president and felt that he represented the Nehru-Indira- Rajiv tradition in political and economic thinking as he is a staunch Congressman whose loyalty has never been in doubt (Attarchand 1991:6). Thus Narasimha Rao became the first South Indian to be sworn in as Primeminister of India (Mani Sankara Iyer 1993:269).

Manipulations in the party came to the fore when Rao proceeded with his plan to democratise the party. The Congress membership usually increases during organisational polls and general elections and registers a decrease during other times. At the time of the Lok Sabha election of 1967 the number of primary members in the party stood at 17,347,043 and that of active members 332,081. In 1992 the Congress primary membership rose to 2.5 crores and the active membership to ten lakhs (Ramesh Kumar 1994:138).

Inspite of strict rules regarding the membership, frequent complaints about bogus membership are often raised. The district level committees of the party are supposed to keep membership lists and the Pradesh committees have the power to examine the lists from time to time. The factional infightings among rival groups at the district and state levels have made the membership issue more acute today than it was before. When the two factions led by Arjun Singh and Sharad Pawar apparently came together to win most of the elective posts in the CWC at the Tirupati Plenary session, Rao upstaged this majority through methods dubbed as anti-democratic (Nagendra Reddy 1993:169).

During the early months of 1992, elections to the PCC's were held. The elections to the PCC's were not smooth. Factionalism raised its head in almost all states. The rival groups fought bitterly for the office of the party chief in each state. Some of the examples were: Somen Mitra vs. Priyaranjan Das Munshi in West Bengal, Jagannath Misra vs. Siddeswar Prasad in Bihar, Nilangekar vs. Deshmukh in Maharshtra and Vayalar Ravi vs. Antony in Kerala.

Organisational elections which were held after a period of two decades were not free and fair. The election rules were flouted and the procedures not followed. The fact was that Congress members were hardly prepared for the organisational elections.

As indicated in the previous chapter, in the 1977 KPCC Presidential election, Antony's nominee the late S.Varadarajan Nair had defeated Karunakran's nominee, the late C.M Stephen[4]. In the post merger politics of the Congress party in Kerala, Karunakaran tightened his control over the party organisation.

A significant feature of the 1992 organisational polls was that though new faces appeared at the district levels, yet at the Pradesh level leadership largely remained unchanged. The status quoists continued to dominate the PCC's. New entrants remained marginal in strength. Though the democratisation of the party could hardly be achieved, yet the herculean task of holding the organisation election was completed.

Both the groups in Kerala engaged in election propaganda. Antony declared, that he did not want to seek, re-election as the President of the KPCC (*Indian express* 27.11.1991). Later he changed his mind when "some people wanted to capture the organisation for themselves with the help of the government which all of us have made possible" (*Indian Express* 11.12.1991). He added that the fight in the state Congress party is quite different from other states where it was either the PCC president trying to become the chief minister or some MLA's aspiring Cabinet berths. Here it is rather a clash of two styles of functioning[5]. In his opinion he was sure that the present phase of mutual distrust and criticisms will end as soon as the organisational elections are over. Oommen Chandy also expressed more or less the same view while inaugurating a district convention of the Antony faction leaders. He said that the practice of nomination has weakened the party. The party leadership should have a close relationship with the rank and file after the elections (ibid).

The organisational elections in Kerala adversely affected the personal relationships among the leaders. A staunch supporter and onetime close associate of Antony decided to contest against him. In the election Vayalar Ravi, representing the Karunakaran faction defeated Antony by a margin of eighteen votes. An executive committee consisting of eighteen members was constituted and all of them were Karunakaran loyalists. Later the committee was expanded on the basis of an understanding between the groups. Another committee was also constituted by the KPCC to look into the problems connected with the organisational elections. The Antony group even demanded an enquiry by a party committee into the police high- handedness in the organisational election. Karunakaran faction scored a runway victory in 11 out of 14 districts. Elections to Thrissur and Kottayam District Committees were postponed due to severe problems. Later the Antony faction won the control of the Kottayam District Congress Committee and the Karunakaran faction wrested the Thrissur DCC. Factionalism reached its peak and Antony said that he could not consider Karunakaran as his leader (*Malayala Manorama* 16-2-1992).

The Suraj Kund meeting of the AICC passed a resolution enabling the offices of the Congress President and the Prime Minister to be presided over by one person (Ralhan 1996:3996). The position of the Prime Minister and the Congress President was never challenged. The power struggle in the Congress party took a decisive turn with the suspension of Arjun Singh from the primary membership of the party. Subsequently some of the senior members of the party namely N.D Tiwari, Madhava Rao Scindia and K. Moopanar left the party and formed their own regional parties. Following a number of allegations and criminal cases the popularity of the Prime Minister declined. In the Parliament elections of 1996 the Congress party under Narasimha Rao lost. By this time Karunakaran had already fallen out with Rao (Narasimha Rao 1998:767).

On September 1996 Kesari succeeded Rao as the Congress President. Antony backed Kesari after realising the ground reality. Congressmen hoped to replace Kesari in the next round (India Today 15th October, 1996:63). In March 1997 the Congress organisational election was due. That was when the party chief's post came for grabs. Later Sitaram Kesari was elected as the President with a thumbing majority (*Hindu* 13-6-1997).

Congress held a three day plenary session at Calcutta on 8 August, 1997. This session elected the members of the CWC (*Malayala Manorama* 11.8.1997). Because of the fall of the National Front headed ministry another round of Parliamentary election was due. For the first time since independence Congress went to the Polls without a recognised leader or a slogan. In the absence of a clear cut political and economic programme, Kesari first announced that secularism would be the party's main plank (India Today 12-1997:23). During the election campaign Sonia Gandhi entered into active politics. There was a move to remove the Congress President Sitaram Kesari, who was by now considered a big liability for the party. Kesari's tenure witnessed a steady erosion of the party's morale and there was no way he could have continued in that place for long. Pressure mounted from all quarters, and ultimately on 14 March 1998, the CWC exercised special powers and removed Sitaram Kesari from the office of the President of the Congress party and Sonia Gandhi became the President. On 16 March, 1998, Sonia Gandhi formally took over as Congress Parliamentary Party chief. The Congress constitution was amended and Sharad Pawar was appointed the party's leader in Lok Sabha and ManMohan Singh in the Rajya Sabha (Janak RaiJai and Rajiv Rai 1999:24). Sonia's efforts to revitalise Congress received acceptance at the Panchamarhi conclave in September 1998. There was criticism at the Panchmarhi session that the Congress leadership was trying to capture power in alliance with the left parties (*Kalakaumudi* 20-9-1998).

In the meantime factional conflict again broke out in the Congress party. Factionalism was nothing but a reflection of individual or group ambition. Three CWC members openly expressed their reservations about the advisability of projecting Sonia Gandhi as the Prime Ministerial candidate because of her foreign origin (Yogesh Atal 2000:64). Sonia Gandhi cleverly confronted her adversaries through resignation. The three were expelled from the party and then Sonia reoccupied her party position. In the ensuing organisational election inner party democracy was the casualty (*The Hindu* 29-10-2000). In the election held to the post of the party President the congressmen gave a thumbing mandate to Sonia Gandhi with 7448 out of 7712 voting in her favour. Her challenger Jitendra Prasad could muster only 94 votes (*Indian express* 16-11-2000). Thus Sonia again became the elected President of the Congress Party.

In this road show of the organisational election the four groups in the Cong (I) in Kerala vied with each other in supporting Sonia. Only a few congressmen from Kerala had voting right due to the failure of the state party to elect AICC members. None in

Kerala was in favour of Jitendra Prasad, who contested to the post of Party President. This raised suspicion among the ordinary congressmen and the opposition parties about the democratic nature of the party.

(b) System of nomination

The end of Nehru era and the process of succession had resulted in the emergence of a collective leadership in the Congress and a decision making process based on consensus. Unlike the centralised pattern under Nehru, the period from 1963-1969 was marked by divergence of views and opinions freely expressed. Lal Bahadur Sastri, had shown a decision making style and temperament that was well suited to the new circumstances (Stanley A Kochanek 2002:77). His successor Indira Gandhi as the new Prime Minister was unwilling to accept the restraints imposed on the Prime Minsiter by the party leadership. The result has been six years of conflict, factional intrigue, and the first major split at the national level since independence. During her struggle for the control of the party and government from 1966 to 1972, Indira Gandhi had challenged every major institutional structure in India, including the central cabinet, the Presidency, the courts, the office of the President of the Congress party, the working committee of the Congress and the chief minister's of states.

The new political process which Indira Gandhi inaugurated, however, proved to be more centralised and personalised and less institutional than Nehru's (ibid:78). It involved an unprecedented centralisation of power in party and government with the Prime Minister at the top of the decision making pyramid. Indira Gandhi made a major effort to modify the federal character of the party and government by strengthening the unitarian tendencies and thereby reinforcing the centralisation of power. She changed the support base of the Congress from above by recruiting unrepresented sections of the society into party organisation and into legislative bodies. The method she adopted was the system of nomination rather than the democratic device of free and fair modes of election.

In order to attain control over the party she had to ensure control over the appointment of the working committee, the parliamentary board, and the central election committee. Collectively, these functionally distinct organs of the party composed of inter- locking and overlapping personnel of the Congress high command. With the energising of these party organs, Indira Gandhi directively intervene in the affairs of the state and district party organisation by adopting a scheme of nominations[6].

Having experienced considerable difficulty in her relations with two of the former Presidents of the Congress party, she herself took over the position of the party President during the time of the split in 1978 (Haridwar Rai and Jawaharlal Pandey 1971:431). She also made sure that only her trusted lieutenants were named to the important posts, and that no one would remain in the position long enough to build an independent base of power[7]. She even started nominating congress chief ministers who were then ratified in office by the state congress legislative party. Although the state congress legislative parties and PCC's dutifully endorsed their new leaders unanimously, they deeply resented the imposition from above.

In the Congress unit in Kerala also the post-merger phase saw the emergence of problems caused by nominations. At the time of the merger of the Antony faction into the Congress (I) led by Karunakaran which had the backing of the National Congress (I) leadership, K.M Chandy was the President of Congress (I) in the state. After the elevation of K.M Chandy as Lt. Governor, K.G Adiyodi the then Vice President of the KPCC wanted to be elevated as the chief of the KPCC. But going by the practice of nomination, the AICC appointed A.L Jacob as KPCC President (*Mathrubhoomi* 14-10-1982). There was a strong group under the leadership of Mullappaly Ramachandran, the Youth Congress(I) President, opposed to chief minister K. Karunakaran. That resulted in the nomination of G. Karthikeyan as the YC(I) President (*Kerala Kaumudi* 31-7-1982). The student wing of the party, the KSU, was also reconstituted in the same way[8]. All the DCC's were reconstituted as an after effect of the merger process. When the central cabinet was reshuffled in January 1983 C.M Stephen was avoided and was nominated the general secretary of the AICC. When C.M Stephen expired on 15 January 1984 Indira Gandhi nominated A.K Antony as one of the general secretaries.

When Karunakaran reshuffled the government in 1983, the KPCC President A.L Jacob, N. Sundaran Nadar and P.K. Velayudhan were inducted to the Ministry (Sreedhar Pillai 1983:38). C.V Padmarajan who belonged to the Karunakaran group was to be the new KPCC chief[9]. According to the chief minister, the changes were made for the sake of finding a young and energetic President for the KPCC (*The Hindu* 26-8-83). It was followed by a deliberate move on the part of Karunakaran to sideline the Antony faction in the KSU and YC. Soon P.T Thomas of the 'A' faction was replaced as KSU President by Joseph Vazhakkan and AIYCC(I) general secretary Ramesh Chennithala of the Karunakaran group was nominated as the KPYCC President.

The infighting in the KSU continued. Two groups of students came to blows in front of the secretariat (*The Sunday* 1985:12). The nomination of a Karunakaran follower Sarat Chandra Prasad as KSU(I) chief created further tensions in Congress politics. When Rajiv Gandhi was unanimously elected as President by the CWC, A.K Antony continued as the AICC general secretary and Karunakaran was nominated as member of the CWC and congress parliamentary board (CPB). The KPCC chief Padmarajan continued till the nomination of A.K. Antony as the new President (*Indian Express* 8-9-87). Antony continued as the President of the KPCC till the organisational election in 1991 when Vayalar Ravi was elected as the President of the KPCC. During this period Congress factionalism in the state acquired new dimension with the entry of a third group. This group known as the 'Thiruthalvadikal' was formerly Karunakaran loyalists. They became a disgruntled lot as they felt that they were being sidelined for making the entry to Karunakaran's son K.Muraleedharan into state politics a smooth affair. On 5 June, 1998 Vayalar Ravi left the office of the KPCC President, a post he held for six years; to make way for a nominated adhoc substitute, Thennala Balakrishna Pillai (Frontline 18-31 July 1998:20). K.C Venugopal, of the III group and J. Joseph belonging to the Antony group continued as Presidents of the YC and KSU respectively [10].

K. Muraleedharan, the Vice President of the KPCC and son of K. Karunakaran replaced Thennala Balakrishna Pillai as the KPCC chief on 17 May 2001. The appointment was facilitated by the incumbent Thennala Balakrishna Pillai's resignation at the behest of the AICC which came in the form of a direction from the

AICC General secretary Gulam Nabi Azad (*The Hindu* 18.5.2001). Due to intense factionalism KPYCC President K C Venugopal resigned from the post after getting direction from the party high command. The KSU President also resigned on May 2001. Both these posts were filled by nominating K.P Anil Kumar of the third group and P.C Vishnunath of the 'A' group (*The Hindu* 15-7-2002). Shanimol Usman of the (I) group replaced Savithri Lakshmanan of the same group in the post of the President of the Mahila Congress by way of nomination.

These nominations however failed to satisfy the groups in the party as is evident from the statements of the leaders belonging to different groups (*Deshabhimani* 15-7-2002). In their responses too, the party office bearers at various levels disapproved the practice of nomination as is seen in following table.

TABLE NO:2
THE ATTITUDE OF THE RESPONDENTS TO THE PRACTICE OF NOMINATIONS BY THE HIGH COMMAND

Position Held	*Whether approve/disapprove*		*Total*
	Approved	*Disapproved*	
DCC President	2	12	14
DCC Secretary	6	33	39
DCC Member	9	22	31
Block President	4	30	34
Block Secretary	4	22	26
Mandalam President	8	30	38
Mandal Secretary	9	24	33
Activists	60	248	308
Others	50	92	142
Total	152	513	665

Those who responded to this question included all the DCC Presidents in the state. But among the other categories this observation is based on the feedback of only those respondents who were selected for answering the questionnaire by the researcher in accordance with the purpose of the study. As such the observations are based on a sample study of the collected data.

The table shows that 513 respondents out of 665 are against the practice of nomination to party posts by the high command. Twelve respondents were unwilling to express their opinion.

Despite the opposition of 77.14% of the Congressmen, the practice still continues resulting in the emergence new factions and frequent shifts in old loyalties as the faction leaders find it difficult to satisfy the old loyalists all the time in the ever changing political contexts and the emerging new equations. Naturally, factional conflicts gets more and more complicated as old time mates try to outmanoeuvre each other through manipulations and by striking new equations.

(C) Candidate selection and elections upto 2001

The Congress party is organised and managed through its units pyramidically arranged. At the national level, the AICC has the power to frame rules relating to the organisational matters which are binding on all the lower units of the party. The AICC has the power to lay down the guidelines for the functioning of the party (Constitution of the INC& Rules: Article XIII:41-47). The Congress working committee (CWC) is the chief decision making body. It consists of twenty members including the President. The CWC possesses a great deal of power. The parliamentary board is another important organ of the Congress. The group interests prevent the PCC's from nominating the commonly accepted candidates. A central election committee (CEC) shall be set up consisting of members of the parliamentary board and nine other members elected by the AICC (ibid:78). The PCC's are authorised to constitute such election committees (Ibid Article XXXV (b)). The CEC intervenes to avoid issues in the processing of nomination of candidates to the various parliamentary bodies.

The nomination of candidates is a very crucial stage in gearing up the party to face the polls. Half of the electoral battle is won, if a candidate is nominated properly by a political party. It is therefore not surprising if the politics of nomination turns out to be a microcosm of election politics in their totality (N.C Mehrotra 1980:61). In Kerala, the nomination process is influenced by a number of factors where a candidate is nominated after several intra- structural considerations. Being a broadly aggregative and secular political party, Congress has deliberately attempted to accommodate different religious, linguistic and caste groups (Marguerite Ross Barnett and others 1975:39). This is a difficult process since different groups remain dissatisfied and they make unacceptable demands at different times.

The Assembly election of 1982 was necessitated as a result of the re-alignment of forces belonging to the two leading fronts in state politics. In the 1982 elections UDF came to power by winning 77 seats out of 140 Assembly seats. The two Congress factions together could win only thirtyfive seats. Congress (A) and (I) together contested in sixtythree seats. The 1984 Lok Sabha election took place in an atmosphere of sympathy generated by the tragic death of Indira Gandhi. In Kerala the party won thirteen seats out of twenty.

The ninth Kerala Assembly Election was held in the year 1987 after five years (K.P Nair 1987:20). A government headed by the CPI(M) assumed office after the election. The process of seat allocation in the UDF and in the Congress party was very difficult. The process of seat allocation among the front partners was not completed even on the last day of filing of nominations (*The Indian Express* 26.2.87). On the basis of the assurance given by the LDF the civic election was held in January 1988. Both the fronts faced problems due to the emergence of rebel candidates. Seat adjustments were made at the district level. A number of local leaders contested against official candidates (*The Kerala Kaumudi* 10-1-88).

Results of the 1989 Lok Sabha election was against the Congress(I) at the centre. However the performance of the UDF was better in Kerala. The District Council election of 1991 witnessed factional fight between rival groups with in the Congress creating problems in the selection of candidates. In the elections the CPI(M) led LDF won a decisive majority (Aravindakshan 1991: 27). The 1991 Assembly and Parliament elections were held together in the background of the assassination of Rajiv Gandhi. The UDF government which came to power completed its term with two chief ministers. The factional fight resulted in Antony taking over as chief minister replacing Karunakaran. In the 1995 local bodies election both the fronts finished evenly.

The 1996 Assembly and Parliament elections were held in the midst of intense factional feud at the centre and in the state. Both at the centre and the state, Congress party was voted out of power. In the mid-term elections to the Lok Sabha in 1998 and

1999, the results were not favourable to the Congress. In the 2000 civic elections in Kerala both the fronts were placed equally. Factionalism remained subdued during this period.

In the 2001 Assembly elections also the candidate selection posed a big problem to the Congress. The senior most leader himself was in the forefront to create issues. For other reasons this did not affect the election results. The two thirds majority that the UDF won this time was the largest any coalition in Kerala had achieved since 1977 (Krishna Kumar 2001:24-25). Clearly there was a wave of antipathy against the LDF government for the mismanagement of finances and corrupt practices (Vinu Abraham 2001:10-24).

An examination of the how candidates are selected by each group to contest different elections is important since it brings out many of the intricacies associated with the factional dynamics in the party, like the respective strength of each group in the legislative wing, the policies and tactics adopted by each group to erode the social and political base of the other and the shifts in group loyalties. The following table examines this with respect to the Assembly elections of 1982, 1987, 1991, 1996 and 2001 and the Lok Sabha elections of 1984, 1989, 1991, 1996, 1998 and 1999.

The following table reveals the respective sway enjoyed by the 'I' and 'A' factions of the Congress party among the three major religious groups. It also helps us to understand the policies and tactics adopted by both groups to breach each others support bases and to evaluate the resultant changes. Such efforts added fuel to the ongoing factional feuds within the party.

At the time of the1982 Assembly elections both factions had not yet merged. As such they fielded candidates separately. Majority of the candidates selected by each group belonged to the Hindu community. This included all the castes and sub castes which were dominant in the respective areas. The Nadar community candidates were given priority in the South Travancore region and the Nairs and Ezhavas in Thiruvananthapuram and Kollam districts. The SC/ST, candidates were included by both groups. Since 1987 the same pattern is followed by two groups. Regional and communal considerations were common in the selection of the candidates.

TABLE NO: 3

THE RELIGION WISE EQUATION FOLLOWED BY THE FOUR CONGRESS GROUPS IN THE SELECTION OF THEIR CANDIDATES FOR THE ASSEMBLY ELECTIONS OF 1982, 1987, 1991, 1996 AND 2001

Religion	*Period*											
	1982		*1987*		*1991*		*1996*		*2001*			
	Cong (I)	*Cong (A)*	*Cong (I)*	*Cong (A)*	*Cong (I)*	*Cong (A)*	*Cong (I)*	*Cong (A)*	*Cong (I)*	*Cong (A)*	*III**	*IV**
Hindu	28 (80%)	15 (53.57%)	40 (86.96%)	18 (60%)	37 (68.52%)	21 (58.33%)	37 (71.15%)	25 (59.52%)	22 (59.46%)	27 (70.97%)	9 (88.89%)	5 (100%)
Christian	5 (14.29%)	8 (28.57%)	4 (8.7%)	7 (23.33%)	11 (20.37%)	9 (25%)	12 (20.08%)	10 (23.81%)	11 (29.73%)	7 (18.92%)	—	—
Muslim	2 (5.71%)	5 (17.86%)	2 (4.34%)	5 (16.67%)	6 (11.11%)	6 (16.67%)	3 (5.77%)	7 (16.67%)	4 (10.81%)	3 (8.11%)	1 (11.11%)	—
	35 100%	28 100%	46 100%	30 100%	54 100%	36 100%	52 100%	42 100%	37 100%	37 100%	9 100%	5 100%

Note: * — The III and IV groups emerged only at the time of the 2001 Assembly election.
(See Appendix No. II for details)

The percentage of Hindus in the 'I' group list registered an all time high of 86.96 per cent in the 1987 election which came down to 59.43 per cent in 2001. The Christians in the 'I' list increased from 14.29 per cent in 1982 to 29.73 per cent in the 2001 poll. This trend of providing more representation to this community in the 'I' list is clearly visible in the elections of 1991 and 1996 also. In the case of the Muslim community the same pattern broadly repeats.

The other major group i.e. the 'A' faction counters this by gradually accommodating more Hindus in its list. From 53.57 per cent in 1982 it rises to 70.97 per cent in the 2001 polls. At present the equation in respect of the Hindu community stands at 54.46 per cent in the 'I' list and 70.97 per cent in the 'A' list. In respect of the Christian community it is 29.73 per cent in the 'I' list and 18.92 per cent in the 'A' list. A comparison of these figures with the 1982 figures will reveal the under currents of the politics of Congress factionalism in Kerala since 1982. The Muslim representation in the 'I' list almost doubled during this period, while in the 'A' list it came down from 17.86per cent to 8.11 per cent. It shows that Karunakaran has successfully expanded his support base among the Christian and Muslim communities as Antony systematically tries to break Karunakaran's Hindu fortress. The reality is that candidate's selection is also used as a tool to beef up factional fights.

The religion wise analysis of the selection of candidates to Lok Sabha elections since 1984 reveals that the Karunakaran group is yet to field a Muslim candidate. It was in 1980 that Karunakaran selected A.A Rahim to contest the Chirayinkeezhu parliamentary constituency. Rahim won the election eventhough the 'A' group was not supporting the Congress(I). The following table presents religion wise details of the candidates belonging to the 'I' and 'A' groups for the Lok Sabha polls since 1984.

The percentage of the Hindu and Christian candidates in the 'I' list for the Lok Sabha polls of 1984 stood at 66.67 per cent and 33.33per cent respectively. It became 71.43 per cent and 28.57 per cent in the 1999 poll. In the 'A' faction list it stood at 50 per cent and 33.33per cent in 1984 and 42.86per cent and 28.57 per cent in the 1999 Lok Sabha poll.

TABLE NO: 4

THE RELIGION WISE EQUATION FOLLOWED BY THE TWO CONGRESS GROUPS FOR THE SELECTION OF CANDIDATES TO THE LOK SABHA POLLS FROM 1984 POLL ONWARDS

	PERIOD														
	1984		*1989*		*1991*		*1996*			*1998*			*1999*		
Religion	*Cong (I)*	*Cong (A)*	*Cong (I)*	*Cong (A)*	*Cong (I)*	*Cong (A)*	*Cong (I)*	*Cong (A)*	*Cong (T)*	*Cong (I)*	*Cong (A)*	*Cong (T)*	*Cong (I)*	*Cong (A)*	*Cong (T)*
Hindus	4	3	7	3	7	3	5	4	1	6	3	1	5	3	2
%	66.67	50.0	77.78	42.86	70.01	50.0	62.5	57.14	100	75.0	42.86	100	71.43	42.86	100
Christi-	2	2	2	3	3	2	3	2	—	2	2	—	2	2	—
ans %	33.33	33.33	22.22	42.86	30.0	33.33	37.5	28.57		25.0	28.57	—	28.57	28.57	
Muslims	—	1	—	1	—	1	—	1	—		2	—	—	2	—
%		16.67		14.28		16.67	—	14.29	—		28.57	—	—	28.57	
Total	6	6	9	7	10	6	8	7	1	8	7	1	7	7	2
%	100	100	100	100	100	100	100	100	100	100	100	100	100	100	100
	K.R. Narayanan without group		K.R. Narayanan without group		K.R. Narayanan without group		K.P. Unnikrishnan without group			P.M Suresh Babu without group			P.M Suresh Babu without group		

(For source and details please see Appendix No.III)

Note: In 1996 a splinter group from the Karunakaran faction emerged and its leader Ramesh Chennithala who is at present one of the secretaries of the AICC contested in 1996 Parliament election. This group at that time was known as 'Thiruthalvadi' (T) group.

It is interesting to note that in the list for the 1999 Lok Sabha elections Hindu candidates dominate in the Karunakaran faction list while in the list for the Assembly polls of 2001 it stands reduced so as to effect a balance. In turn, the 'A' faction list for the Lok Sabha polls of 1999 contains more Christians. But there is a decreasing trend in the number of Christian candidates in its list for the Assembly polls. Among the Muslim community also the percentage figure of the 'A' faction goes up in 1999. It is a fact that the Congress high command has high stakes in the Lok Sabha elections. Hence the high command has a greater say in the selection of candidates to the Lok Sabha polls than in the Assembly polls. As such the factions have only limited freedom in the selection of candidates. Still it is worthwhile to take note of the politics of factionalism being pursued by different groups in the party in the selection of candidates to contest the Lok Sabha polls.

2. The Nature of the UDF and the Leadership Role of the Congress

Religion, nationality, race, education, profession or economic interest, individually or in combination may be the vital factors determining party affiliations. India with her huge size, the existence of innumerable communities and caste and other problems like linguistic differences and regional contrasts has found it necessary to evolve a party system consistent with these facts. These differences exist in no small measure in Kerala too (John P. John 1983:9).

Since the formation of Kerala there have been thirteen general elections to the legislative assembly. In all the elections except one in 1957, coalitions of parties have played a major role (Jose Chander 1997:117). Really the transformation of the caste system into a set up of political interest groups began during the last part of the nineteenth Century when the British rulers in India set up a modern system of administration (Johari 1973:206). The role of communal and regional groups in the coalition politics of Kerala is worth examining.

(a) Communal – regional parties and the coalition setup

Communal or regional groups make identification with the major political parties-the Congress and the Communists. When they are unable to fit in with these parties they gravitate to other political parties. The various splits in the Praja Socialist Party (PSP) were due to communal and regional factors. The Kerala Congress is another party which became a considerable force by exploiting the communal and religious factors. Muslim League is exploiting the religious label as well as regionalism to a considerable extent (John P. John:117). The origin of the National Democratic Party (NDP) and Socialist Republican Party (SRP) was part of caste mobilisation efforts. So the caste-communal underpinning of the coalition setup is important for the Congress party which provides leadership to the UDF.

Coalition politics in the state went through three stages of development; the experimental, the search for identity and the stage of political stability (Jose Chander 1997:118). The 1960's can be considered the experimental stage when both the Congress and the Marxists were experimenting with coalition tactics. In the 1965 election, the Kerala Congress, a splinter group from the Congress and the CPI(M) appeared on the political scene. The CPI(M) attracted the Socialists and the Muslim League to its fold to form a three party alliance. The CPI, the Congress and the Kerala Congress fought independently. In 1967 the CPI(M) formed a *Sapta Munnani*, with communal and socialist elements within its fold and came to power[11]. The Kottayam session, of the KPCC decided to form a *'Jana Munnani'* to face the Marxist front. The inner contradictions within the Marxist front led to its down fall and to the formation of the CPI led ministry under C. Achutha Menon. This alliance of the Congress, the CPI and few others came to be known as the Ruling Front and the CPI(M) and others, the Opposition Front. In the 1970 election with the support of the Congress the CPI came to power. Differences of opinion emerged in the party regarding Congress member's participation in the ministry[12]. The KPCC President K.K Viswanathan and K. Karunakaran left for Delhi for consultation with Indira Gandhi. Finally she permitted the state Congress party to join the ministry. There emerged a group of congressmen openly supporting K. Karunakaran who became the powerful home minister in that cabinet. That ministry continued till the 1977 election. This coalition again came to power in Kerala with K. Karunakaran as the chief minister with a thumping majority. But Karunakaran had to resign in connection with the verdict in the Rajan case and Antony replaced Karunakaran as the chief minister.

The 1980's witnessed further consolidation under new titles-the United Democratic Front (UDF) and the Left Democratic Front (LDF). At the national level, the Congress(I) had split into two – Urs and Indira. The UDF included Congress(I) led by K.M Chandy and K. Karunakaran, Kerala Congress (Joseph Group), IUML and the newly emerged National Democratic Party (NDP) of the Nairs and the Socialist Republican Party (SRP) of the Ezhavas and some others. The LDF consisted of CPI(M), CPI, Cong (Urs) under Antony, Kerala Congress (Mani), RSP and others.

In 1982 there was further shift in the alliances. The Congress (A) faction and KC(M) came out of the LDF and supported the UDF. A small splinter group of the 'A' faction remained in the LDF. A political polarisation of the right and left parties occurred. The 1970-82 period saw unprincipled alliances between parties and factions which were ideologically poles apart. In the post 1982 period the Congress allies were trying to gain maximum through bargaining tactics. Psychologically, they were searching for an identity and stable political relationship (Jose Chander 1997:120).

Vested economic interests are well entrenched in the communal-regional parties aligned with the UDF and the LDF. In the different Congress factions also these interests are well entrenched. Naturally the Congress factions monitor the inner party politics of the allies and takes often, opposite sides in the inner party struggles. Each Congress faction competes to win over the confidence of the allies since it will enhance the claims of a faction leader to lead the UDF. Inspite of the dominant role of the Congress party in the UDF, the coalition set up demands that the UDF leader should be acceptable to all the partners. So the politics of factionalism in the allies spills over to the Congress party and vice-versa.

(b) Divergence of approach regarding the functioning of the UDF

The spill over politics created problems for the UDF and its leader, the Congress party. Congress groups, differed among themselves in dealing with the above parties. In Kerala, as years went by the 'left' and the 'right' parties lost their significance as community based choices gained an upperhand in the survival of various ministries. The Catholics, who were against the atheists, joined the communist headed coalitions. The Congress, who branded the Muslim league as communal, readily accepted them. The class ideology became less and less significant and community identity became more and more relevant.

The UDF being a combination of political and caste-communal forces did not have any coherent ideology or programme as there were inherent contradictions within it due to the presence of different vested interests. The major differences that surfaced in the UDF and the Congress party on account of this is worth examining Karunakaran first as home minister and later as the chief minister proved to be more successful in leading the party in a coalition set up which necessitated a delicate balancing act as it consisted of strong caste-communal forces in the form of KC, ML, NDP and SRP. Moreover during the emergency period his position as the powerful home minister helped him win the respect, loyalty and allegiance of the caste-communal leaders. Naturally many of the highhanded actions of Karunakaran with the help of central and state government machinery antagonised the other group as they did not have any say in the running of the government or the party. All these created bitterness between him and the leaders sidelined by him. In short Karunakaran's imposing position as the architect and leader of the UDF and his bulldozing of opposition within the party precipitated factionalism in the party. Naturally differences regarding the functioning of the UDF arose in the Congress party.

The course of the differences are sequentially examined below by taking the four Assembly elections since 1982 as the base and by dividing them into four phases i.e.1982-87, 1987-91, 1991-96 and 1996-2001 for convenience sake.

The 1982-1987 period

An important element in Congress party's strength was its ability to form coalitions of caste and communal groups. The tremendous social diversity makes caste and communal coalitions essential in Kerala. The Congress has been able to draw support not only from the dominant castes but from other communities as well, because of this coalition set up. Due to this reason allocation of seats in the assembly and parliament elections remains a hurdle to be overcome by coalition partners. In the 1982 elections Mani group Kerala Congress demanded twentytwo seats and they were given eighteen. The Joseph group also came with similar demands (Kala Kaumudi 6-6-82). Most of the partners in the coalition took the same attitude at the time of seats sharing including Cong(A), a partner at that time.

Ministry formation in 1982 also became a ticklish problem. The size of the ministry went up to nineteen to accommodate all sections. Congress groups were to be satisfied with less important portfolios other than the home portfolio and chief ministership. Only seven ministers were inducted from both the Congress groups. Vayalar Ravi, belonging to the Antony faction was given the very important portfolio of home. K. Karunakaran as chief minister was only in charge of Harijan welfare and general administration.

The UDF since its formation in 1982 was a divided front. This was due to factors like lack of cohesion, conflict over sharing of spoils and communal pressures. In the meantime Cong(A) merged with Cong (I). Inspite of this the Antony supporters felt that they were being humiliated by the other faction. When A.L Jacob the President of the KPCC was inducted into the ministry every congressmen felt that Antony would be made the President of the KPCC(I) (*Kerala Kaumudi* 8-1-1983). Also a strong loyalist of 'A' faction, Cyriac John was dropped from the ministry. Later Antony became the general secretary of the AICC when the vacancy arose due to the death of C.M Stephen. A strong Karunakaran loyalist C.V Padmarajan was made the President of KPCC.

Meanwhile Cong(I) in Kerala started preparations for parliament elections. Karunakaran became a member of the CWC and parliamentary board during this period and he had an upper hand in the organisational matters also. As factionalism was at its top, Antony and Padmarajan submitted two lists to the Congress high command for the selection of candidates to contest the parliament seats. Congress(I) decided to field sixteen candiates with out consulting other partners in the front. The IUML demanded three seats and the KC(M) and KC(Joseph) claimed two seats each. Other partners were also in the fray. Finally after hectic consultations the list was finalised (*Malayala Manorama* 18-11-84). The election result was in favour of the UDF which won seventeen out of twenty seats (Parameswaran 1985:29). The two Kerala Congress parties and the NDP faction led by Upendranatha Kurup criticised the big brotherly attitude of the leading party (Krishnakumari 1994:154).

Meanwhile V.M Sudheeran of the 'A' group became the speaker of the legislative assembly in place Vakkom Purushothaman, who was elected to Lok Sabha. Sudheeran's assumption of office as speaker widened the factional rivalry between Antony and Karunakaran. Sudheeran gave a ruling on the misuse of the provision relating to ordinances. His ruling stunned the treasury benches. He said, "It is unhealthy to misuse the provisions to issue ordinances so as to make legislature a rubber stamp" (*Malayala Manorma* 25-7-1986). Along with this Sudheeran reconstituted the privileges committee with the deputy speaker as chairman, in place of the chief minister who was occupying the post. This resulted in the resignation of the privileges Committee. Thus the Sudheeran issue resulted in a major tussle between the 'I' group and 'A' group in the assembly.

Karthikeyan, the President of the Youth Congress, charged that Congress was being bullied by communal parties whose mismanagement of sensitive portfolios had cast a shadow on the "image" of the Congress (I) government in Kerala (*Mathrubhumi* 7.3.85). The youth wing of the Kerala Congress questioned the propriety and motives of Karthikeyan. Karthikeyan also propagated one party rule in Kerala (Kalakaumudi 21.4.85). Another problem which developed in the UDF was the one centering on the speech delivered by R. Balakirhsna Pillai in which he called for a 'Punjab Model' agitation against the central negligence of Kerala (Front Line 15-18 June 1985). Balakrishna Pillai was forced to resign from the ministry and was re-inducted after one year. According to the 'A' group, it was the Karunakaran loyalists who inflated a small issue into a big event which caused much embarrassment to the UDF. Another issue centered on the visit of some Kuwaiti nationals whose request for entry permit was rejected by the Central government. Vayalar Ravi was the home minister when this incident happened. Antony group flashed the news that Karunakaran had a hand in this (Kalakaumudi 6.4.86). All these aggravated the personal rivalry between Karunakaran and Vayalar Ravi within the Cabinet (*Indian Express* 14-2-86). The chief minister came up with an 'image building exercise' which resulted in the shifting of Mani from finance to irrigation and Vayalar Ravi from home to agriculture. It resulted in the resignation of Vayalar Ravi. In support of Vayalar Ravi, Oommen Chandy too resigned from the convenorship of the UDF(Venugopalan 1992:162). In these reshufflings Cong(A) was with the Mani group. The 'A' faction considered the whole exercise as aimed at giving more powers to the chief minister. The chief minister took over the home portfolio and inducted Thachadi Prabhakaran and Ramesh Chennithala as ministers in his cabinet (ibid). The rift between 'A' and 'I' factions widened during this period. The ruling front could carry on only because of the divisions in the opposition front.

The 1987-1991 period

When the assembly elections for 1987 were announced both the Congress groups were against selecting candidates on the basis of communal considerations (*Mathrubhumi* 3-1-87). Candidate's selection became a crucial issue between the two groups in the party. The office bearers of the Youth Congress resigned to register their protest against seat allocation. Along with the elders, who were denied tickets like Thachady Prabhakaran and M.P Gangadharan, the youngsters were also posing problems. Cherian Philip, a staunch loyalist of Antony vehemently criticised the UDF leadership. The split in the Kerala Congress (M) brought into existence a new one known as the 'Pillai group'. Most of the backward caste leaders including the Muslim league leader and minister U.A Beeran and M.K Raghavan, the President of the SNDP Yogam were against the decision of the government to grant 15 per cent reservation on the basis of economic criteria (Kalakaumudi 1.2.87). In the midst of intense factional feud between Congress groups and rivalry among UDF partners the elections were held. The election saw the marginalisation of small parties like NDP and SRP (Frontline 10.1.87).

The infighting within UDF and factional fight between Karunakaran and Antony caused the failure of the UDF. To revamp the party for the Lok Sabha elections Rajiv Gandhi nominated Antony as the chief of the KPCC. The Youth Congress under its new President, Ramesh Chennithala conducted a 'Kerala March' from Kasargod to Thiruvananthapuram which attracted the attention of Kerala as a whole. Factional fight within the Congress(I) remained subdued during this stage.

Elections to the ninth Lok Sabha was held on 22 November, 1989. The UDF secured seventeen seats. The Congress(I) won 14 out of the 17 seats it contested (Lok Sabha Election Reportage 1999:7). The victory was due to the cooperation between the organisational wing and the parliamentary wing along with the active involvement of the youngsters. The LDF chief minister Nayanar soon declared elections to the District Councils which went in favour of the LDF. The candidate selection to the district council seats intensified the group rivalry and those who were denied candidature contested as rebels.The Nayanar government recommended that the assembly be prematurely dissolved and fresh elections be held immediately (*The Hindu* 27-10-2002).

During the 1987-91 period the Congress party was in opposition. This explains why during this period factionalism scaled down. Moreover the victory in the 1989 Lok Sabha poll taught Congressmen the lesson that only through unity can they overcome the LDF challenge.

The 1991-1996 period

Candidate selection during the 1991 Assembly election did not pose any serious threat, due to the fact that Congress(I) was out of power at the centre and in the state. Seat allocation to the partners was made on the basis of an understanding to please all of them and even the small parties were given due consideration. In the selection of Congress candidates Karunakaran dominated the scene and accommodated a good number of his loyalists. This created some issues within the Antony faction. Ministerial allocation did not produce any hurdle due to the undue influence of Karunakaran at the centre. There were certain complaints raised by the Kerala Congress and Muslim League on the chief minister's style of functioning.The League publicly criticised the functioning of the UDF. The relation between IUML and Congress(I) further worsened on the reported remark that the IUML would pull out of the Congress(I) led UDF (*The Indian Express* 7-8-92). There was also allegation that Karunakaran was secretly helping the Islamic Seva Sangh (ISS) to check the growth of IUML. Hence they were more intimate with the 'A' faction (*The Kerala Kaumudi* 11-8-92).

Kunhalikutty representing the League said that the interference of the UDF partners in the Congress(I) infighting is aimed at finding a solution to the waning image of the UDF and that it was done with the knowledge and concurrence of the Congress(I) leadership in the state. Vayalar Ravi expressed displeasure over the interference of the UDF partners in the internal affairs of the party (*Indian express* 10-5-92). Relationship further deteriorated after the demolition of the Babri Masjid when Ibrahim Sulaiman Sait asked the IUML to quit the UDF (*Malayala Manorama* 18-2-93). In the Ottappalam by-election when the Congress(I) candidate failed miserably, it was attributed to the secret understanding that the Muslim League had with the LDF leadership (*Mathrubhumi* 20-9-93).

Muslim League leaders and followers were of the view that the demolition of Babri Masjid may be with the knowledge of Karunakaran, who at that time was in the inner circles of Delhi coterie. Following the Masjid issue the Muslim league's power declined due to the split. All these introduced a strong element of communalism in Kerala politics (Pradeep Mandav 2000:28).

Affairs in the UDF reached such a stage that the 'A' faction and some of the partners demanded a change of leadership in the government. When Antony left the union ministership, political conditions became favourable to effect a leadership change. Oommen Chandy had been nurturing a grudge with Karunakaran ever since 1991, when he was deliberately denied by the leader a chance to discharge the duties of the chief minister when Karunakaran was away in USA for medical treatment. Later in a dramatic situation he resigned from the cabinet. The 'I' group demand for the withdrawal of nomination of M.A Kuttappan of the Antony group to the Rajyasabha seat to accommodate Vayalar Ravi became a prestige issue for the Antony group. Oommen Chandy was able to wean away some Congress legislators from the 'I' group in favour of Antony. He also won over the support of front partners, mainly the Muslim League and the Kerala Congress (Mani) group. Muslim league leader Kunhalikutty and K.P.A Majeed demanded a change of leadership in the UDF (*Kerala Kaumudi* 17-1-95). Kerala Congress leader Mani who was also entertaining a grudge with Karunakaran joined hands with Kunhalikutty-Oommen Chandy axis for a leadership change (*Kerala Kaumudi* 24-1-95). Due to the pressure from the high command and the growing factional feud within the legislature party, the leadership change was effected and Antony replaced Karunakaran as the chief minister (*Deshabhimani* 12.3.95).

After this leadership change, the NSS fell out with the UDF leadership. Though the immediate provocation was the *Mannam Samadhi Issue*, the real intention was to punish the UDF for disregarding the NSS policy of reservation. As a matter of fact the UDF lost considerably in the Nair segments in the 1996 Lok Sabha and Assembly elections (Yamuna Devi 1998:257).

In brief the KC(M) and Muslim league were with Antony group to oust Karunakaran from the chief ministership whereas KC(B) and CMP were in favour of Karunakaran. Jacob group from the beginning was silent on this issue and later joined with the Antony faction. The KPCC leadership was in support of Karunakaran (*Kerala Kaumudi* 27.2.95). Apart from this, thirty one out of the fifty seven Congress legislators in a joint statement declared that the demand of the 'A' faction is an insult to democratic practices (*Malayala Manorama* 27-2-95). Karunakaran faction alleged that Oommen Chandy resorted to horse trading to topple Karunakaran (*Kerala Kaumudi* 28-2-95).

Trends since 1996

Antony's assumption of office as chief minister in 1995 was not a smooth affair. After the resignation, Karunakaran took initiative to oust Narasimha Rao from his posts, since Rao had a role in Antony's elevation as chief minister.

Seat sharing to the Assembly and Lok Sabha elections was

not a smooth affair in the UDF and the Congress in 1996. Kunhalikutty himself took the lead for an amicable settlement between the warring Kerala Congress factions (*The Hindu* 24-3-96). The relationship of Kerala Congress (Pillai) group with the Antony faction was not cordial since Balakrishna Pillai was in favour of Karunakaran during the period of leadership change. As a protest against leadership change and reservation policy the NDP left the UDF and decided to stay out of the electoral fray. The NDP chairman said that "we were part of the coalition for the past many years. There were ups and downs in the relation. However, the UDF attitude towards NSS drastically changed under Antony" (*Mathrubhumi* 29-3-96). Antony faction suspected that Karunakaran had a role in this policy change.

SNDP also turned against Antony, when he gave permission to the police to enter the holy Sivagiri mutt premises in connection with a dispute. Thus the two main Hindu groups became enemies of the UDF. Karunakaran faction demanded more seats for his loyalists. It was with the intervention of the high command that the UDF completed the seat sharing process (*The Hindu* 30-3-96). The elections to the Assembly and Lok Sabha were a great blow to the UDF. It was alleged that it was due to cross voting that Karunakaran and his son was defeated. Antony group alleged that Karunakaran was responsible for the election debacle. Karunakaran expressed his displeasure over the performance of the UDF (*Deshabhimani* 17-11-96).

Karunakaran blamed Antony for the UDF defeat in the 1996 election as some of his actions had alienated communities like the Nairs and Ezhavas which had traditionally adopted a pro-Congress attitude. Karunakaran did ultimately succeed in making Narasimha Rao resign from the Presidentship of the party. In the meantime his group suffered a split. The new group declared itself as the real 'I' group and joined hands with the 'A' group (*The Hindu* 23-1-1996). The third group leader Ramesh Chennithala in a veiled attack on Karunakaran said; "some persons were indulging in a futile exercise to create the impression that the party central leadership was behind them" (*Kerala Kaumudi* 26-11-96).

The groupism in the Congress (I) faction raised its head again with the controversy over Karunakaran's failure to contest the elections to the Congress working committee. As a fall out of this Vayalar Ravi and P.C Chacko came out of the 'I' faction.

With the fall of the National Front government at the centre, mid term polls to the Lok Sabha were announced. Though the candidate selection remained a mystery till 22 January 1998, Karunakaran succeeded in securing safe constituencies for him and his son at Thiruvananthapuram and Thrissur respectively. Some of his loyalists were also accommodated. Karunakaran also saw to it that P.C Chacko who had fallen out with him was shifted to Mukundapuram from the Idukki Lok Sabha seat (*The Hindu* 31-1-98). Antony remained silent in all these. These incidents irked the Christian community which resulted in the defeat of Muraleedharan from Thrissur. The differences between Antony and Karunakaran were patched up for the time being. But the rift between Karunakaran and the PCC President Vayalar Ravi widened with the undue interference of Muraleedharan in the organisational matters as general secretary of the KPCC(I). By Ravi's own admission the KPCC and its President were reduced to being rubberstamps (Frontline 31-8-98:21). A bitter Vayalar Ravi relinquished the office on 5 June 1998. Thus Thennala Balakrishna Pillai became the President of the KPCC(I) and K. Muraleedharan was appointed the only Vice-President as desired by Karunakaran. The subsequent events prompted Vayalar Ravi to form a group of his own known as the fourth group.

After the Kargil war elections to the Lok Sabha were to be held again in 1999. Party leadership issued a direction to all its state units that it need not consider a candidate who failed to win for two consecutive terms. Karunakaran decided to shift from Thiruvananthapuram to Mukundapuram by shifting A.C Jose to Thrissur. Karunakaran also succeeded in allotting the Kozhikode Lok Sabha seat to his son K. Muraleedharan in violation of the above direction. As a tactician Karunakaran proved his ability when his nominee won the Thiruvananthapuram constituency which was vacated by him this time.

In the meantime the central leadership's relations with Karunakaran touched a new low. He stated that he has lost faith in the high command. He added that it has become difficult to believe the words of the high command on the issue of reorganisation of the Youth Congress leadership (*The Hindu* 25-2-2000). On several occasions Karunakaran criticised Antony's role as the opposition leader.

Election to the Kerala Assembly was declared in the year 2001 in the midst of intense group rivalry. Differences over seat distribution in the Congress party plunged the party into a serious crisis. The denial of seats to Karunakaran's daughter Padmaja and some of his close confidants signalled a shift in the policy of the Congress high command. This provoked a revolt against the Congress high command (The Week 22.4.2001). In protest Karunakaran resigned his position as the permanent invitee to the CWC. The revolt of Karunakaran was settled by the decision to allot the Aranmula, Vadakkekara and Peravoor assembly seats to the 'I' faction. Antony was forced to accept the high command decision inorder to save the day for the UDF (*The Hindu* 16-4-2001). Factionalism asserted again after the UDF victory at the time of the cabinet formation. Events have reached such a stage that the 'I' group is now asking for a cabinet reshuffle.

3. Personal Factors

Personal factors are often incorporated in group goals. Democratic leadership stresses upon individual personality as the ultimate seat of all values (Kundu and Tutoo 1988:478). Individual personality and its impact have the capacity to influence the functioning of particular groups within a political party. The success and popularity of a leader depends on his personal integrity and political capability. One such leader's style of functioning may conflict with the style of functioning of another similarly placed leader. This results in personal rivalry and personality clashes.

Congress politics in Kerala promotes an 'unfriendly friendship' between the leaders in place of 'unfailing friendship'. Both factions followed the same attitude from the 1970's onwards. Changing situations has also brought together bitter rivals in an effort to regain strength (Jose Chander 1986:204). Post independent history of the Congress party in Kerala is the history of personal rivalry and jealousy[13]. From the early days onwards Karunakaran distanced himself from the Youth Congress style of functioning and their demands. His style of functioning is not democratic.

Those who praise and worship him will be unduly elevated to high positions without considering the quality of the persons. While analysing the style of functioning of the Congress party second line of leadership, it is seen that most of them are parochial and communal. The style of functioning of the top leadership is not transparent. It is directed towards obtaining power and position. It was alleged that in the early 1970's "Antony instigated T.O Bava, the then President of the KPCC to suspend M.A John from the party[14]. Ideology as such has no bearing on their thoughts and actions.

(a) Generation gap

Generation gap is one of the personal factors responsible for the divide in the Congress party in Kerala. When K.K Viswanathan was appointed as the governor of Gujarat A.K Antony became the KPCC President. Antony gave too much importance to the lower levels of the organisation and discussed the policies of the party from the lower strata onwards. As the leader of the legislature party, Karunakaran was against this type of functioning. Many senior leaders including C.M Stephen and A.A Kochunni shared this view. Youth Congress was fully in support of the organisational stand adopted by the KPCC leadership. This naturally created a rift between the elders and youngsters in the party.

(b) Differences in style of functioning

Differences in style of functioning also constitute one of the personal factors abetting factionalism. The leadership styles projected by the faction leaders are mainly meant for public consumption. Congressmen identify their interests either with Karunakaran's leadership style or with that of Antony's. Based on the respondents feedback data the chief qualities of Karunakaran's style of functioning as seen by Congressmen are his concern for the group loyalists, his role as the protector of partymen's interest, his effective leadership of the UDF, the effective handling of caste-communal forces and his abilities in meeting the Marxist challenge. He has deliberately and openly projected the image of a godfather to those partymen who are loyal to him. His flamboyant style is countered by Antony by projecting the image of a democrat, who is impartial, transparent in dealings, honest, flexible and straight forward in approach. The two contradictory styles of leadership have enough followers among the public. It is quite natural that in the absence of any visible ideological differences, leadership styles deliberately built up over years becomes a chief cause for factional differences.

4. Indiscipline and Public Statements

Indiscipline and public statements are the natural outcome of frustration when one group dominate the entire party at all levels as in the case of the Congress party in Kerala during the heydays of Karunakaran. The above observation is applicable today also. Leaders from top to bottom irrespective of their positions and responsibilities indulged in acts of grave indiscipline and often issued provocative statements to the detriment of the party itself.

In 1983 P.T Thomas, the KSU President and a loyalist of Antony, criticised the government for permitting the private managements to start too many schools (*Kerala Kaumudi* 13-6-83). Following this a serious act of indiscipline came from the KSU when the education minister visited Kottayam to inaugurate the office of the Gandhi University. The KSU(I) and YC(I) activists shouted 'go back' against the minister (*The Hindu* 12-7-83). P.T Thomas was suspended from the KSU. P.T Thomas alleged that the suspension was at the behest of the chief minister K. Karunakaran[15].

The socialist cultural forum was formed by the dissidents to pressurise the government from entering into alliance with communal interests. Youth Congress President Karthikeyan, a loyalist of Karunakaran at that time criticised the government for its lack of collective responsibility. The KSU(I) participation in the medicos strike, the criticism of the KSU for the failure of the education department to supply text books, formation of district level committees to discuss students problems and the YC(I) general secretary, Cherian Philip's corruption charges against some ministers were instances of indiscipline (*The Hindu* 9-10-84). When the chief minister dismissed the statements as 'immature' the opposition created much embarrassment to him by pointing to the fact that the KPCC general secretary had justified the statement of YC(I) leader by saying that YC had always acted as a corrective force in the organisation (*Kerala Kaumudi* 31-10-84). Karunakaran faction believed that these were the activities of the Antony faction to tarnish the government.

When Karthikeyan said that it was better for the Cong (I) to leave the ministry than to remain in power by appeasing communal elements,Karunakaran said that people who were in responsible positions should not have made such frivolous statements before ascertaining facts. There had been accusations and counter accusations of induction of bogus members during the time of membership campaign in the party. This practice was more in vogue when the party was running the government.

Antony wanted a 'code of conduct' to be implemented for the UDF leaders and ministers for the smooth functioning of the system(*The Deepika* 21-11-91). To this Vayalar Ravi responded that, "we would not permit party leadership to have a remote control like that of the Marxist party (*Mathrubhumi* 23-11-91). Muraleedharan in a dig at the opposite faction leader thundered that "such people should be publicly flogged" (*Kerala Kaumudi* 26-11-91). While replying to the ongoing controversy Antony asked "how can the office bearers of the KPCC remain silent when they were also responsible for the attainment of power by the party" (*Malayala Manorama* 26-11-91). In another public meeting Ravi said that Karunakaran alone was responsible for the victory of the UDF (*Mathrubhumi* 4-12-91). Following this Antony wanted the UDF partners to see to it that Karunakaran changes his style of functioning (*Kerala Kaumudi* 4-2-92).

Oommen Chandy remarked that "if the chief minister decides his colleagues it is the MLA's who determine the chief minister". This was a reaction to the reported speech of K. Muraleedharan that the chief minister possesses the constitutional prerogative of selection of his colleagues. Oommen Chandy was emphatic in saying that 'expression of opinion is not indiscipline' (*Malayala Manorma* 22.2.92).Sudheeran lambasted Karunakaran for trying to politically wreck the party and the ruling front by his actions, which according to him, were solely motivated by his personal interest (*The Indian Express* 26-2-92). He added that wide ranging consultations with like minded Congress(I) men and UDF partners will be held and that an action plan would be chalked out against the authoritarian and partisan ways of the chief minister which was helping the opposition (*The Deepika* 26-2-92). It was decided to move against Karunakaran collectively to democratise the party.

To air their views in public, Antony faction loyalists formed 'Kerala Deseeya Vedi', under the chairmanship of Cherian Philip. Ravi viewed the functioning of such forums as an act of indiscipline in the party (*Kerala Kaumudi* 25-4-92) and warned that there may be disciplinary action against those violating party direction. To this the senior party member of the Antony faction, Aryadan Mohammed retorted: "if it is so let the KPCC President hang me" (*Malayala Manorama* 28-4-92).

When the reformist group in the Karunakaran faction became active, the troika of Karthikeyan, Ramesh and Shanavaz accused that a coterie was in charge of cliff house, the official residence of the chief minister, when Karunakaran was hospitalised (*Kerala Kaumudi* 16-9-92). Mullappally Ramachandran also criticised Karunakaran's leadership of the government. (*Mathrubhumi* 27-9-92). Vayalar Ravi issued suspension notices and show cause notice to senior party leaders including Aryadan Mohammed (*Malayala Manorama* 1-12-92). In the meantime V.M Sudheeran had called upon the government officials to ignore 'all illegal and verbal orders' issued by the ministers. He added that the verbal orders issued by the ministers often provided enough room for corruption and the ministers escape scot free as they are not on record (*The Indian Express* 22-3-93).

After the defeat in the 1996 Assembly election, the small Reformist Group leader Karthikeyan demanded that the KPCC President and his team should resign owning up the moral responsibility for the humiliating defeat (*The Hindu* 15-10-96). The faction feud had assumed the dimension of a power struggle in view of the impending organisational elections (*The statesman* 18-10-96). When factionalism attained high pitch, K. Sudhakaran, the Kannur DCC President, accused Mullappally Ramachandran as a 'Marxist Spy' (*The Kerala Kaumudi* 1-12-96). To Oommen Chandy such a remark was 'not in tune with Congress culture'. To this Sudhakaran replied that Oommen Chandy was not the fit person to talk about Congress culture (*The Mathrubhumi* 3-12-96). Antony in a press conference criticised Karunakaran's style of functioning and said that he was responsible for the failure of the UDF in the last election (*The Malayala Manorama* 15-3-97).

The Indian Youth Congress organised the 'Aao Bharath Banaye' *Padayathra* which started from Kanyakumari on 20 January 1997. When the *padayathra* entered the Kerala border at Kaliyikkavila the rival factions clashed on 22 January, 1997 interrupting the programme (*The Malayala Manorama* 23-1-97). The factional clash reached a new dimension when rival factions again took it as an issue. To Oommen Chandy, it was proper for the KPCC President Vayalar Ravi to initiate disciplinary action. Vayalar Ravi described it as unfortunate that a senior leader like Chandy should have made such a statement (*The Kerala Kaumudi* 24-1-97).

Groupism in the Congress raised its ugly head again with the controversy over Karunakaran's failure to contest the CWC election (*The Kerala Kaumudi* 14-8-97). Muraleedharan openly held Vayalar Ravi and P.C Chacko responsible for this. But those in the rival 'A' group and the 'third' group felt that the whole thing was stage managed by Karunakaran group as an 'act of escape' from being defeated in the contest. Karunakaran replied that he was saddened by the events in Calcutta. "This type of experience is nothing new in my long political career. However, I have not fallen into any trap". He said that it was "his own mistake which resulted in his not contesting in the elections" (*The Hindu* 17-8-97).

Irritated by certain issues Karunakaran decided to prove his strength in the Congress party by organising a rally of the Youth Congress on 14 November, 1997 to coincide with the birth anniversary of Jawaharlal Nehru. The euphemistically termed *Nehru Jayanthi Swathantrya Suvarna Jubilee Yuvajana Prakadanam* was a milestone in the chequered history of the veteran. This was really intended to politically resurrect him and reinforce his reported clout with the grassroots. While addressing the rally at the Marine drive grounds at Cochin, Karunakaran wanted the Youth power to come to the fore and enable the historic Congress party to capture power at the centre (*The Statesman* 15-11-97). While addressing another rally of the 'A' faction Youth wing at

Kozhikode, Oommen Chandy urged Congress men with different views to unite for political stability at the centre. All the anti-Karunakaran faction leaders of the second row were present at the Muthalakulam meeting of the Cong(A) (*The Mathrubhumi* 15-11-97).

Loyalties and friendships shifted again. Vayalar Ravi, T.H Musthafa and P.C Chacko became enemies of their mentor Karunakaran. Karunakaran demanded the resignation of the KPCC President. Vayalar Ravi said that Karunakaran persuaded him to take steps to appoint Murali, his son as the President of the KPCC (*The Malayala Manorama* 19-7-98). Musthafa criticised that Karunakaran is against giving leadership positions to the minority community leaders (*The Madhyamom* 3-11-98). Chacko demanded that it is high time that the Karunakaran makes way for others (*Kerala Sabdam* 1998:12-16). Hassan in his statement said that the state Congress party is not the ancestral property of any leader (*Kerala Kaumudi* 23-8-98).

M.A John pointed out that both Antony and Karunakaran were responsible for the destruction of the Congress party (*Kerala Kaumudi* 24-1-99). Muraleedharan, the KPCC Vice President said that Antony should take the initiative urgently to settle the ongoing factional feuds in the party. He added it was Karunakaran who had created the present Congress(I) in the state when there was a split in the party and some sections had taken shelter in the AKG centre after deserting Indira Gandhi. Nobody could dream the possibility of kicking out Karunakaran from his *Tharavadu* (*The Hindu* 6-8-2000). Various anti Karunakaran groups in the Congress(I) took out an impressive Youth Congress march at Thrissur on 6 August, 2000 as a move to counter the proposed rally of the 'I' group on 9 August, 2000. On 9 August 2000 the Karunakaran group held a mammoth rally at Thrissur. While addressing the rally Karunakaran said "Youth Congress would be led by youngsters themselves and nobody should try to indulge in back seat driving" (*The Hindu* 10-8-2000).

The candidate selection and the finalisation of assembly seats in the 2001 Assembly elections came to the advantage of Karunakaran faction. At the time of the 2001 Assembly election, Cherian Philip took cudgels against the party seniors, Oommen

Chandy, Aryadan and Thankachan by advocating a 'Kamaraj Formula' so as to make way for the youngsters (The Hindu 13.4.2001). KPCC President, Muraleedharan openly expressed his dissatisfaction of the appointment of Anil Kumar as the Youth Congress President. One of the major issues raised by the KPCC President was the need to have a Youth Congress President with whom he could share a working relationship (*The Hindu* 15-7-2002). The affairs of the Congress party in Kerala is facing a major challenge with Antony and Karunakaran gearing up for a direct confrontation, the first one of its kind since the Congress led UDF came to power in 2001. Antony alleged that a section in the Congress had hatched a conspiracy to topple the government (The Hindu 12.8.2002). 'Immature' was the term used by Karunakaran to describe Antony's theory of conspiracy.

Karunakaran strongly opposed the government's decision to hike electricity tariff and demanded a roll back of the rates (*The Kerala Kaumudi* 3-9-2002). Some KPCC office bearers and certain ministers in the coalition publicly criticised the hike in electricity tariff (*Mathrubhumi* 4-9-2002). Differences between Karunakaran and Antony have taken an irreconcilable course. Antony also reacted sharply to the leader's criticism when he said that Karunakaran had always been a vehement critic of his actions and that no one expected him to utter a good word about his government" (*The Hindu* 10-9-2002). In the midst of all these the Karunakaran group demanded a cabinet reshuffle. Ambika Soni, the AICC general secretary said that it is the prerogative of the chief minister to reshuffle the cabinet. Muralidharan and Antony ruled out the possibility of a reshuffle now.

Anxious to prevent the party's image in Kerala from being further damaged because of the 'war of statements', the high command announced that certain measures would be taken. Congress President Sonia Gandhi accepted the state unit's request for the formation of a disciplinary committee to deal with such acts of indiscipline (*The Hindu* 27-9-2002). However experience tells us that adoption of such disciplinary mechanisms cannot prevent indiscipline either at the top, or at the bottom. The loyalists placed at the lower and middle level leaderships of their groups who often bear the brunt of disciplinary action get rewarded at a later stage with plum party or government positions. This has been the pattern prevalent among different groups. So institutionalisation in this sphere becomes meaningless as groups are a reality in the state Congress party.

It is impossible to strike a perfect harmony among the different Congress groups in Kerala since the basis of groupism is not overtly ideological or for the larger good of the society. Naturally, efforts at consensus gets narrowed down to sharing of the 'spoils of office'. When it comes to this, a group's aspirations are insatiable and it conflicts with the aspirations of another group. Inspite of the talk of unity, it is seen that one group always has an upper hand in Congress politics in the state. The upper hand that a group has depends on many factors, but the most important is its closeness and credibility with the party high command. So depending on this, the 'I' & 'A' factions interchange their roles during intervals. The group that gains an upper hand argues for party discipline and a full stop to irresponsible statements while the other group stands for freedom of criticism and inner party democracy. The net result is that nobody can claim to be 'angels of party discipline'. This infact is the paradox of the politics of Congress factionalism in Kerala.

In Kerala elections, it is only a few lakhs of votes that separate the victor from the looser. As such what is required is accommodation of the interests of the different groups without forcing them out of the party. Infact this is what the Congress high command is doing at present in its unit in Kerala.

5. The Weakening of the High Command:-

During the pre-independence period, it was the organisational wing in the party which controlled its governmental wing while after independence it was the governmental wing of the party that controlled the organisational wing. Nehru once stated that the cabinet was primarily responsible to the parliamentary board, and that the parliamentary wing and cabinet were only secondary to the party (Ramesh Kumar 1994:81).The dominance of governmental wing over the organisational wing was a substantial reversal of the pre-independent party-government relationship. Another development was the dominance of central government wing over the provincial one, resulting in the dominance of the centre over the states.

The chief ministers were infact nominated by the central leadership and the state legislative party approved it. Such a tendency promoted centre-state tensions. The emergence of regional parties is the fallout of this tendency. In the absence of a strong opposition, Nehru was able to keep up the umbrella image of the Congress during his period. After Nehru's death, the 'Syndicate' managed party affairs on the basis of collective responsibility, collective leadership and collective approach. This was the Lal Bahadur Shastri period. The Indira- Morarji team functioned for a short period and then followed the split. For a while the ideological division seemed apparent. The leftists rallied round Indira Gandhi and the rightist forces aligned with the Syndicate Congress (Ibid:83). Indira Gandhi wrested the control of the Congress party and Congressmen all over the country saw Indira Gandhi as the true representative of the Gandhi-Nehru tradition.

Congress affairs during Indira's and Rajiv's period had remarkable similarities as well as differences. In both periods, the leader-party relationship is the same; the leader's personality controlled the party. The suppression of internal democracy in the party and suspension of elections in the party were features common to both Indira and Rajiv regimes. State party chiefs were appointed by the centre, not elected. The convention of the Prime Minister or the Party President nominating Congress chief ministers stems from the same period. But Rajiv did reaffirm the principle of the state party choice via his 'doctrine of consensus' (Lyold L. Rudolph and Susannett Rudolph opcited:99).

After two decades Rao conducted party elections from bottom to the top. The practice of nomination of chief ministers of the Congress ruled states continued. Dissident activities continued and some of the senior leaders including Arjun Singh were suspended from the party (Verinder Grover and Ranjana Arora:285). The highhandedness of Narasimha Rao and his coterie was challenged by the regional satraps who had played a dominant role in the Congress affairs at the national level during Indira-Rajiv periods.

N.D Tiwari in Uttar Pradesh and Madhava Rao Scindia in Madhya Pradesh formed separate regional organisations, just like Mooppanar in TamilNadu and Mamta Banerjee in West Bengal. Battle for the leadership was eventually fought in the AICC. CWC was split into two for selection of a predecessor. Finally Sitaram Kesari became the President. He copted youngsters and tried to capture the power of the country. The functioning of the official bodies of the party gave the impression that there was no co-operation between the different wings of the party. The Congress(I) soon shed all its pretensions to real internal democracy and went back to the Nehru-Gandhi family for guidance and leadership by electing Sonia as the President of the AICC.

For long the Congress President retained the moral and political authority to manage factional conflicts in the manner that was deemed best for the party. The decline in the Congress(I) fortunes began increasingly with the adoption of the ad-hoc course of appeasing factions (Frontline 8-5-98:5). This tendency increased during Rajiv's time and Narasimha Rao indulged in much politicking in state units through his policy of checks and balances which also included replacement of different leaders so as to thwart challenges to his leadership of the party and government from other powerful and senior leaders. Sonia Gandhi continues this practice even today. It is an irony of history that all her close associates are those who had left the party at one time or other. The collapse of the central authority in the Congress (I) is a matter of serious concern today.

Earlier the high commands diktats were obeyed as the party was running the central government and there was no credible alternative to Congress at the centre and in a large number of states. The changed socio-economic configuration and the resultant political realignments has brought into existence an alternative to Congress rule in the traditional bastions of the party, especially in the Hindi belt. The net result of this change is that the dominant party role that it played once is difficult to be re-enacted. The factional infighting in the state units can turn its apple cart for formation of governments in the states and at the centre. Moreover, the factions in each state are led mostly by party veterans who have systematically nurtured and developed a constituency of their own in their states.

In Kerala, the Congress (A) faction in 1980 proved that inspite of walking out of the parent organisation it could still retain its base. In the Kerala context where the party has to grapple with the powerful CPI(M) for power, the high command knows too well that the best guarantee for this lies in somehow accommodating the various factional demands. This dwindling authority of the Congress high command to strike at the roots of factionalism has made the factional leaders bold enough to openly challenge the decision of the high command.

Faction fights took place in all state units after the organisational election of 1992. Elected PCC chiefs were removed for the sake of appeasing the opposition faction in Tamil Nadu, Karnataka, Maharashtra and Kerala. In Kerala KPCC President Vayalar Ravi was sacked and in his place Thennala Balakrishna Pillai was nominated as the Chief. In 1998 Karunakaran faction was firm in their demand that they should get the presidentship of the KPCC. Karunakaran's son K. Muraleedharan was incorporated as the only Vice President of the KPCC to pacify that faction. Vayalar Ravi's successor Thennala Balakrishna Pillai was also ousted from the Presidentship more or less in the same manner for elevating K.Muraleedharan as the KPCC President to placate Karunakaran's demands. The AICC general secretary Gulam Nabi Azad refused the allegation that the incumbent Thennala has been unceremoniously packed off[16]. He said that Pillai had been inducted as PCC chief as an interim arrangement, but had been asked to continue since the party was not able to complete organisational elections along with other states due to faction fights (*The Hindu* 18-5-2001).

Due to the weakening of the high, command the different Congress factions found it convenient to align even with the opposition parties to embarrass the opposite group. When Karunakaran was the chief minister the opposing factions frequently demanded the resignation of the chief minister. It was a shot in the arm for the opposition LDF, when immediately after the organisational election Antony asked the UDF partners to examine whether the style of functioning of the chief minister adversely affected the stability of the front (*Kerala Kaumudi* 24.2.92). Internal strife continued throughout the period of the chiefministership of Karunakaran. During the time of the 'espionage case', Sudheeran, a strong Antony loyalist demanded the "resignation of the chief minister as he was protecting the accused police officers and denigrating the image of the Congress party" (*Mathrubhumi* 7.1.95). This was highly embarrassing to the chief minister as even the opposition had not gone that far. The same attitude continued even after the change of leadership at the government level. When the police action on Sivagiri mutt took place, Antony, the new chief minister complained that a section of Congressmen along with the opposition was trying to topple his government (*Malayala Manorama* 19-10-95).

The factions have also found a novel way of doing this through directing the feeder organisations loyal to them to openly join with similar groups owing allegiance to the opposition parties in opposing the controversial government policies and decisions. In the general strike of the state government employees and teachers from 6 February to 10 March, 2002 the pro-Congress organisations played a leading role with the full support of the 'I' faction and its leader K. Karunakaran. This was infact an important political challenge to the Antony government since its inception. In this context Karunakaran remarked: "the strike was a success from a trade union perspective, proving that the government cannot behave like a company management while handling issues related to its employees" (*The Hindu* 11.3.2002). The differences between K Karunakaran and A.K Antony have now taken an irreconcilable course. The divide has come quite unbridgeable as could be seen in Karunakaran's statement harping on the lack of collective responsibility in the cabinet. Antony hit back by stating that his ministry was not the first to occupy office in the state (*The Hindu* 10-9-2002).

Similarly the factions find it easy today to openly hobnob with caste- communal forces. The issues connected with the demand for the release of Madani, the PDP leader is being a cleverly exploited by the 'I' faction to embarrass A.K Antony and his group.

The eroding position of the high command has also emboldened the faction leaders to promote their kith and kin to important organisational and parliamentary positions. This adds fuel to the ongoing factional feud. It is pertinent here to note that this tendency increased in the 1990's, the decade during which the high command lost much of its credibility.

The above determinants and causes worked together; some more prominently than others at different points of time, and all aided by the course of political events and factional tendencies inherent in the social nature of man, took the factional conflict in the Congress party to new heights.

Notes

1. In this election Karunakaran contested from two constituencies one at Nemom in Thiruvananthapuram and the other at Mala in Thrissur. In both the seats he won.
2. The UDF included several parties namely, the Cong (I), the Cong(A), the IUML, the KC(M), the KC(J), the NDP, the SRP, the Janata (G), the RSP(S) and the NRSP. The DLP also declared support to the front. (Assembly Election Reportage 1996, PRD, Government of Kerala:12).
3. When Antony was the chief minister S. Varadarajan Nair was elected as the President of the KPCC as an Antony loyalist in 1977. During that period Kadannappally Ramachandran, A C Shanmughadas and Vayalar Ravi were the loyalists of Antony. In the late 1970's C M Stephen was the candidate of Karunakaran faction for the KPCC President's post. When Stephen became the leader of opposition in Lok Sabha in 1978, another Karunakaran loyalist K.M Chandy became the President of the KPCC. M.M Jacob, A A Kochunni and T.H Musthafa also belonged to the Karunakaran faction.
4. The Election to the KPCC in 1977 witnessed the first open clash between Antony and Karunakaran after Karunakaran resigned from the chief ministership in 1977. S. Varadarajan Nair defeated the Karunakaran loyalist C M Stephen. (The Hindu 13-11-1977).
5. Antony advised the party cadres that every one should follow the style of functioning of Prime minister P V Narasimha Rao, who takes important decisions only after consulting party colleagues and even the opposition leaders (Indian Express 27-11-1991).
6. See for details the *Constitution of the Indian National Congress & Rules*, AICC New Delhi, as approved by the CWC at its meeting on 16th January and 17th of March 1999.
7. After the 1978 split, the Congress(I) headed by Indira Gandhi

nominated K M Chandy as the President of the KPCC and K. Karunakaran as the leader of the legislature party in Kerala. Antony who was chief minister at that time was with Brahmananda Reddy. Indira Gandhi was then out of power.

8. Ramesh Chennithala, of the Karunakaran faction was nominated as the President of the KSU(I).
9. During the time of party reshuffle many Congressmen believed that Antony was going to be appointed as the chief of the KPCC. Newspaper reports also gave such an impression.
10. K.C Venugopal was nominated as President of the Youth Congress as a Karunakaran loyalist. Later he shifted his loyalty to the third group. J. Joseph is continuing in the 'A' faction.
11. The Front consisted of seven parties having contradictory views. It was formed by the CPI(M) under the leadership of EMS Namboodiripad. Interview with Aryadan Mohammed on 7-12-2001.
12. K. Karunakaran was in favour of joining the UF ministry headed by C AchuthaMenon, whereas A K Antony and Vayalar Ravi were against this view.
13. Interview with M.A John at Kuravilangad, Kottayam.
14. *Ibid.*
15. Interview with P.T Thomas MLA, at the MLA Hostel, Thiruvananthapuram
16. Thennala Balakrishna Pillai in an interview on 24-12-2002 at his residence in Thiruvananthapuram revealed that the nominee of the High command did not inform him of the decision to remove him even on the previous day of his exit from office.

References

Government Publications

Government of Kerala, (Undated) *Assembly Election Since 1951*, Thiruvananthapuram, Department of Public Relations.

Government of Kerala, (1991): *Backgrounder To Lok Sabha/Assembly Elections*, Trivandrum, Department of Public Relations.

Government of Kerala (1991): *Report on the Election to Kerala Legislative Assembly and Lok Sabha*, Trivandrum, Department of Public Relations.

Government of Kerala (1999): *Lok Sabha Election Reportage 1996,'98,'99*, Thiruvananthapuram, Department of Public Relations.

Government of Kerala (2001): *Assembly Elections Reportage 1996*, Trivandrum, Department of Public Relations.

Election Guides

Kalakaumudi (1979): *Kalakaumudi Election Guide (I) 1980*, Trivandrum, Laisa publication.

Kalakaumudi (1980): *Kalakaumudi Election guide (II) 1980*, Trivandrum , Laisa Publication.

Malayala Manorama (1982): *Manorama Election Guide 1982*, Kottayam, Manorama publication.

Malayala Manorama (1991): *Manorama Election Guide 1991*, Kottayam, Manorama publications.

Malayala Manorama (1996): *Malayala Manorama Election Guide 1996*, Kottayam, Manorama Publication.

Malayala Manorama (2001): *Malayala Manorama Election Guide 2001*, Kottayam, Manorma Publication.

Books

All India Congress Committee (1999): *Constitution of the Indian National Congress & Rules*, New Delhi.

Attarchand(1991): *Prime Minister P.V. Narasimha Rao: The Scholar and Statesman* , New Delhi, Gyan publishing house.

Barnett Marguerite Ross and others (1975): *Electoral Politics in the Indian States: Party systems and Cleavages*, New Delhi, Manohar Book service.

Bhabani Sengupta (1989): *Rajiv Gandhi: A Political Study*, New Delhi, Konark Publishers.

Chakraborty Bidyut (1993): *Whither India's Democracy*, Calcutta, K.P. Bagchi & Com.

Engineer Asghar Ali (1995): *Kerala Muslims*, New Delhi, Ajanta Publication.

Janak Rai Jai & Rajiv Jai,(1999): *Revival of Two Party System in India Ruling Vs Combined Opposition*, New Delhi, Regency.

John P John (1983): *Coalition Politics in Kerala*, Thiruvananthapuram, Institute for the Study of Public Policy and Management.

Jose Chander (1986): "Politics of Merger" In Jose Chander (ed) *Dynamics of State Politics: Kerala*, New Delhi, Sterling.

Jose Chander N (1997): "Coalition Politics: Kerala Model", in Subhash C Kashyap (Ed), *Coalition Governments and Politics in India*, New Delhi, Uppal Publishing House.

Kalim Bahadur & M.C. Paul (2000): *Contemporary India*, New Delhi, Netaji Institute of Sub continental Studies.

Kochanek A Stanley (1968): *The Congress Party of India: The Dynamics of One Party Democracy*, New Jersey, Princeton University Press.

Kochanek A Stanley (2002): "Mrs. Gandhi's Pyramid: The New Congress" in Zoya Hasan (Ed), *Parties and Party System in India*, New Delhi, Oxford University Press.

Krishna Kumari S (1994): *Coalition Politics in Kerala 1970-85*, (PhD Thesis) Thiruvananthapuram, University of Kerala.

Kundu C L & D N Tutoo (1988): *Educational Psychology*, New Delhi, Sterling.

Mani Sankar Aiyar (1993): *In Rajiv's Foot Prints: A Year in Parliament*, New Delhi, Konark.

Manor James (1997): "Parties and Party Systems" In Partha Chatterjee (Ed) *State Politics in India*, New Delhi, Oxford.

Mehrotra N.C (1980): *Political Crisis and Polls in India*, New Delhi, Deep & Deep.

Mekhala Kulapati (1999): *Political Disputes and Controversies*, New Delhi, Kanishka.

Merchant Minhaz (1991): *Rajiv Gandhi*, New Delhi, Penguin Books.

Nagendra Reddy, M Venkal Taò & P. Venkareswara Rao (Ed) (1993): *P.V. Narasimha Rao: Years of Power*, New Delhi, Har Anand Publication.

Narasimha Rao P V(1998): *The Insider*, New Delhi, Viking.

Om P.Gautham (1985): *The Indian National Congress*, New Delhi B.R. Publishing Corporation.

Ralhan O P (1996): *Encyclopedia of Political Parties*, New Delhi, Anmol.

Ramesh Kumar (1994): *Congress and Congressism in Indian Politics*, New Delhi, Deep & Deep.

Rudolph L Lloyed and Susanne H Rudolph (1990): "Organisational Adaptation of the Congress under Rajiv Gandhi's Leadership" in Richard Sission and Ramshray Roy (Ed) *Diversity and Dominance in Indian Politics: Changing Bases of Congress Support*, New Delhi, Sage.

Shubhabrata Bhattacharya (1985): "Kerala Fragile Coalition", *The Sunday*, 6-12 October.

Subrata Mukherjee (2000): "Crisis of the Congress: From Mass Consensual Origins to Restrictive Politics" in S R Chakravarty and others (Ed) *Contemporary India*, New Delhi, Netaji Institute of Sub Continental Studies.

Thomas E J (1985): *Coalition Game Politics in Kerala*, New Delhi, Intellectual Publishing House.

Verinder Grover and Ranjana Arora, *India: Fifty Years of Independence*, New Delhi, Deep & Deep.

Vrindavan G Venugopalan (1992): *K Karunakaran* (M), Aluva, Islamiya Book Stall.

Wood R John (1984): *State Politics in Contemporary India*, USA West View Press.

Yogesh Atal (2000): *Mandate for Political Transition: Re-emergence of Vajpayee*, New Delhi, Rawat.

Periodicals

Anoop C (1999): "Closeup: Thiruvananthapuram" (M), *Kalakaumudi*, VOl.1253, 12 September.

Aravindakshan P (1991): "Hit With Poll Axe", *The Week*, 10 February.

Frontline (1987): "Kerala at the Polls", *Front Line*, April 18- May 1.

Gauridasan Nair . C(1992): "Nebulous in Kerala", *Front Line*, September 11.

Kalakaumudi (1982): "Chaarem Moodiya Kanal Kattakal" (M), *Kalakaumudi*, vol.349, 9 May

Kalakaumudi (1982): "Eeni Vijayathinte Parajayam" (M), *Kalakaumudi*, vol.353, 6-June.

Kalakaumudi (1982): "Bharanakakshi Managerude Chiri" (M), *Kalakaumudi*, vol.357, 4-July.

Kalakaumudi (1998): "Edathottu Kanneriyunna Sonia",(M) *Kalakaumudi*, vol.1202, September 20.

Kalakaumudi (1984): "Joseph Groupinte Uriyadi", (M) *Kalakaumudi*, vol.433, 1 January.

Kalakaumudi (1985): "Karthikeyante Poovedi" (M), *Kalakaumudi*, vol.501, 21 April.

Kalakaumudi (1986): "Delhiyil Mani Nirathiya Fayalukal", *Kalakaumudi*,(M), vol.547, 9-March.

Kalakaumudi (1986): "Karunakarante Puthiya Kallakkali", (M), *Kalakaumudi* , vol.551, 6 Apirl.

Kalakaumudi (1986): "Sreenivasante Vyangyam" (M), *Kalakaumudi*, vol.561, 15 June.

Kalakaumudi (1986): "Ee Yudham Eniyum Neelum", (M), *Kalakaumudi*, vol.573, 7 September.

Kalakaumudi (1987): "A Tale of Two Parties", *Kalakaumudi*, vol.594, 1-February.

Krishna Kumar R (1998): "Adhoc Arrangement", *Front Line* Vol.15, No.15, July 18-31.

Krishna Kumar R (2001): "A Record of Sorts", *Front Line*, Vol.18, No.11, May 25-June 8.

Nair K.P (1985): "Kerala's Unholy Coalition Politics", *Front Line* 15-28 June.

Nair K P (1987): "Kerala- A Water Shed", *Front line*, Vol.4, No.7, April 14-27.

Nair K P (1989): "Kerala: Fight of the Fronts", *Front Line*, 11-24 November.

Nair K P (1992): "Kerala Politics in the Cauldron", *The Hindu*, 29 February.

Nair K.P (1992): "Cong (I) Charade: In Kerala Karunakaran under siege", *Front Line*, Oct 23.

Narendran (1998): "Jayikkunna Antonyum Thakarunna Antony Groupum" , *Malayalam*, Vol. 1, No. 38, 30 January.

Sajeevan A (2000): "Leaguea, Leaguea Koodevide", *Kalakaumudi*, Vol. 1300, 6 August.

Sankar M (2001): Antoniyum Oommen chandyum Yuvakkale Kuruthikoduthu", *Malayalam*, Vol. 4, No. 41, 13 April.

Sarat Lal K S (2001): "Karunakarante Thriptiyum Poorna Thriptiyum" (M), *Kalakaumudi*, Vol. 1343, 27 May.

Sasikumar V. (1983): "Antony Muthal Antulay Vare" (M), *Kalakaumudi*, Vol. 425, 6 November.

Sreedhar Pillai (1983): "Surprise Move", *India Today*, Vol. 8, No.17, September.

Sreedhar Pillai (1984): "Patching Up", *India Today*, VOl. 9, No. 15, August 15.

Sreedhar Pillai (1986): "Truce Time", *India Today*, Vol.11, No.1, 15 January.

Sreedhar Pillai (1986): "Compromise Formula", *India Today*, Vol. V, No. 11, 15 June.

Sujathan P (2000): "Pankuvaippukar Nanichu: Congressil Thiranjeduppu"(M), *Kalakaumudi*, Vol. 1272, 23 January.

Sujathan P (2001): "Kerala Congressile Kolilakkom", *Kalakaumudi*, Vol. 1345, 10 June.

Sukumar Muralidharan (1999): "A Kargil Election", *Front Line*, Vol. 16, No. 19, 11-24 September.

Swapan Dasgupta (2001): "Two winners And A Photo Finish ", India Today, Vol. 35, No. 20, 8-14 May.

Venu Menon (1985): "For God's Sake", *Illustrated Weekly of India*, 15 July.

Vinu Abraham (2001): "Foul Start", *The Week*, Vol. 19, No. 19, 22 April.

Vinu Abraham (2001): "Left with Bloody Nose", *The Week*, Vol. 19, No. 24, 27 May.

Newspapers

Deepika
Deshabhimani
Kerala Kaumudi
Madhyamom
Malayala Manorama
Mathrubhumi
The Hindu
The New Indian Express
Times of India

Four

Approach to Empirical Analysis

As stated already, the practice of maintaining proper records systematically is non-existent as far as Congress party in Kerala is concerned. This compels the researcher to go for data obtained through field study. As such primary data and statistics connected to the present study had to be obtained from selected Congress activists spread over the fourteen districts of Kerala. The interview schedule for this purpose was prepared in such a way that it touched upon all the important socio-economic and political background of the respondents. Though the feedback is restricted to a select group of 677, the data has the potential for examining the issue in the larger context. It is presumed that the data thus obtained will be of help to the future students of Congress politics in the state.

With the above general purpose in mind and for specifically enabling us to undertake an empirical analysis of the data in the next two chapters of the thesis, various tables containing the gender, age, religion, caste, education, income and leadership wise details of the Congressmen are given below. This is essential since it reveals the strength and weaknesses of our analysis. These tables remain an original source of data as far as studies on Congress party in the state are concerned.

Universe and Sample Size

The interview schedule covered all the fourteen districts in the state. The researcher had selected all the 14 DCC presidents. 39 DCC secretaries, 31 DCC members, 34 Bloc presidents, 26 Bloc secretaries, 38 Mandalam presidents, 33 Mandalam secretaries and 462 congressmen performing various leadership roles in the party at different levels including the leaders of the feeder organisations as respondents. Multi stage random sampling technique has been used to select the respondents from among the office bearers. A sample of 677 Congressmen was chosen for the study. Random selection of sampling unit is practically impossible due to the lack of proper official sampling frame (non availability of proper membership details at the bottom level). Inorder to ascertain that the respondents are genuine Congress workers, the researcher conducted cross checking at various levels. Due care was taken to make the sample representative by giving due weightage to different factors such as gender, region, rural-urban divide, different factions, different age and income groups, religion and caste. Based on the interview schedule fifty respondents each were interviewed in twelve districts except in Waynad and Idukki, where it was thirty eight and thirty nine respectively.

Data Collection

The data for the study were gathered from the records maintained in the KPCC offices in Trivandrum and Ernakulam and all DCC offices in the State. The researcher conducted personal interviews with the chosen respondents. Tools of data collection include:

(a) Interview Schedule

Interview schedule was the main tool used for data collection because of its relative advantage in gathering descriptive data from the respondents. This method was chosen for avoiding non response and irrelevant response and also to hasten the data collection process. Further, this method is capable of facilitating the collection of supplementary data through observation. For interviewing the respondents, a schedule was prepared in English. The schedule was pre tested before it was finalised. The schedule contained questions to obtain information as to the socio-economic background of the respondents. It was also devised in such a way as to understand and interpret the nature and dynamics of Congress factionalism as discussed in the conceptual framework. On an average an interview lasted for about 1 to 1.30 hour per respondent.

(b) Interview Guide

Apart from the interview schedule an interview guide was also prepared to interview top leaders of the Congress party in Kerla. Using the interview guide, K. Karunakaran, K. Muraleedharan, Thennala Balakrishna Pillai, A.C Jose, George Eden, M.I. Shanavas, P.P Thankachan, M.K Raghavan, N. Venugopal, Rajmohan Unnithan, Ajay Tharayil, K.K Vijaya Lakshmi, P.K Velayudhan, Rosakutty Teacher, JosephVazhakkan, Ajeeba M Sahib, N.K Abdul Rahman, Shanimol Usman, C. N Balakrishnan, Aryadan Mohammed, M.A John, P. Balan, N.P Moideen, I Rama Rai, P.T Thomas, Prathapa Varma Thampan, K.C Joseph, Ezhukone Narayanan, E. M Augusty, Khader Mangad, K. Prathapan, Punalur Madhu, V.V Prakash, K.P Anil Kumar, Peeliphose Thomas, K.P. Noorudeen, V. Sathyaseelan, Karumalil Sukumaran, A.K Hafees, A.A Samad, Vasudeva Sarma and Palode Ravi were interviewed.

Framework of Analysis

As the data, to a large extent, were qualitative in nature, simple statistical correlation was found possible in most cases. In several tables the data clearly revealed the trend and as such no statistical correlation has been worked out. In few other cases X^2 have been calculated.

Gender-wise Profile

The social set up prevailing in the state provides almost equal status to women in all fields of life. Women are fully aware of their rights and privileges. Though the national movement brought to the forefront of political struggle a few women from the elite sections, it was the left movement that politically organised a large number of women from the downtrodden sections of the society. Eventhough they have been guaranteed thirty three per cent reservation in the election to the local bodies in Kerala, their participation in leadership roles at different levels in different parties, is negligibly low. Particularly it was very low in the Congress party compared to the left parties. The data collection also indicates this.

TABLE NO. 1
THE GENDER-WISE RATIO OF THE RESPONDENTS AND ITS PERCENTAGE

Gender	*Frequency*	*Percent*
Male	651	96.16
Female	26	3.84
Total	677	100.0

As the table shows only 26 out of the 677 (3.84%) respondents belong to the female category. The abysmally low participation of women in Congress party activities is clear from the following Pie chart.

DIAGRAM — 1
PIE DIAGRAM SHOWING GENDER-WISE RATIO OF RESPONDENTS

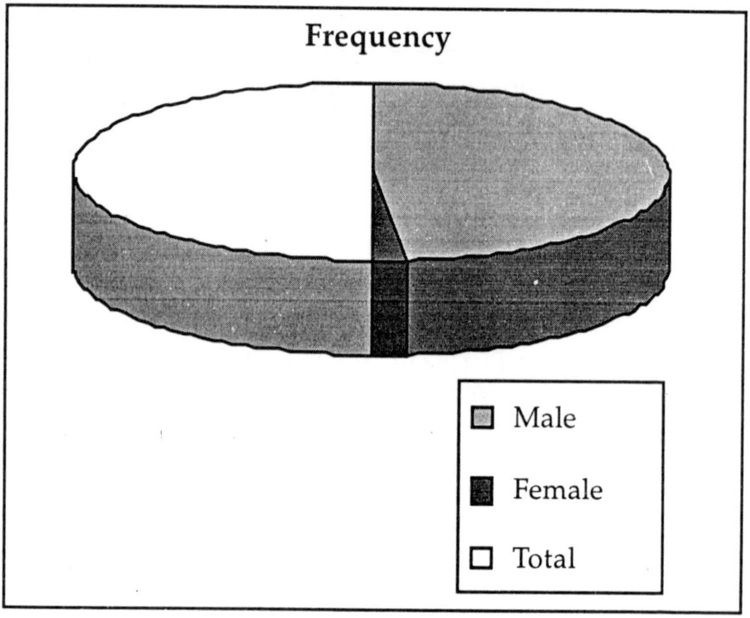

A further religion wise classification of the female respondents can be seen below.

TABLE NO. 2
THE RELIGION-WISE CLASSIFICATION OF THE FEMALE RESPONDENTS

Religion	*No. of respondents*
Hindu	16
Christian	6
Muslim	4

DIAGRAM — 2
BAR DIAGRAM SHOWING THE RELIGION-WISE CLASSIFICATION OF THE FEMALE RESPONDENTS

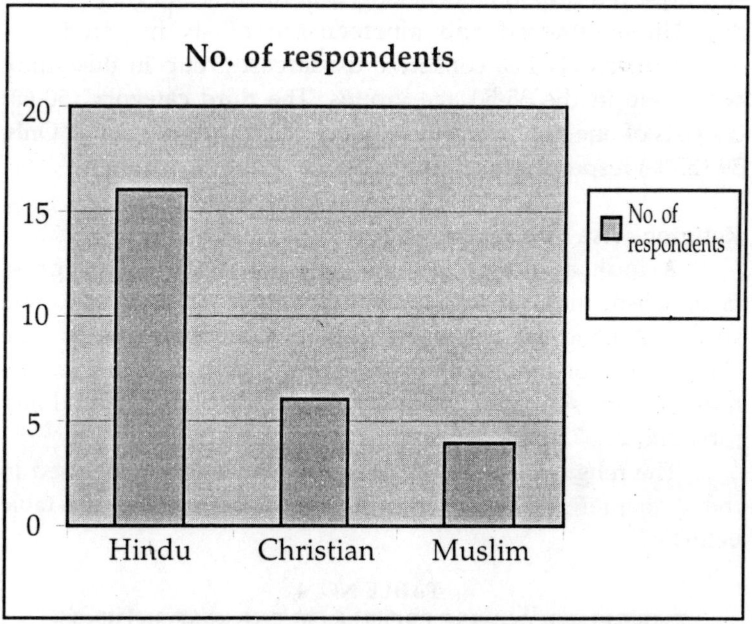

Among the Hindus eight belong to the higher castes, four to the Ezhava and one to most backward community. Three respondents are from the SC/ST category.

Age-wise Profile

For facilitating the age based analysis, the respondents are grouped into four categories.

TABLE NO. 3
THE AGE-WISE PROFILE OF THE RESPONDENTS

Age	*Frequency*	*Percent*
18/35	158	23.4
35/50	319	47.1
50/65	161	23.8
Above 65	39	5.7
Total	677	100.0

One hundred and fiftyeight out of sixhundred and seventyseven respondents belonged to the first category i.e. (18-35). Three hundred and nineteen out of six hundred and seventyseven (47.1%) constitute the largest group in this study who were in the 35-50 age groups. The third category (50-65) consists of one hundred and sixty one (23.8%) respondents. Only 39 (5.7%) respondents are in the above sixtyfive category.

Religion-wise Profile

A look at the religion wise orientation of Congress factionalism more or less corresponds to the pattern of Kerala society. Among the respondents three hundred and sixty nine (54.51%) out of six hundred and seventy seven are Hindus, one hundred and sixty two Christians (23.9%) and one hundred and forty six (21.57%) are Muslims.

The religious context of Congress factionalism analysed in the V chapter is based on the responses as shown in the table below.

TABLE NO. 4
THE RELIGION-WISE PROFILE OF THE RESPONDENTS

Religion	*Frequency*	*Percent*
Hindu	369	54.51
Christian	162	23.93
Muslim	146	21.57
Total	677	100

Caste-wise details

In India, caste has played a key role in the socio-economic life of the people. Besides being an ascriptive system of status hierarchy the caste system has defined and controlled the social, economic and political relationship of individuals in Indian society. Caste is a sub-classification of religion. The number of sub-classification in the form of various castes is very high in the Hindu religion. The classification of castes into 'backward' and 'forward' is based on the relative social status of the members belonging to these castes as determined by the government of Kerala for official purposes.

TABLE NO. 5
THE CASTE-WISE DETAILS OF THE RESPONDENTS

Caste	*Frequency*	*Percent*
FC	278	41.06
OBC	356	52.58
MBC	4	.59
SC/ST	39	5.76
Total	677	100

As the table shows two hundred and seventyeight respondents out of six hundred and seventy seven (41.06%) are Forward Castes, three hundred and fiftysix (52.58%) are members of the Other Backward Castes and Four (0.59%) out of 677 (0.59 %) belong to the Most Backward Castes and thirty nine (5.7%) respondents are in the SC/ST category.

Education-wise details

Based on the level of education attained by each respondent, they were classified into seven categories. The respondents whose level of education was below SSLC were treated as having low level of education. Twenty three (3.4%) out of 677 were placed in this category. Eventhough they did not possess any formal schooling they were literate and could read and write in the mother tongue.

TABLE NO. 6
THE EDUCATIONAL BACKGROUND OF THE RESPONDENTS

Education	*Frequency*	*Percent*
Below SSLC	23	3.4
SSLC	276	40.8
Under Graduate	103	15.2
Graduate	163	24.1
Post Graduate	59	8.7
Professionals (diploma)	37	5.5
Professionals (Graduate & above)	16	2.4
Total	677	100.0

Those up to SSLC constitute the largest category i.e., two hundred and seventysix (40.8%). Under graduates number one hundred and three (15.2%), graduates one hundred and sixty three (24.1%) and post graduates 59 (8.7%). Thirty seven (5.5%) out of 677 were professionals (Diploma holders) and sixteen (2.4%) were professionals (Graduates and above). The education wise categorisation of the respondents reveals the ability of the Congress party to recruit cadres from different section of the society.

Income-wise Profile of the Respondents

The details of the income of the respondents from all sources are given in the table below:

TABLE NO. 7
THE DETAILS OF THE INCOME OF THE RESPONDENTS

Income	*Frequency*	*Percent*
Below 1000	148	21.9
1000-5000	366	54.1
5000-8000	61	9.0
8000-10000	43	6.4
10000 & above	59	8.7
Total	677	100.0

Majority of the respondents comes under the income category of Rs. 1000-5000 i.e three hundred and sixty six (54.1%) out of six hundred and seventy seven. The low income category, i.e., below Rs.1000/- comprises of one hundred and fortyeight respondents (21.9%) out of six hundred and seventy seven. Other three categories constitute only one-fourth of the total respondents.

Profile of Congress Party Respondents based on their Leadership Roles

Inorder to have an understanding of the factional dynamics, it is necessary to have religion wise, caste wise and gender wise data on the leadership patterns. There is no such data available in the party archives. This compels us to go for sample data directly collected from party activists. Based on such data and available records, various tables have been prepared which indicates the religious wise, caste wise and gender wise composition of the different factions.

TABLE NO. 8
THE LEADERSHIP POSITIONS HELD BY THE DIFFERENT RELIGIONS AND CASTE GROUPS IN THE CONGRESS PARTY

Position held	*Christian*	*Muslim*	*Nair*	*Ezhava*	*MBC*	*SC/ST*	*Total*
DCC President	4	2	5	3	-	-	14
DCC Secretary	7	4	13	10	-	5	39
DCC Member	6	4	10	7	1	3	31
Bloc President	12	4	9	8	1	-	34
Bloc Secetary	7	2	6	9	1	1	26
Mandal President	17	5	8	7	1	-	38
Mandal Secretary	10	4	9	8		2	33
Total	63 (29.30%)	25 (11.63%)	60 (27.91%)	52 (24.19%)	4 (1.85%)	11 (5.12%)	215

Though the sample survey consists of 677 respondents only those occupy leadership roles from the District Committee President down to the Mandalam Secretary is relevant for this table. Their number comes to two hundred and fifteen. Among the remaining, three hundred and eight are party activists and one hundred and fiftyfour are working in the feeder organisation affiliated to the party.

The following four tables (Table 9(a), (b), (c) & (d)) depicts the leadership positions of the Congress respondents belonging to Nair, Ezhava, SC/ST and MBC communities and their group affiliation.

TABLE NO. 9 (A)
THE LEADERSHIP POSITIONS HELD BY THE RESPONDENTS BELONGING TO THE NAIR COMMUNITY AND THEIR GROUP AFFILIATION

Position Held	*Group*			
	AK	*KK*	*GK*	*VR*
DCC President	1	4	-	-
DCC Secretary	4	4	2	1
DCC Member	3	4	1	1
Bloc President	1	5	2	1
Bloc Secretary	3	3		
Mandalam President	2	3	1	
Mandalam Secretary	3	6		
Total	17	29	6	3

TABLE NO. 9 (B)
THE LEADERSHIP POSITIONS HELD BY THE RESPONDENTS BELONGING TO THE EZHAVA COMMUNITY AND THEIR GROUP AFFILIATION

Position Held	*Group*			
	AK	*KK*	*GK*	*VR*
DCC President	2		1	
DCC Secretary	3	6	0	1
DCC Member	3	4		
Bloc President	2	5		1
Bloc Secretary	2	5	1	1
Mandalam President	2	4		1
Mandalam Secretary	2	3		1
Total	16	27	2	5

TABLE NO. 9 (C)
THE LEADERSHIP POSITIONS HELD BY THE RESPONDENTS BELONGING TO THE SC/ST COMMUNITY AND THEIR GROUP AFFILIATION

Position Held	*Group*			
	AK	*KK*	*GK*	*VR*
DCC President	-	-	-	-
DCC Secretary	1	2		
DCC Member	1	2		
Bloc President	-	-	-	-
Bloc Secretary	1	-	-	-
Mandalam President	-	-		
Mandalam Secretary		2		
Total	3	6		

TABLE NO. 9 (D)
THE LEADERSHIP POSITIONS HELD BY THE RESPONDENTS BELONGING TO THE HINDU-MBC COMMUNITY AND THEIR GROUP AFFILIATION

Position Held	*Group*			
	AK	*KK*	*GK*	*VR*
DCC President	-	-	-	-
DCC Secretary				
DCC Member		1		
Bloc President		1		
Bloc Secretary		1		
Mandalam President	1			
Mandalam Secretary				
Total	1	3		

The following two tables show the Christian and Muslim representation at different leadership positions (DCC President to Mandalam Secretary) in the Congress party. It also indicates their group preference.

TABLE NO. 10 (A)
THE LEADERSHIP POSITIONS HELD BY THE RESPONDENTS BELONGING TO THE CHRISTIAN COMMUNITY AND THE GROUP TO WHICH THEY BELONG

Position Held	*Group*			
	AK	*KK*	*GK*	*VR*
DCC President	1	2		1
DCC Secretary	2	4		
DCC Member	2	3		
Bloc President	3	7		
Bloc Secretary	4	3		
Mandalam President	3	7		
Mandalam Secretary	4	4	1	
Total	19	30	1	1

TABLE NO. 10 (B)
THE LEADERSHIP POSITIONS HELD BY THE RESPONDENTS BELONGING TO THE MUSLIM COMMUNITY AND THE GROUP TO WHICH THEY BELONG

Position Held	*Group*			
	AK	*KK*	*GK*	*VR*
DCC President	1	1	-	-
DCC Secretary	2	2		
DCC Member	1	3		
Bloc President	1	3		
Bloc Secretary	1	1		
Mandalam President	2	2		
Mandalam Secretary	1	1		
Total	9	13		

TABLE NO. 11
THE AREA OF ACTIVITY OF THE FEMALE RESPONDENTS

S. No	*Area of activity*	*No.*
1	MLA's	3
2	Mahila Congress Office bearers (State level)	4
3	DCC Secretary's	3
4	District Panchayat Member	1
5	Block Congress President	1
6	Block Panchayat Member	1
7	Panchayat Vice President	1
8	Councillors (Corporations and Municipalities)	5
9	Activists (contested candidate)	7
	Total	26

It would also be worth while to provide the details regarding the women representation at different leadership levels in the party. Most of the women respondents work as members of local bodies. Their representation in the leadership roles in the party is insignificant.

In this chapter, the socio-economic profile of the respondents has been described. Of the total respondents 26 (3.8%) are females. Majority of the respondents are Hindus. Of these the majority consists of the OBC's. Majority of the respondents studied up to SSLC. Income wise the majority comes under the Rs.1000-5000/- category. Of the total 677 respondents, 215 are office bearers in the organisational hierarchy. Majority of the respondents favoured the 'I' group. Majority of the female respondents held official positions such as MLA's and members of the local self government institutions. From the above, it is clear that the profile of the respondents reflects the true nature of Kerala society.

In the light of the above, the social base of Congress factionalism in Kerala is analysed in the next chapter.

Five

Social Base of Factionalism

The state of Kerala was formed out of three political units each of which had a separate identity in British period, namely, the Travancore state, the Cochin state and the Malabar province which formed part of Madras Presidency of British India. Two thirds of the present day Kerala is composed of Travancore and Cochin; each with its distinct history and cultural background. While the Indian National Congress directly operated in Malabar, Travancore and Cochin had their own separate organisation to fight for responsible government. Politics in Travancore and Cochin was for a long period built around interest groups based on caste and religion. The unique feature of the politics of Malabar was that it always had an ideological content. Ideologically, 'right' and 'left' groups emerged in the Congress and each of these tried to capture the party and organisation to give it a new ideological orientation (Sadasivan Nair 1970:1-2).

For a logical understanding of the electoral politics of Kerala and the Congress party's compulsions, it is essential to have an understanding of the peculiarities that the region has inherited in the form of its demographic composition and geography. In Kerala as per the 1991 census the Hindus constitute 57.28% of the population. Muslims (23.33%) and the Christians (19.32%) together constitute 42.65%. It means that 2/5 of the population is non Hindus. Social stratification on caste lines in Kerala is similar to what exists elsewhere in the country. Among the Hindus, Ezhavas constitute 22.19% and Nairs 14%. The SC population consisting of 68 groups makes up 8%, while ST, found scattered in about 35 officially identifiable groups, form 1.5% of the state population [1]. Nairs and Ezhavas are a political force to be reckoned with due to their concentration in the southern region of the state where they are sizeable in number. The Nair Service Society (NSS) established in 1914 has played a dominant role in consolidating Nair votes (Muraleedharan Nair 1996:252-96). The Ezhavas, more numerous than Nairs, have same kind of influence in the southern districts and a sizeable presence in Thrissur and in north Kerala. Christians and Muslims cannot be considered as minorities in Kerala if due allowance is made to the existence of several castes and sub-castes in the Hindu fold. Moreover in Kerala, one can see the existence of a Muslim belt and a Christian belt during elections. These 'minority belts' assure them a sizeable representation in the state legislature. As such nobody can overlook nor ignore the political clout that these two communities wield in the electoral politics of Kerala (Suresh Kumar 2001:189-99). Likewise, caste is also predominant in Kerala politics. It has also been a potential source of factionalism in all political parties. Caste and communal support very often decides the outcome of an election. The Congress led UDF always project itself as an umbrella under which all caste-communal groups find shelter.

In the 1977 and 1980 Assembly elections the CPI (M) led LDF also consisted of a section of Muslim League and a splinter section of the Church dominated Kerala Congress. This policy was continued during 1991, 1996 and 2001 elections. In short, the Congress, the CPI(M) and the two combinations led by them remain the prisoners of this demographic and geographical syndrome. The social formations that played a pivotal role in establishing the bi-party pattern of equilibrium has already fixed the orbit of both the fronts and its constituent parties (Mohanan 1999:111-29).

The Congress party's emotional appeal extends to all religions and communities. Traditionally majority of the Christians are pro-Congress. The NSS and SNDP representing Nair and Ezhava interests respectively often come to the help of the Congress party since it was more accommodative to the economic and educational interests of these social formations[2]. The Muslim and Christian communities have their own political parties which serve their general anti-communist stand. The geographical and demographic composition of Kerala compels the LDF also to accommodate the interests of the above communities.

The social base of the Congress party in Kerala remains intact from 1957 onwards. This shows its ability to adapt itself to the compulsions of coalition politics. This is evident from the following table which also enables a comparison with the CPI (M)'s performance during the same period.

TABLE NO. 1
THE NUMBER OF SEATS WON AND THE PERCENTAGE OF VOTES POLLED BY THE CONGRESS PARTY AND THE CPI(M) IN THE KERALA ASSEMBLY ELECTIONS SINCE 1957

1957	*1960*	*1965*	*1967*	*1970*	*1977*	*1980*	*1982*	*1987*	*1991*	*1996*	*2001*
Cong 43 (38.0)	Cong 63 (34.4)	Cong 36 (33.0)	Cong 9 (34.2)	Cong 32 (18.3)	Cong 38 (19.4)	Cong 17 (17.3)	Cong 35 (22.0)	Cong 33 (25.0)	Cong 55 (32.0)	Cong 37 (30.0)	Cong 62 (31.4)
CPI 60+5 (47.5)	CPI 26 (36.7)	CPM 40 (19.9)	CPM 52 (22.6)	CPM 28 (23.4)	CPM 17 (21.4)	CPM 35 (19.3)	CPM 26 (18.7)	CPM 38 (22.8)	CPM 29 (22.5)	CPM 41 (21.5)	CPM 23 (21.3)

(*Source:* R.K Suresh Kumar: 2001).
The Figures in brackets denote percentage.

Except the CPI(M), all parties in Kerala has at one time or other aligned with the Congress party. There was an alliance between the Antony led faction of the Congress and the CPI(M) led LDF in 1980. Eventhough the Congress offered the chief ministership to the CPI during the 1970-77 period, Congress was the dominant party in the alliance. A look at the electoral pattern reveals the ability of Congress to stage a comeback after loosing an election. As opposed to the cadre nature of the CPI(M), the Congress Party machine functions mainly through the factional groups. The group leaders act as the protectors of multiple interests of their supporters, who in turn act as a link between the party and different religions, caste and sub-caste groups.

The period of the present study witnessed the peak of factionalism in the party. During this period the party came to power three times viz, 1982, 1991 and 2001. In the two decades, the party was in power for nearly twelve years. During this period, groupism prevailed throughout. Congress groupism during the first decade (1982-1991) was mainly bi-factional in nature, while it became multi-factional in the latter period. At present there are four groups in the Congress party in Kerala, each known by the factional leader's name. They are the groups led by Karunakaran, Antony, Karthikeyan and Vayalar Ravi. The two major groups have been in existence since the 1970's. The other two groups are of recent origin and they emerged from the 'I' group. In the 2001 Assembly elections and in the subsequent formation of the ministry, the spoils of office was shared according to an accepted formula which took into account the relative strength of the groups as understood by the Congress high command. This shows that groupism in the Cong(I) in Kerala is a concrete reality and accepted as such by the party and the general public.

A faction is a vertical group as it brings together individuals from different economic categories and castes. They forged strong bonds between unequal partners and provided yet another countervailing force to the horizontal ties of caste and class. Membership in it was voluntary unlike caste and lineage (Srinivas 1976:226). The Congress groups project a secular image and an egalitarian outlook. This is evident from the policy of accommodating loyalists from different classes, castes and communities in the leadership hierarchy[3].

Intra-party conflicts and factions may arise in a variety of ways. Factions may emerge in a party on the basis of differences among the party leaders on overall ideology. Even if there is general agreement on ideology, disagreement may arise on the issue of strategy and tactics to be used to realize the ideological objective. Factional conflict may draw their rationale from and get intertwined with socio-economic cleavages, regional disparities or state interests. The leaders involved in factional conflicts always "endeavor to cover factional feuds with the mantle of theory so that personal dislikes and personal hostilities pompously masquerade as differences of views and tactics" (Mahendra P. Singh 1975:6). The authoritative party elite often lend a certain amount of indirect recognition to such sub groups by bargaining with and mediating and arbitrating with them (ibid :5).

In this chapter we take a look at the dynamics of Congress factionalism since 1982 from the position of the three major sociological determinants- namely; gender (sex), caste and religion. They act as the bedrock of Kerala politics. The role of these factors in Congress factionalism is thoroughly examined. The relevance and importance of these factors lies in the fact that they are the inborn characteristics of individuals. The group preferences of the three social groups can provide a general understanding of the nature of factionalism in the Congress party in Kerala.

The responses testify to one of the major hypotheses of the study that all the four Congress groups projects a secular image. This is the most natural and practical outcome of the demographic compulsions of Kerala politics. As is evident from all other determinants discussed elsewhere in this work the Karunakaran faction is indicated as the predominant group in the Congress party in Kerala. A detailed analysis of the gender, caste and religion-wise data is necessary to understand the social base of Congress factionalism in Kerala.

I. Gender and Factionalism

In all societies gender is related to political activity; men are more active than women. And of course, in all societies male-female distinction is measurable. Sex related issues find little attention in politics due to the lesser political role of women (Sydney Verba, Norman H. Nie & Joe 1978:235). Inspite of a high literacy rate, women in Kerala generally shy away from politics. The low representation of women in the parliamentary bodies, in party leaderships and among ordinary workers is an accepted fact in Kerala. Male-female differences in political activity reflect the fact that women possess fewer socio-economic resources. This explains the gap in participation levels. Even when men and women have comparable levels of individual and institutional resources, female political activity rates remain well below to those of their male counterparts (ibid :251).

In the case of the present study, the two gender groups are unanimous in their view that groups exist in the state Congress (Table No. 2). Both groups also take the position that groups are not inevitable in the state Congress (Table No. 3). The following tables indicate this.

TABLE NO. 2
TABLE SHOWING WHETHER GROUPISM EXISTS IN THE CONGRESS IN KERALA (GENDER-WISE)

Gender	*Yes*	*No*	*Total*
Male	607	13	620
Female	24	2	26
Total	631	15	646

TABLE NO. 3
TABLE SHOWING WHETHER GROUP IS INEVITABLE TO CONGRESS (GENDER-WISE)

Gender	*Yes*	*No*	*Total*
Male	112	494	606
Female	2	22	24
Total	114	516	630

The two groups also opine that personality factors constitute the main cause of factionalism since 1969 (Table No. 4), while it was policy oriented before 1969 (Table No. 5). It is important here to note that a large number of respondents failed to answer the question posed in the two tables.

TABLE NO. 4
WHETHER CONGRESS FACTIONALISM IS PERSONALITY ORIENTED SINCE 1969 (GENDER-WISE)

Gender	*Yes*	*No*	*Total*
Male	363	4	367
Female	16	2	18
Total	379	6	385

TABLE NO. 5
WHETHER CONGRESS FACTIONALISM WAS POLICY ORIENTED BEFORE 1969 (GENDER-WISE)

Gender	*Yes*	*No*	*Total*
Male	374	17	391
Female	16		16
Total	390	17	407

The two gender groups also agree that factionalism is becoming less and less ideological in nature (Table No. 6) over the years.

TABLE NO. 6

WHETHER CONGRESS FACTIONALISM IS BECOMING LESS AND LESS IDEOLOGICAL AFTER THE 1969 SPLIT: (GENDER-WISE)

Gender	*Yes*	*No*	*Total*
Male	383	17	400
Female	7		7
Total	390	17	407

The ideological rift constituted the major reason for the All India split in 1969. It was after the 1969 split that personality factors emerged as the major cause for factionalism in the party. The leaderships of all the present factions in the state Congress unit were behind the Indira faction of Congress during the 1969 split. It was during the 1970's that groups came to be organised around personalities. The fact that 270 respondents out of 677 did not answer this is an indication that a large number of congressmen are not bothered about the ideological moorings of the Congress party.

The following table examining the Christian support base (gende-rwise) of the Antony faction conveys the message that his group does not enjoy the overwhelming support of the Christian community. 84.62% of the female respondents agreed with their male counter parts (87.08%) the above view. It is significant here to note that the majority of the women Congress respondents were Hindus.

TABLE NO. 7

TABLE EXAMINING WHETHER 'ANTONY' GROUP HAS A PREDOMINANT CHRISTIAN SUPPORT BASE (GENDER-WISE)

Gender	*Yes*	*No*	*Total*
Male	80	544	624
Female	4	22	26
Total	84	566	650

The gender-wise rating of K. Karunakaran as the leader of opposition, as chief minister and as protector of party men is attempted in the following three tables. (Tables 8(a), 8(b) and 8(c)). In spite of the gender differences majority of the respondents place Karunakaran in the topmost category in all these.

TABLE NO. 8 (A)
I. KARUNAKARAN AS OPPOSITION LEADER

Gender	*VG*	*G*	*A*	*B*	*Total*
Male	505	87	23	7	622
Female	22	3			25
Total	527	90	23	7	647

TABLE NO. 8 (B)
II. KARUNAKARAN AS CHIEF MINISTER

Gender	*VG*	*G*	*A*	*B*	*Total*
Male	495	86	26	7	614
Female	22	3			25
Total	517	89	26	7	639

TABLE NO. 8 (C)
III. K.KARUNAKARAN AS PROTECTOR OF PARTYMEN

Gender	*VG*	*G*	*A*	*B*	*Total*
Male	509	79	23	7	618
Female	22	3	1		26
Total	531	82	24	7	644

VG - Very Good; G - Good; A - Average; B - Bad

Since every individual is inescapably male or female, society becomes automatically divided based on gender. Biological groupings in nature can be a base for a particular orientation. Sex is indeed in many societies a divisive factor of first rate importance, but by itself it rarely, if ever, splits a society into two antithetical halves (Robert H. Lowie 1950 :4). Sex based social and political assertion happens mostly when coupled with age or some other factor. This is evident in the rating of A.K. Antony on the three counts as opposition leader, as chief minister, and as protector of party workers.

TABLE NO: 9

THE RATING OF A.K ANTONY AS OPPOSITION LEADER, CHIEF MINISTER AND AS PROTECTOR OF PARTY MEN

TABLE NO. 9(A)

I. ANTONY AS OPPOSITION LEADER

Gender	*VG*	*G*	*A*	*B*	*Total*
Male	179	155	222	35	591
Female	11	7	4	-	22
Total	190	162	226	35	613

TABLE NO. 9(B)

II. ANTONY AS CHIEF MINISTER

Gender	*VG*	*G*	*A*	*B*	*Total*
Male	180	155	215	35	585
Female	11	7	4	-	22
Total	191	162	219	35	607

TABLE NO. 9(C)

III. AS PROTECTOR OF PARTYMEN

Gender	*VG*	*G*	*A*	*B*	*Total*
Male	166	134	210	76	586
Female	11	7	4	-	22
Total	177	141	214	76	608

While the majority of the male respondents place A.K. Antony in the average category, nearly 50% of the female respondents place A.K. Antony in the very good category. This is not unexpected since irrespective of caste-communal differences women in Kerala whole heartedly welcomed Antony's policy of prohibition. In the personal interviews with them, they openly declared their unconditional support to the above policy.[4]

The following comparative leadership rating of the four faction leaders also confirms that 61 per cent of the Congress respondents consider Karunakaran as the most suitable person to provide effective leadership to the UDF.

TABLE NO. 10
TABLE EXAMINING THE COMPETENCY OF ANTONY, KARUNAKARAN AND OTHERS IN PROVIDING LEADERSHIP TO THE UDF (GENDER-WISE)

Gender	*Name of leader*				
	AK	*KK*	*GK*	*VR*	*Total*
Male	157	293	15	14	479
Female	9	12			21
Total	166	305	15	14	500
%		(33.2)	(61.0)	(3.0)	(2.80)

AK-A.K Antony; KK-K.Karunakaran;
GK - G.Karthikeyan; VR - Vayalar Ravi

Only 33.2 per cent think that Antony can provide effective leadership to the UDF. The other two faction leaders pale into insignificance with 2.22 per cent and 2.06 per cent respectively. In both male and female category Karunakaran's leadership ability is placed high. While among the male respondents Karunakaran enjoy a lead of 27.8 per cent, in the case of female respondents it is only about half of that (14.28 %). Here also 42.86 per cent of the female respondents vote in A.K Antony's favour while it was only 32.64 per cent in the case of men. This shows that gender differences when coupled with other factors may affect ones preferences.

II Caste Based Analysis

Social configurations influence and shape the political processes operating in any region and an understanding of the traditional social hierarchy gives a proper perspective of political processes. The Indian caste system is a unique system of social stratification. It is characterized by rigidity, codes of behaviour and set attitudes. Each region in India has different castes which play a significant role in its social and political life (Sirsikar 1994:59). In every region there are some castes which dominate the others.

Numerically the major castes in Kerala are the Nairs and the Ezhavas. There are innumerable other castes in the Hindu fold which have their own peculiarities but it is impossible to explain the role of each one of them here. Apart from this, the role of various Christian and Muslim sects/groups is also important.

The process of politicisation of caste acquired a great deal of sophistication in the politics of the Congress party. Those who yielded to the appeal of the caste and voted for candidates of their own caste, could not have thought that it was a bad thing to vote according to caste. By and large the intelligentia showed an ambivalent attitude. They were troubled by casteism in politics eventhough they might support some one from their own caste. In Indian politics one could not afford to be too idealistic if one wishes to remain in business (Andre Beteille 1996:168-69). But the caste has been changing in their character and outlook in tune with other areas (Peter Ronald De Souza 2000:250). These changes have the potential of providing similar outlook, including in politics.

In the factional politics of the Congress party each group has to satisfy their supporter's aspirations. The privileged in different castes try to further their interests through party groups. When the different groups champion these interests, it adds to their self importance (Srinivas 1994:119). Each factions in the state Congress saw to it that different castes and communities get adequate representation in leadership positions.

Caste-wise examination of group preference reveals that the Karunakaran group enjoys the support of 54.89 per cent forward castes, 59.19 per cent OBC's, 50 per cent MBC's and 60 per cent Congressmen belonging to the SC/ST groups.

TABLE NO. 11
THE GROUP AFFILIATION OF CONGRESS RESPONDENTS (CASTE WISE)

Caste	*Group to which you belong*				
	AK	*KK*	*GK*	*VR*	*Total*
FC	94	129	6	6	235
OBC	100	161	6	5	272
MBC	1	2	1		4
SC/ST	11	21	2	1	35
Total	206	313	15	12	546

As the table shows 313 (57.33 %) out of 546 respondents belonging to various castes are supporters of the Karunakaran group; while Antony faction has the support of 37.73 per cent and the remaining two groups together commands a very low 5 per cent support. The OBC's top in the Karunakaran faction closely followed by the SC/ST communities. The forward caste's top in the Antony faction with 40.0 per cent of the F.C. Congress respondents identifying themselves with that group, followed by OBC's (36.76 %). In the case of the MBC and SC/ST group the Karunakaran group has overwhelming support than the 'A' faction. It is significant here to note that third and fourth groups practically enjoys no support from the MBC and SC/ST groups. This is indicative of the growing polarisation between the OBC's and the MBC's and the SC/ST communities. However, the fact that one hundred and thirty one respondents (19.35 %) did not divulge their group orientation indicates that they are wary of the ongoing factional fight in the party.

Similarly, 73.17 per cent of the Congressmen belonging to the above four categories consider Karunakaran group as the dominant group in the party. This is evident from the following table.

TABLE NO. 12

CASTE WISE TABLE SHOWING THE PREDOMINANT GROUP IN THE CONGRESS PARTY IN KERALA

Caste	*Predominant group*				
	AK	*KK*	*GK*	*VR*	*Total*
FC	73	186	2	1	262
%	(27.86)	(70.80)	(0.76)	(0.38)	
OBC	75	245	2	3	325
%	(23.08)	(75.38)	(0.62)	(0.92)	
MBC	1	3			
%	(25.0)	(75.0)			4
SC/ST	11	27	1		
%	(28.21)	(69.23)	(2.56)		39
Total	160	461	5	4	630
%	(25.41)	(73.17)	(0.79)	(0.63)	

This shows that even some of those who are Antony's supporters have openly accepted the reality that the majority of the rank and file is with Karunakaran. The chi-square test also confirms the assertion since the calculated chi-square value 4.55 is less than the table/value of chi-square 16.919 at 5 per cent level of significance and 9 degrees of freedom. (For details of chi-square see Appendix IV). Here also one hundred and forty six (21.57%) out of six hundred and seventy seven respondents failed to indicate the predominant group in the party.

The following table examining the caste-communal basis of factionalism in the party (caste-wise) shows that 63.86 per cent of the respondents do not believe in such a base, while 36.14 per cent does so.

TABLE NO. 13
THE CASTE COMMUNAL BASIS OF CONGRESS FACTIONALISM

Caste	*Yes*	*No*	*Total*
FC	110	167	277
OBC	106	229	335
MBC	2	2	4
SC/ST	18	19	37
Total	236	417	653

But among the most backward castes (MBC) and the SC/ST groups a considerable number of respondents i.e. 50 per cent and 48.65 per cent respectively believed in the existence of a caste-communal basis of Congress factionalism in Kerala. This can not be brushed aside as insignificant since these sections could never occupy the chairs of the KPCC President or the chief minister. In the interview with SC/ST Congressmen they expressed their concern in this matter.

The accusation that one caste or religion is behind a particular faction is examined in the following four tables. (Tables 14-17)

Table probing the Nair community support to 'I' group that the 'I' faction enjoys no such support from the community. Among the 643 respondents 576 (89.58 %) holds that view. Only 67 (10.42 %) out of 643 believes that the Nair community extends a special support to the 'I' faction. That the support enjoyed by this faction does not have any caste basis is also proved on the basis of the chi-square test (For details Appendix V)

While examining the 'A' faction's support base (Table 15), it is seen that 12.92 per cent believes that the 'A' group has a Christian support base.

TABLE NO. 14
THE NAIR COMMUNITY SUPPORT TO THE 'I' GROUP

Caste	*Supporting K.K from Nairs*		
	Yes	*No*	*Total*
FC	25	249	274
%			
OBC	38	292	330
%			
MBC	1	3	4
%			
SC/ST	3	32	35
%			
Total	67	576	643
%	(10.42)	(89.58)	

TABLE NO. 15
TABLE EXAMINING THE CHRISTIAN SUPPORT TO THE 'A' GROUP

Caste	*Yes*	*No*	*Total*
FC	46	223	269
%			
OBC	31	307	338
%			
MBC	1	3	4
%			
SC/ST	6	33	39
%			
Total	84	566	650
%			

Here the calculated value of chi-square 9.1205 is greater than the table value 7.815 at 5 per cent level of significance and 3 degrees of freedom. This shows that there is in fact a slight Christian consolidation behind the 'A' group (See Appendix VI). Likewise 19.92 per cent feel that Karthikeyan has a Nair support base (Table 16) and 22.37 per cent of the respondents point out to the Ezhava support base of Vayalar Ravi (Table 17).

TABLE NO. 16
THE NAIR COMMUNITY SUPPORT OF G. KARTHIKEYAN

Caste	*Yes*	*No*	*Total*
FC	40	152	192
%	(20.83)	(79.17)	
OBC	57	234	291
%	(19.59)	(80.41)	
MBC	2	2	4
%	(50)	(50)	
SC/ST	2	18	20
%	(10)	(90)	
Total	101	406	507
%	(19.92)	(80.08)	

TABLE NO. 17
THE EZHAVA COMMUNITY SUPPORT TO VAYALAR RAVI

Caste	*Group to which you belong*		
	Yes	*No*	*Total*
FC	66	157	223
%	(29.6)	(70.4)	
OBC	45	231	276
%	(16.3)	(83.7)	
MBC	1	3	4
%	(25)	(75)	
SC/ST	9	29	38
%	(23.7)	(76.3)	
Total	121	420	541
%	(22.37)	(77.63)	

A comparison between K. Karunakran and A.K. Antony regarding their respective ability to manage the numerous and powerful caste-communal interest groups in Kerala is attempted in the two tables below.

TABLE NO. 18
THE CASTE-WISE ASSESSMENT OF THE ABILITY OF K. KARUNAKARAN TO DEAL WITH THE CASTE-COMMUNAL GROUPS

Caste	*VG*	*G*	*A*	*B*	*Total*
FC	186	31	14	4	235
OBC	287	49	13	5	354
MBC	3	1			4
SC/ST	30	5	1	1	37
Total	506	86	28	10	630

TABLE NO. 19
THE CASTE-WISE ASSESSMENT OF THE ABILITY OF A.K ANTONY TO DEAL WITH THE CASTE–COMMUNAL GROUPS

Caste	*VG*	*G*	*A*	*B*	*Total*
FC	72	82	64	14	232
OBC	103	66	140	18	327
MBC	3		1		4
SC/ST	13	6	11	6	36
Total	191	154	216	38	599

A total of 506 respondents out of 630 places Karunakaran in the very good category (Table No.18), while it was only 191 (31.89 %) out of 599 in the case of A.K. Antony (Table No.19). Among the respondents, 216 (36.06 %) places Antony in the average category and 38 (6.34 %) in the bad category. The responses clearly prove that K. Karunakaran is considered as the most effective Congress leader in dealing with the numerous caste-communal interest groups in Kerala.

The assumption that the practice of nomination by the high command to party posts has helped to maintain the caste-communal equations in the party is examined in the following table (Table No. 20). The table below probing the caste wise response to the practice of nomination by the Congress high command reveals that a vast majority belonging to the four caste categories are of the opinion that this has not helped to maintain caste-communal equation in the party.

TABLE NO. 20
TABLE EXAMINING WHETHER THE PRACTICE OF NOMINATIONS HAS HELPED THE PARTY TO MAINTAIN CASTE-COMMUNAL EQUATIONS

Caste	*Yes*	*No*	*Total*
FC	14	213	227
OBC	16	268	284
MBC	1	3	4
SC/ST	1	36	37
Total	32	520	552

The above table conveys the message that nominations by the high command have not helped the four caste wise categories to gain party positions as they want it to be. So the displeasure is over choice rather than against the principle of nomination.

III. Nature of Congress Factionalism: Religious Context

Man needs religion to give him a sense of place in the world, a sense of his own identity, an idea of himself that satisfies him; for without it he, who differs from other animals in being self-conscious, is intolerable to, and seeks to escape from, himself. Religion satisfies an essential need of a creature that is an object of thought to itself, and therefore aware to itself as a finite being in an infinite world (John Plamentaz 1970:86). Religion, atleast for the educated, sheds its grosser superstitions and becomes more coherent, or it loses its hold together. Montesquieu, was more concerned with the social functions and the social conditions that favour or impede the growth of particular religions. There are traces of the idea of religion in the writings of Rousseau. Rousseau spoke of religion in such a way as to suggest that man's need of it goes deeper than his need of science. Kant held that there are three beliefs necessary to man if he is to be moral and happy: he must believe in God, in freedom of the will, and in immortability. Hegel says that the course of human history is the self revelation of spirit at the levels of self-consciousness and reason. Religion as he saw it, expresses figuratively what philosophy seeks to make explicit. Marx spoke of religion as a fantasy of alienated man. His ideas about alienation and religion do not fit nicely together into a consistent whole (ibid :91).

The connection between religion and politics arises as a problem only in nations, which are not religiously homogeneous. Even classical thinkers such as Aristotle took it for granted that religious homogeneity was a condition of political stability, and they were right. Where opposing beliefs about ultimate values enter the political arena, they exacerbate struggles by preventing compromise (Robert A. Alford 1964:49). In modern non-homogenous societies, three changes have moderated conflicts over ultimate values. They are (i) the secularization and weakening of the religious belief in general; (ii) the compartmentalization, the separation of religion from other areas of life; and (iii) homogenization, the convergence of many religions upon a vaguely-defined consensus on teaching and practice. Actually all these processes, or contradictory forms of them, may be going on simultaneously (ibid :50). It is paradoxical when religious apologists declare that the teachings of all religions are same when on many issues at least they are at very great variance with each other (Sheshadri 1999:22).

Hinduism is caste-based and hierarchically ordered. In India whoever were the rulers, the people had accepted them irrespective of their religious beliefs. Political independence and nationalism in twentieth century sense meant nothing to the twelfth century Hindus and Muslims. Constant strife had sapped the energy of the people who were disgusted with the conditions of unrest and wanted peace at any cost. This sort of feeling was shared by the common man whether he was a Hindu or a Muslim. The historic fact is that neither Christianity nor Judaism could co-exist in great harmony with each other and with Islam though all these three religions have so much in common (Ibid:42).

But as things shaped, there is now politicisation of religion in India. Growth of fundamentalism among the believers and the pursuit of vote bank politics by the political parties have assigned a premier role for religion in India. The Congress being an umbrella organisation providing shade to all religions is very much concerned about its secular image. But the party is vulnerable to the pulls and pressures of religion. The religious interests get articulated in the Congress through the leaders deriving support from religious establishments. As such the religious context of the factional dynamics in the party assumes importance. By relying on the sample data obtained from congressmen at all levels belonging to the three major religious groups, an empirical study of the relationship, if any, between religious identity and Congress factionalism is attempted below.

The responses of the Congress party respondents belonging to the Hindu, Muslim and Christian communities on the indispensability of factionalism in the party can be seen in Table No. 21 given below.

TABLE NO. 21
TABLE SHOWING WHETHER GROUPS ARE INEVITABLE

Religion	*Yes*	*No*	*Total*
Hindu	65	276	341
Christian	28	122	150
Muslim	21	118	139
Total	114	516	630
%	(18.1)	(81.9)	

The figures in the table indicate that congressmen irrespective of their religious affiliations ardently believe that groupism is not inevitable to the functioning of the party in the state.

A large number of leaders in modern India considered religion to be the source of their inspiration and the sustaining force in their public and personal life. In this country political movements have been organized explicitly to press the claims of religious communities to share power and to fashion the state in a manner that would assure the performance of community based politics. All this was inevitable given the plural character of Indian society (Gopalakrishna 1981:49).

But as mentioned earlier the umbrella nature of the Congress party prevents it from articulating any particular religious interest. Since the Congress consists of a cross section of the Kerala society, different religious interests gets articulated through the party. This "exotic Congress culture" overrides the religious identities of the party members at least in theory.

The religious basis of group affiliation of the respondents is examined in the table below.

TABLE NO. 22
THE RELIGIOUS CONTEXT OF GROUP AFFILIATION

Religion	*Name of the faction to which you belong*				
	AK	*KK*	*GK*	*VR*	*Total*
Hindu	96	175	7	6	284
%	(33.8)	(61.62)	(2.46)	(2.11)	
Christian	56	76	5	3	140
%	(40)	(54.29)	(3.57)	(2.14)	
Muslim	54	62	3	3	122
%	(44.26)	(50.82)	(2.46)	(2.46)	
Total	206	313	15	12	546
%	(37.73)	(57.33)	(2.75)	(2.2)	

Out of the total 546 respondents 313 (57.33 per cent) are in the Karunakaran faction, which places that group above the Antony group by a clear margin of over 19.6 per cent. Among the Hindus the margin is 27.8 per cent. Among the Christians and Muslims it is 14.39 per cent and 6.56 per cent respectively. Eventhough the margin of difference is showing a downward trend among the last two categories; here also Karunakaran faction has more support. It is of significance that 33.8% of the Congressmen belonging to the Hindu community identify themselves with the Antony faction, which roughly corresponds to his total support base in the party. 131(19.35 per cent) out of 677 expressed their unwillingness to respond by saying that they do not belong to any group.

Apart from confirming the above facts, the following table clearly shows that the Karunakaran faction emerges as the predominant one in the religion wise analysis also.

TABLE NO. 23
TABLE INDICATING THE PREDOMINANT FACTION IN THE PARTY

Religion	*Predominant group*				
	AK	*KK*	*GK*	*VR*	*Total*
Hindu	76	263	2	4	345
Christian	48	103	2		153
Muslim	36	95	1		132
Total	160	461	5	4	630

Eventhough 47 respondents (6.92%) refrained from answering this question, 461 (73.17%) out of 630 respondents consider the Karunakaran faction as the predominant one in the Congress party in Kerala. Only 160 (25.40 %) respondents consider the Antony faction as the predominant one. They are the hardcore loyalists of the Antony faction. In this table, the percentage of support to the Karunakaran faction further increases and that of Antony faction decreases when compared with the previous table (Table 23). This is because of the fact that many in the Antony faction consider the other group to be the predominant one.

A religion wise look at the ideological base of Congress factionalism is necessary as "ideology often becomes a powerful instrument of manipulation" (Zenab Banu 1999:43). The impact of ideology on political and social change has long been a matter of dispute in the study of politics. Ideology is a symptom and a remedy. It is also a mask and a weapon (Rod Hague, Martin Harrop and Shaun Breslin 1992:91). The following table looks into the ideological basis of Congress factionalism.

TABLE NO. 24
TABLE EXAMINING WHETHER CONGRESS FACTIONALISM HAS IDEOLOGICAL ROOTS

Religion	*Yes*	*No*	*Total*
Hindu	181	176	357
%	(50.7)	(40.3)	
Christian	98	58	156
%	(62.82)	(37.18)	
Muslim	54	88	142
%	(38.03)	(61.97)	
Total	333	322	655
%	(50.84)	(49.16)	(100)

Most of the activists in the party are confused on the Congress party's ideology in the Kerala's context. Earlier the party was against aligning with the communal groups and parties. The party also took a consistent anti-communist stand. In the economic realm the party stood for self sufficiency and Congress socialism. But all these have changed over the years. Naturally the responses indicate an equal division. However the chi-square test confirms the ideological basis of Congress factionalism. An analysis of the data gives the calculated value of chi-square as 18.29 and the table value 9.21 at 1 per cent level of significance and 2 degrees of freedom (See Appendix VII).

However, the responses in the following table indicates personality clash also as one of the major reasons of Congress factionalism.

TABLE NO. 25

RELIGION WISE TABLE EXAMINING PERSONALITY CLASH AS ONE OF THE REASONS FOR FACTIONALISM

Religion	*Yes*	*No*	*Total*
Hindu	309	48	357
Christian	141	16	157
Muslim	122	19	141
Total	572	83	655
%	(87.33)	(12.67)	

An overwhelming majority i.e 87.33 per cent of the respondents confirmed personality clash also as one of the reasons for factionalism.

The religion-wise responses in the following table show that 36.14 per cent of the respondents believe that factionalism in the party has a caste-communal angle also while 63.86 per cent deny this.

TABLE NO. 26
THE CASTE-COMMUNAL ORIENTATION OF CONGRESS FACTIONALISM

Religion	*Caste-communal basis*		
	Yes	*No*	*Total*
Hindu	136	221	357
%	(38.1)	(61.9)	
Christian	66	91	157
%	(42.04)	(57.96)	
Muslim	34	105	139
%	(24.46)	(75.54)	
Total	236	417	653
%	(36.14)	(63.86)	

However, the statistical analysis shows that there is infact a close relationship between caste or community and Congress factionalism. Here the calculated value 11.17 is greater than the table value 9.21 at 1 per cent level of significance and 2 degrees of freedom (See Appendix VIII).

In the table below an attempt is made to find out whether the Hindu community constitutes the major support base of the Karunakaran group.

TABLE NO. 27
TABLE EXAMINING WHETHER THE HINDU COMMUNITY CONSTITUTES THE MAJOR SUPPORT BASE OF THE KARUNAKARAN GROUP

Religion	*Yes*	*No*	*Total*
Hindu	41	309	350
%	(10.11)	(88.29)	
Christian	18	136	154
%	(11.69)	(88.31)	
Muslim	8	131	139
%	(5.76)	(94.24)	
Total	67	576	643
%	(10.42)	(89.58)	

The responses suggest that there is no consolidation of Hindus behind the Karunakaran faction.

Similarly, Table No. 28 attempts to find out whether the Christian community constitutes the major support base of the Antony group.

TABLE NO. 28

TABLE EXAMINING WHETHER THE CHRISTIAN COMMUNITY CONSTITUTES THE MAJOR SUPPORT BASE OF THE ANTONY GROUP

Religion	*Yes*	*No*	*Total*
Hindu	54	302	356
%	(15.17)	(84.83)	
Christian	22	132	154
%	(14.29)	(85.91)	
Muslim	8	132	140
%	(5.71)	(94.29)	
Total	84	566	650
%	(12.92)	(87.08)	

The statistical analysis of Christian support base of the Antony group shows that the 'A' faction enjoys such a support. Here the calculated value of chi-square 8.32 is greater than the table value 5.99 at 5% level of significance and 2 degrees of freedom (see Appendix IX).

Though insignificant at present, the groups centering round G.Karthikeyan and Vayalar Ravi are generally believed to derive their support from the Nair and the Ezhava communities respectively.

However the religion wise data deny the existence of such a support base for the two groups. There are two reasons for this contradiction; first, the insignificance of these two groups in the politics of Congress factionalism and second, the general image of the leaders of these groups as 'fortune seekers'. Moreover, it is natural for the vast majority of the respondents belonging to the 'A' & 'I' groups, to consider these groups as incapable of drawing any support from the two dominant Hindu communities. It shows that in the context of the 'Antony-Karunakaran factional contest, Congressmen does not regard the third and fourth groups as a lasting reality.

A religion wise assessment of the four faction leaders in dealing with the CPM challenge is presented in the table below.

TABLE NO. 29
TABLE SHOWING THE RATING OF FACTION LEADERS TO FACE THE CPI(M) CHALLENGE

Religion	*AK*	*KK*	*GK*	*VR*	*Total*
Hindu	89	221	10	5	325
%	(27.38)	(68)	(3.08)	(1.54)	
Christian	55	82	3	3	143
%	(38.46)	(57.34)	(2.1)	(2.1)	
Muslim	50	81	2	2	135
%	(37.08)	(60)	(1.48)	(1.48)	
Total	194	384	15	10	603
%	(32.17)	(63.68)	(2.49)	(1.66)	

Congressmen irrespective of the religious divide rate Karunakaran's potential in this regard as the highest. It is highest among the Hindus with 68%. The existence of Kerala Congress and Muslim League with strong anti-communist views may have influenced Christian and Muslim Congressmen to consider these parties as effective anti-dote to the CPI(M).

The same kind of response is returned with regard to the ability of the four faction leaders to meet the BJP challenge.

TABLE NO. 30
THE RATING OF THE ABILITY OF FACTION LEADERS TO FACE THE BJP CHALLENGE

Religion	*AK*	*KK*	*GK*	*VR*	*Total*
Hindu	104	170	10	5	289
%	(35.99)	(58.82)	(3.46)	(1.73)	
Christian	53	64	3	2	122
%	(43.44)	(52.46)	(2.46)	(1.64)	
Muslim	51	69	2	2	124
%	(41.13)	(55.65)	(1.61)	(1.61)	
Total	208	303	15	9	535
%	(38.88)	(56.64)	(2.80)	(1.68)	

The rating as seen in the table is slightly more in the case of A.K. Antony when compared with the earlier table. This is due to the fact that the two minority communities consider Antony to be more efficient in dealing with the BJP than the CPI(M). Antony's personal rapport with Sonia Gandhi, who heads the party at the centre, may be one of the factors responsible for this.

The rating of the respondents as to who can provide effective leadership to the UDF is given in the following table.

TABLE NO. 31
THE RATING OF THE FACTION LEADERS IN PROVIDING EFFECTIVE LEADERSHIP TO THE UDF

Religion	*AK*	*KK*	*GK*	*VR*	*Total*
Hindu	76	173	10	9	268
Christian	48	64	3	3	118
Muslim	42	68	2	2	114
Total	166	305	15	14	500
%	(33.2)	(61)	(3)	(2.8)	

The same pattern is repeated in the responses regarding the choice of the most effective person to lead the UDF. According to 61% of the respondents Karunakaran is the leader most suited for this job. This may also be because of his position as the chief architect of the UDF.

Certain skills may inherently be present in leaders whether they are in opposition or in the government. As such it is pertinent here to examine the performance of Karunakaran and Antony as opposition leaders. The following two tables examine this.

TABLE NO. 32 (A)
THE RATING OF K. KARUNAKARAN AS OPPOSITION LEADER

Religion	*VG*	*G*	*A*	*B*	*Total*
Hindu	295	47	11	1	354
Christian	116	30	6	2	154
Muslim	116	13	6	4	139
Total	527	90	23	7	647
%	(81.45)	(13.91)	(3.55)	(1.08)	

TABLE NO. 32 (B)
THE RATING OF A.K. ANTONY AS OPPOSITION LEADER

Religion	*VG*	*G*	*A*	*B*	*Total*
Hindu	85	91	135	15	326
Christian	57	40	44	11	152
Muslim	48	31	47	9	135
Total	190	162	226	35	613
%	(31.0)	(26.43)	(36.86)	(5.71)	

VG: Very good; G: Good; A: Average; B: Bad

A comparison of the above two table's reveals that K. Karunakaran is well ahead of A.K. Antony with an undoubted 50% lead in the very good category. Among the respondents 36.86 per cent places Antony in the average category while 5.71 per cent place him in the bad category.

In the context of intense factionalism, a faction leader should also have the ability to protect the interests of his followers. The two tables below shows the religion-wise comparative rating of the two leaders as protectors of party workers interests.

TABLE NO. 33 (A)
THE RATING K. KARUNAKARAN AS PROTECTOR OF PARTYMEN

Religion	*VG*	*G*	*A*	*B*	*Total*
Hindu	292	47	11	1	351
Christian	123	22	7	2	154
Muslim	116	13	6	4	139
Total	531	82	24	7	644

TABLE NO. 33 (B)
THE RATING A.K.ANTONY AS PROTECTOR OF PARTYMEN

Religion	*VG*	*G*	*A*	*B*	*Total*
Hindu	81	77	124	43	325
Christian	50	33	42	23	148
Muslim	46	31	48	10	135
Total	177	141	214	76	608

VG - Very good; G - Good; A - Average; B - Bad

While 82.45 per cent of the Congress respondents belonging to the three religious groups place Karunakaran in the very good category, this is 29.11 per cent in the case of A.K. Antony. Out of 351 Hindu respondents, 292 (83.19 per cent) places Karunakaran in the very good category whereas only 81 (24.92 per cent) out of 322 places Antony in this category. Similarly, 123 (79.87 per cent) out of 154 Christian respondents accepts Karunakaran as a very good protector of party wokers interests, while this is only 50 (33.78 per cent) out of 148 in the case of Antony. Among the Muslims, 116 (83.45 per cent) out of 139 places Karunakaran in the first category while only 46 (34.07 per cent) out of 135 places Antony in this category. The above tables prove that Karunakaran has the greatest appeal among congressmen belonging to the three communities.

The analysis of the social base of the politics of Congress factionalism in Kerala since 1982 brings out the following aspects—

(i) The empirical analysis suggests that there is no relationship between caste and groupism in the factional politics of the Congress party. This is mainly evident from the tables 13 and 14. Similarly the analysis reveals that the support base of Karunakaran is not caste based. Though the analysis deny the existence of a Nair support base for the Karthikeyan group and an Ezhava support base for the Vayalar Ravi group, a perusal of the candidates list of these two groups during the last assembly elections reveals that they do in fact cater to the interests of the above castes. In the case of Vayalar Ravi group this is more evident as four out of the five candidates fielded by that group belonged to the Ezhava community. This does not mean that Congressmen belonging to the Ezhava community constitute the support base of this group. It only indicates the attempt of this group to attract the Ezhavas in to its fold and to secure a political mileage. Vayalar Ravi was nominated as the General Secretary of the AICC inorder to placate the Ezhava community.

(ii) The analysis does not rule out the possibility of a Christian community support base for the 'A' group.

The statistical analysis of table 15 reveals that there is a slight Christian consolidation behind the 'A' group. The responses in different tables show that even among the Christian respondents, the Karunakaran group is more favoured than the 'A' group. But it is to be understood that having a Christian support base among Congress party members is different from deriving such a support from the Christian community in the state. The table only reveals the existence of such a consolidation outside the party, however small it may be, behind the 'A' faction.

(iii) The analysis shows that group affiliation is independent of religion. This is evident from Table 22. Eventhough the 'I' group enjoys a majority among the Hindu, Muslim and Christian communities, the margin of difference with the 'A' group in the case of the Muslim community is comparatively low; pointing to the possibility of a growing preference of that community for Antony's leadership of the UDF.

(iv) The ideological orientation of Congress factionalism is confirmed in the analysis. At the peripheral level, it may seem foolish to look for the ideological fault lines separating the factions in the Congress party. But the crystalisation of a powerful socio-economic-regional group centering around a section of the Christian community is discernible in the Kerala society since the advent of parliamentary democracy and coalition governments. It is this socio-economic-regional group that compelled the 'A' faction to come out of the CPI(M) alliance in 1982 and to rejoin the UDF. This section was longing for political power to further their economic, educational and religious interests. Their political aspiration which is closer to the neo-liberal idology gets articulated through the 'A' group and some of the regional and communal parties. It was the historic necessity of realizing their economic, educational and religious interests that made this section to seek the leadership of the democratic camp headed by the Congress (I). Actually the merger of the 'A' faction with the Congress (I) in 1982 was the first step in this direction.

(v) Congress factionalism is not rooted in personality clash as is tried to be projected by the religious, educational and economic interest-group having a decisive say in the affairs of the 'A' faction. Eventhough the data also indicate personality clash as one of the reasons (Table 25), this has to be understood in the background of the efforts by the above section to deliberately reduce the politics of factionalism in the party to the level of a mere personality clash. This section fails to see or deliberately conceal the differences in the ideological perceptions between them and others. The authoritarian style of functioning of Karunakaran also contributed to strengthen the view. So it is wrong to reduce the politics of Congress factionalism to the level of a mere personality clash.

Notes

1. The present census indicates no considerable changes in the composition of the demographic structure of Kerala. As per the census report 2001, Kerala's population is 3,18,38619. In this 1,54,68664 are males and 1,63,69955 females. The rural population comes to 2,15,71484 and the urban population strikes a figure of 82,67135 (Sheela Thomas 2001)
2. The decision to grant 15% reservation for the economically backward sections from among the forward communities taken by the Karunakaran government in 1987 is an example of this policy.
3. Out of the three ministers of the 'A' faction in the present Antony ministry, two are Hindus and one a Muslim. Similarly two Christians namely K M Chandy and A L Jacob who became the Presidents of the KPCC were the nominees of K. Karunakaran.
4. The Antony government declared prohibition as the policy of the government and issued orders prohibiting the sale of arrack.

References

Alford R. Robert (1964): *Party and Society: The Anglo American Societies*, USA, Rand McNally &Com.

Beteille Andre (1996): 'Caste in Contemporary India' Fuller C.J (ed), *Caste Today*, Delhi, Oxford University Press.

De Souza Peter Donald (2000): "Caste Secularisation Process in India", DL Sheth (Ed) *Contemporary India*, New Delhi.

Gopalakrishna (1981): "Religion and Politics" in a project sponsored by the ICCSR *Political Dynamics* Vol.III, New Delhi.

Hague Rod, Martin Harrop and Shaun Breslin (1992): *Comparative Government and Politics: An Introduction*, London, Macmillan.

Lane E Robert. (1972): *Political Man*, New York, The Free Press.

Lowie H Robert. (1950): *Social Organisation*, London. The Free Press.

Mahendra P Singh (1989): *Cohesion in a Predominant Party: In the Pradesh Congress and Party Politics in Bihar*, New Delhi, S. Chand.

Mohanan B (1999): "Verdict of Kerala Elections 1998", *ISDA Journal*, 9(2).

Muraleedharan Nair V (1996): "Nair Service Society and 1996 Kerala elections", *ISDA Journal*, 7(4).

Plamentz John (1970): *Ideology*, London, Pall Mall.

Ramakrishnan Nair. R (1964): "Government and Politics in Kerala" In V.K Sukumaran Nayar (Ed) *Kerala Society and Politics*, Trivandrum: Department of Politics, University of Kerala.

Raman Pillai K. (1998): "Moonu Desakangal Pinnitta Kerala Rashtreeyam", In N. Vijayan (ed) *Keralathinte Moonu Deskangal* (M), TVPM, State Institute of Languages.

Sadasivan Nair K. (1970): *The Congress Party in Kerala 1947-63* (PhD Thesis), Trivandrum: Department of Politics, University of Kerala.

Seshadri K. (1999): *Stagnancy and Change in Indian Society and Politics*, Jaipur, Aalekh Publishers.

Sheela Thomas (2001): *Census of 2001 services 33 Kerala.* Thiruvananthapuram: Department of Census.

Sirsikar V.M (1994): *Politics of Modern Maharashtra*, Bombay, Orient Longman.

Srinivas M.N (1976): *The Remembered Village* Delhi Oxford University Press.

Srinivas M.N (1994): *The Dominant Caste*, New Delhi, Oxford University Press.

Suresh Kumar R.K. (2001): "Ideological chimera, Peoples verdict and the Left Debacle: Kerala Assembly Election 2001". *The Indian Journal of Political Science* vol. 2, No.2 June 2001.

Sydney Verba, Norman H. Nie & Joe - on Kim (1978): *Participation and Political Equality: A Seven-Nation Comparison*, Cambridge: Cambridge University Press.

Varghese T.C (1970): *Agrarian Change and Economic consequences: Land Tenures in Kerala 1850-1960*, Delhi.

Zenab Banu (1999): *Decline and Fall of Indian Politics*, New Delhi, Kanishka.

Six

Political and Economic Context of Factionalism

In this chapter, the political and economic context of the factional dynamics in the Congress party is empirically analysed. Here it is proposed to examine the relationship between factionalism and factors like age, education, economic status and leadership role of the respondents.

Age is one of the crucial factors in understanding the nature and functioning of a party organisation. S.M. Lipset emphasised that age differences imply variations in life experiences and affect the political behaviour in two ways: through generational differences and through differences in typical patterns of social experience associated with different age groups (Lipset1960:264). Also prestige and authority is commonly found with the elders, who have more exposure and experience than younger ones. Maturity of age contributed to elite status in the tribal community (Panigrahi1998: 106). There are psychologically based age related changes in political orientations and behaviour. Generational or age group differences in political socialisation and certain consequences of the aging process are the factors most commonly cited. It is widely felt that increasing integration of older cohorts into social system leads them to acquire a greater stake in the system and in the maintenance of status quo (Barry Stacey 1978:132).

In Democracies education provides training in good citizenship and produces leaders at all levels of human activity. Self expression, judgement and independence of thought come from a sound educational background. The ultimate aim of education is liberation through knowledge and wisdom (Hollins 1964:120). Education prepares one for the dual role of leadership and followership. Education appears to broaden man's view and enables him to understand the need for rules of tolerance. With a higher education, one is more likely to believe in democratic values and support of democratic practices (Lipset 1960: 21). Educational level has served to hinder the rise or growth of other anti-democratic forces. The democratic administration of grading or grouping of pupils therefore, indicates that grouping should be kept flexible that they should be reviewed whenever the educational purpose of the group shifts (John S. Brubacher 1962:139). In developing societies education is an index of modernisation. Formal education is a point of modernisation take off in certain attitudinal variables, such as the level of aspiration. So there is an inherent correlation between education and political elite (Panigrahi:110). It is not necessary that individuals with similar educational background should develop identical political orientation, but a close bond exists between the two.

Along with age and education, economic status too, often determines the political orientation of a class or a group. Different rates of industrial growth and increase in the number of industrial workers, and the concentration of industry in cities, however, were accompanied by differences in the development of political groups or parties (Lipset 1960:27).

It is also seen that group preferences are often based on the leadership role that one has in a party organisation. One's perception of groupism changes according to the leadership role that they play in the party. Those at the top of the party pyramid are unwilling to take 'sides openly, while it is those at the middle and bottom levels who act as crusaders of their groups.

I. Age and Factional Orientation

The strength of the Congress party lies in its ability to draw supporters more or less equally from all age groups (Sheth 1975:142). Irrespective of the age groups, 606 (93.81 per cent) out of 646 respondents believed that groupism is a concrete reality in the Congress party in Kerala. 93.38% per cent of the respondents in the age group 18-35, 94.84 per cent in the age group 36-50, 94.23 per cent in the 51-65 age group and 82.78 per cent in the age group of above 65 affirmed this. The following table contains the details.

TABLE NO. 1
WHETHER GROUPISM EXISTS IN THE PARTY

Age	*Yes*	*No*	*Total*
18-35	141	10	151
36-50	294	16	310
51-65	147	9	156
Above 65	24	5	29
Total	606	40	646

But surprisingly a vast majority of 516 (81.90%) out of 630 do not consider that groups are inevitable as revealed in the table below.

TABLE NO. 2
WHETHER GROUPISM IS INEVITABLE

Age	*Yes*	*No*	*Total*
18-35	27	118	145
36-50	54	249	303
51-65	28	124	152
Above 65	5	25	30
Total	114	516	630

Most of the respondents were very much aware of the Marxist design in Kerala to repeat the Bengal pattern where the CPI(M) has been in power continuously for over twentyfive years after relegating the Congress party to a poor third position. The Congressmen hailing from the minority communities in particular were very much apprehensive of the Marxist threat to their economic and educational interests. The Congressmen also realise that power alternates between the two fronts in Kerala. As such ideally they would like the Congress party to face the Marxist challenge unitedly.

Among all the age groups, the Karunakaran faction enjoys maximum support. Out of the 546 respondents, 313 (57.33%) support his faction as is revealed in the table below.

TABLE NO. 3
DIFFERENT AGE GROUPS AND THEIR FACTIONAL ORIENTATION

Age	*Name of Group You belong*				
	AK	*KK*	*GK*	*VR*	*Total*
18-35	45	71	5	5	126
%	(35.71)	(56.35)	(3.97)	(3.97)	
36-50	98	146	8	6	258
%	(37.98)	(56.59)	(3.10)	(2.33)	
51-65	56	77	2	1	136
%	(41.18)	(56.62)	(1.47)	(0.74)	
Above 65	7	19			26
%	(26.92)	(73.08)			
Total	206	313	15	12	546
%	(37.73)	(57.33)	(2.74)	(2.20)	

As is evident the Antony faction is the second largest with 37.73 per cent support. The other two groups are insignificant. Among the above 65 age group Karunakaran enjoys an enviable 73.08 per cent support. His association with the Congress politics from the days of the freedom movement and his consistent anti–CPI(M) stand has helped him gain the confidence of the elder Congressmen. Among the youngsters (18-35), contrary to the commonly held view that the Antony faction is the strongest, the Karunakaran faction emerges as the largest registering a considerable lead of 20.64 per cent than the 'A' faction. In the two other age groups also Karunakaran group emerges a clear winner. The collected age-wise data (Table not given) further reveals that 73.17 per cent of the respondents agree that Karunakaran faction is the predominant one among the existing groups.

A sizeable majority of 63.86 per cent belonging to the four age groups answered in the negative to the enquiry whether Congress factionalism has a caste-communal basis as is seen in the table below.

Statistical analysis of Table.4 also establishes that factionalism has no caste-communal roots. Since the calculated chi-square value 5.229 is less than the table value of chi-square 7.82 at 5 per cent level of significance and 3 degrees of freedom (See appendix X).

TABLE NO. 4
THE RESPONSES OF DIFFERENT AGE GROUPS REGARDING THE CASTE-COMMUNAL ROOTS OF CONGRESS FACTIONALISM

Age	*Caste communal root*		
	Yes	*No*	*Total*
18-35	63 (41.45%)	89 (58.55%)	152
36-50	107 (34.74%)	201 (65.26%)	308
51-65	50 (31.45%)	109 (68.55%)	159
Above 65	16 (47.06%)	18 (52.94%)	34
Total	236 (36.14%)	417 (63.86%)	653

In the responses regarding the ideological underpinnings of Congress factionalism the opinion is clearly divided. Those who believe that ideology is a dominant factor in Congress factionalism has only a slight edge of 1.6 per cent as the following table illustrates.

TABLE NO. 5
WHETHER CONGRESS FACTIONALISM IS IDEOLOGY ORIENTED

Age	*Yes*	*No*	*Total*
18-35	82 (53.95%)	70 (46.05%)	152
36-50	149 (48.06%)	161 (51.94%)	310
51-65	80 (48.73%)	81 (51.27%)	161
Above 65	22 (59.38%)	10 (40.62%)	32
Total	333	322	655

While among the two age groups viz, the youngest and the oldest this edge is considerably visible, in the second and third age groups, non ideological causes have an edge. Twenty two out of six hundred and seventy seven respondents (3.25 %) refrained from divulging their views on the ideological base of Congress factionalism. On employing the chi-square test of significance it is confirmed that factionalism is ideologically oriented since the calculated value of chi-square 5.7314 is less than the table value of chi-square 7.82 at 5 per cent level of significance and 3 degrees of freedom (Appendix XI).

Sajal Basu in his study of the West-Bengal CPI(M) opined that the ideological factor was less influential in shaping factionalism, whereas personal factors had maximum influence in the formation of factions. Mere ideology rarely influenced the decision making in alignment pattern. It could gain power only when personal factors were mixed with it (Sajal Basu :21).

An overwhelming 87.33 per cent of Congressmen between the age group 18-65 classified into four age groups, maintained the view that personality clashes also contribute to factionalism as is seen in the table appearing below.

TABLE NO. 6
THE RESPONSES REGARDING PERSONALITY CLASH AS A CAUSE OF FACTIONALISM

Age	*Yes*	*No*	*Total*
18-35	135	17	152
36-50	274	35	309
51-65	135	24	159
Above 65	28	7	35
Total	572	85	655

The responses in the above two tables are contradictory. While only a little above 50 per cent of the respondents (Table No.5) believe in the ideological moorings of Congress factionalism, in the latter table (Table No.6), 87.33 per cent agrees that personality clash is the major cause of factionalism. This may be due to the fact that ideological differences often get reflected through different styles of functioning. It is also true that Congressmen have no clear perception of the official Congress ideology.

The veiled criticism from certain quarters that the support base of K. Karunakaran is rooted in the Nair community is again proved wrong in the age wise analysis as is seen below.

TABLE NO. 7
THE AGE WISE RESPONSE REGARDING THE NAIR COMMUNITY BASE OF THE KARUNAKARAN GROUP

Age	*Yes*	*No*	*Total*
18-35	18	130	148
36-50	25	278	303
51-65	16	140	156
Above 65	8	28	36
Total	67	576	643

89.58 per cent of respondents belonging to all groups in the case of K. Karunakaran brushed aside this criticism.

The two age-wise tables below shows the comparative assessment of K. Karunakaran and A.K Antony in their roles as protector of party men's interest.

TABLE NO. 8
THE RATING OF KARUNAKARAN AS PROTECTOR OF PARTYMEN

Age	*Protector of Party men*				
	VG	*G*	*A*	*B*	*Total*
18-35	121	19	9	2	151
36-50	251	40	10	3	304
51-65	129	17	5	2	153
Above 65	30	6			36
Total	531	82	24	7	644

A total of 531 (82.45 %) respondents out of 644 place K. Karunakaran in the very good category while in the case of A.K. Antony (Table No.9), it is a poor 29.11 per cent. The uniform support for Karunakaran among all age groups indicates that his support base remains intact over the years.

TABLE NO. 9
THE RATING OF A.K. ANTONY AS PROTECTOR OF PARTY MEN

Age	*Protector of Party men*				
	VG	*G*	*A*	*B*	*Total*
18-35	27	37	53	24	141
36-50	87	68	104	32	291
51-65	53	30	50	13	146
Above 65	10	6	7	7	30
Total	177	141	214	76	608

In the age wise responses assessing the ability of K. Karunakaran and A.K.Antony to maintain working relationship with the caste-communal groups in Kerala politics, Karunakaran emerges as a clear winner with 80.32% rating him 'very good'. The following tables present the details of the dominant position enjoyed by Karunakaran.

TABLE NO. 10
KARUNAKARAN'S RATING IN MANAGING CASTE-COMMUNAL GROUPS

Age	*Working relationship*				
	VG	*G*	*A*	*B*	*Total*
18-35	116 (78.38%)	21	9	2	148
36-50	242 (80.94%)	41	13	3	299
51-65	126 (81.82%)	19	6	3	154
Above 65	22 (75.86%)	5		2	29
Total	506 (80.32%)	86	28	10	630

TABLE NO. 11
A.K. ANTONY'S RATING IN MANAGING CASTE-COMMUNAL GROUPS

Age	*Working relationship*				
	VG	*G*	*A*	*B*	*Total*
18-35	29 (21.32%)	38	56	13	136
36-50	96 (33.1%)	72	105	17	290
51-65	54 (37.76%)	35	48	6	143
Above 65	12 (40%)	9	7	2	30
Total	191 (31.89%)	154	216	38	599

As per the table above, only 31.89 per cent places A.K. Antony in the very good category. It is important here to note that among the youth (18-35), only 21.32 per cent consider Antony to be very good in managing the caste-communal groups, while it is 78.38 per cent in the case of Karunakaran. It is this ground reality that compels the 'I' faction to sack the Presidentship of the Youth Congress. The age wise rating in this regard shows the increasing relevance of K. Karunakaran for the party in the years ahead in the context of the growing caste-communal polarisation in Kerala politics. That an overwhelming majority (78.38%) belonging to the age wise category of 18-35, who are going to be the decisive force in the party in the coming decades and who at present work at the grassroot levels, admit to this inspite of Karunakaran's old age is a pointer in this regard. It is significant here that only 21.32 per cent in the above category see in Antony the potential for this. This naturally caste aspersions on his factions desire to play the role of the leader of the UDF in the coming years.

As opposition leader K.Karunakaran is again ranked high by 527 (81.45 %) out of 647 respondents. This is uniform among all age groups. Here also only 31 per cent includes A.K. Antony in the first category. The details are available in the two tables given below.

TABLE NO. 12
AGE-WISE RATING OF K.KARUNAKARAN AS OPPOSITION LEADER

Age	*Opposition Leader*				
	VG	*G*	*A*	*B*	*Total*
18-35	118	22	9	2	151
36-50	249	44	9	3	305
51-65	128	19	5	2	154
Above 65	32	5			37
Total	527	90	23	7	647

TABLE NO. 13
AGE WISE RATING OF A.K ANTONY AS OPPOSITION LEADER

Age	*Opposition Leader*				
	VG	*G*	*A*	*B*	*Total*
18-35	32	41	60	13	146
36-50	94	75	109	16	294
51-65	54	38	47	4	143
Above 65	10	8	10	2	30
Total	190	162	226	35	613

Here also, in the very good category Karunakaran has a lead of 56.23 per cent over Antony among the 18-35 age group, indicating a positive nod to the 'I' group's style of functioning from the younger generation of Congressmen.

The pattern repeats in the comparative estimate of K. Karunakaran and A.K. Antony in their performance as chief minister. This is revealed from the following two tables. Here, 80.91 per cent (Table No. 14) places K. Karunakaran in the very good category. This is only 31.47 per cent (Table No. 15) in the case of Antony. Those who place Antony in the average category come to 36.08 per cent.

TABLE NO. 14
AGE WISE RATING OF K. KARUNAKARAN AS CHIEF MINISTER

Age	*VG*	*G*	*A*	*B*	*Total*
18-35	119	20	10	2	151
36-50	246	45	10	3	304
51-65	127	19	6	2	154
Above 65	25	5			30
Total	517	89	26	7	639

TABLE NO. 15
AGE WISE RATING OF A.K.ANTONY AS CHIEF MINISTER

Age	*A.K. Antony as CM*				
	VG	*G*	*A*	*B*	*Total*
18-35	31	39	56	14	140
36-50	93	78	108	15	294
51-65	55	37	47	4	143
Above 65	12	8	8	2	30
Total	191	162	219	35	607

The following combined table grades the ability of the four faction leaders to provide effective leadership to the UDF. Naturally in all age groups K. Karunakaran scores high grade. This Table also shows the insignificance of the third and fourth groups in the politics of Congress factionalism.

TABLE NO. 16
THE RATING OF THE FOUR FACTION LEADERS IN PROVIDING EFFECTIVE LEADERSHIP TO THE UDF

Age	*Rating of AK*	*Rating of KK*	*Rating of GK*	*Rating of VR*	*Total*
18-35	34	65	6	4	109
36-50	81	148	7	7	243
51-65	44	73	2	3	122
Above 65	7	19			26
Total %	166 (33.2)	305 (61.00)	15 (3.00)	14 (2.8)	500

AK - A K Antony; KK - K. Karunakaran;
GK - G.Karthikeyan; VR - Vayalar Ravi

The pattern slightly deviates in the rating regarding their ability to face the BJP and the CPI(M) challenge as can be seen in the following tables

TABLE NO. 17
THE RATING OF THE FOUR FACTION LEADERS IN MEETING THE BJP CHALLENGE

Age	*Rating of AK*	*Rating of KK*	*Rating of GK*	*Rating of VR*	*Total*
18-35	42	68	6	3	119
36-50	96	150	7	5	258
51-65	59	69	2	1	131
Above 65	11	16			27
Total %	208 (38.88)	303 (56.64)	15 (2.80)	9 (1.68)	535

TABLE NO. 18
THE RATING OF THE FOUR FACTION LEADERS IN MEETING THE CPI(M) CHALLENGE

Age	*Rating of AK*	*Rating of KK*	*Rating of GK*	*Rating of VR*	*Total*
18-35	38	89	7	3	137
36-50	102	179	6	5	292
51-65	45	97	2	2	146
Above 65	9	19			28
Total %	194 (32.17)	384 (63.68)	15 (2.49)	10 (1.66)	603

Here also Karunakaran is considered as the most suitable person to lead the party in meeting the BJP and CPI(M) challenge. Antony is considered more effective in dealing with the BJP challenge than the Marxist challenge.

II. Educational Status and Factional Orientation

Here we look at the educational background of the respondents to determine the bond, if any, between their educational level and the factional orientation.

Persons having different educational background fill the ranks of all groups and this is not unusual to the Kerala situation. In Kerala, the rate of unemployment among matriculates is higher than that of the graduates. The highest difference in the rate of unemployment between matriculates and graduates was observed in the case of rural males (Mathew 1999:102).

The following table shows the factional orientation of the respondents according to their educational background.

TABLE NO. 19
FACTIONAL ORIENTATION OF THE RESPONDENTS ACCORDING TO THEIR EDUCATIONAL QUALIFICATIONS

Education	*Name the group you belong*				
	AK	*KK*	*GK*	*VR*	*Total*
Below SSLC	8	12			20
SSLC	75	123	7	5	210
Under Graduate	31	53	2	2	88
Graduate	54	74	1	4	133
Post Graduate	23	26	1	1	51
Professional (Diploma)	10	17	2		29
Professional (graduate & above)	5	8	2		15
Total	206 (37.73)	313 (57.33)	15 (2.74)	12 (2.2)	546

One of the puzzles of the Kerala model of Development is the presence of a large number of educated unemployed people. Providing jobs or promise of jobs constitute one of the major items in the election manifestos of political parties. They constitute an important section in every political party. The Congress resurgence of the 1970's in Kerala was led by the educated youth and they are still active in the Congress party. Majority of the Congressmen in the education wise categorisation also favours K. Karunakaran.

The comparatively high educational background of a large number of respondents resulted in 97.76 per cent of them (Table not given) accepting the existence of groups and faction rivalry in the party irrespective of the party leadership's public posture of denying its existence.

It is wishful thinking with a pinch of idealism that prompted 81.90 per cent of the respondents to say that groupism in Congress is not inevitable. This view is dominant among all categories as is clear from the following table.

TABLE NO. 20
THE OPINION OF THE SEVEN EDUCATIONAL CATEGORIES REGARDING THE INEVITABILITY OF GROUPISM

Education	*Group inevitable*		
	Yes	*No*	*Total*
Below SSLC	15	6	21
SSLC	49	202	251
Under Graduate	14	86	100
Graduate	24	129	153
Post Graduate	3	55	58
Professional (Diploma)	8	25	33
Professional (Degree)	1	13	14
Total	114	516	630

In the post-independent period and in particular since the 1970's, the Congress party assimilated the monarchic value system whereby even constructive criticism was neither appreciated nor tolerated. In the absence of free criticism and debate within the party, leaders are denied opportunity to learn facts and correct themselves. Congress party always find scapegoats for its failures and shortcomings (Sethi 1975:214). The existence of groups in the party is essential to give protection to the critics. As such it is not surprising that even the educated takes shelter under the roof of a leader and his group. The opinion that groupism is not inevitable is to be understood in the above context.

The educated in all categories consider the Karunakaran group to be the most dominant one with 73.17 per cent in its favour relegating the Antony group to a modest 25.4 per cent as is reflected in the following table.

TABLE NO. 21
THE PREDOMINANT GROUP IN THE CONGRESS PARTY (EDUCATIONAL QUALIFICATION WISE)

Education	*Name of group*				
	AK	*KK*	*GK*	*VR*	*Total*
Below SSLC	6	12			18
SSLC	45	204	2	2	253
Under Graduate	33	65	1	1	100
Graduate	46	103	2	1	152
Post Graduate	17	39			56
Professional (Diploma)	9	27			36
Professional (Degree)	4	11			15
Total	160	461	5	4	630
%	(25.4)	(73.17)	(0.80)	(0.63)	

The figures in this table contradict the figures in Table No.19 dealing with the factional orientation of the respondents according to their educational background. In Table No.19 while 38.25 per cent of the respondents are oriented towards the Antony faction, in Table No. 21, only 25.4 per cent considers the 'A' faction as the predominant one. It only means that even among the supporters of Antony, 12.85 per cent accept the reality that the 'I' group is the predominant one.

Educational cross tabulation to find whether Congress factionalism was policy and ideology oriented before 1969, reveals that it was so with 95.82 per cent of the respondents subscribing to this view as is seen in Table No. 22 below.

TABLE NO. 22
THE NATURE OF CONGRESS FACTIONALISM BEFORE 1969

Qualification	*Before 1969 policy & ideology oriented*		
	Yes	*No*	*Total*
Below SSLC	12		12
S.S.L.C	136	10	146
Under Graduate	60	2	62
Graduate	104	4	108
Post Graduate	46		46
Professional (Diploma)	18	1	19
Professional (Graduate)	14		14
Total	390	17	407

It also shows that 270 (39.88%) out of 677 respondents were ignorant about the history of the party before 1970 as they failed to answer the question.

Another analysis shows that it is more persónality oriented and less ideological in nature after 1969 as is seen in the table below.

TABLE NO. 23
WHETHER CONGRESS FACTIONALISM WAS MORE PERSONALITY ORIENTED AND LESS IDEOLOGICAL AFTER 1969

Qualification	*After1969 more personality & less ideological*		
	Yes	*No*	*Total*
Below SSLC	5		5
S.S.L.C	139	4	143
Under Graduate	60	1	61
Graduate	102	1	103
Post graduate	44		44
Professional (Diploma)	19		19
Professional (Graduate)	10		10
Total	379	6	385

Here also 292 (43.13%) out of 677 did not answer this question, since they were unaware of what actually constitute the Congress ideology today.

The difference in educational levels does not come in the way of most of them denying any link between economic interest groups and Congress factionalism.

TABLE NO. 24
TABLE EXAMINING THE LINK BETWEEN ECONOMIC INTEREST GROUPS AND CONGRESS FACTIONALISM

Qualification	*Yes*	*No*	*Total*
Below SSLC	8	4	12
S.S.L.C	51	213	264
Under Graduate	17	82	99
Graduate	35	123	158
Post Graduate	14	45	59
Professional (Diploma)	9	28	37
Professional (Graduate)	4	12	16
Total	138	507	645

In this table only 21.4 per cent of the respondents agree that Congress factionalism is linked to economic interest groups. Since we cannot ignore the opinion of the 21.4 per cent, it is necessary for us to identify the major interest groups, if any, behind the four Congress factions. This is done with the help of two tables (table Nos. 25 & 26) which identify the economic interest groups behind K. Karunakaran and A.K Antony

The following table provides figures of the feed back data regarding the major interest groups behind the Karunakaran faction.

TABLE NO. 25
THE MAJOR INTEREST GROUPS BEHIND THE KARUNAKARAN FACTION

Interest group	*Qualification*							
	Below SSLC	*SSLC*	*Under Graduate*	*Graduate*	*Post Graduate*	*Professional (Diploma)*	*Professional (Degree)*	*Total*
Abkari contractor		3		2				5
Businessmen & industrialists				2			1	3
Planters / Agriculturists		6	1	6				13
Trade Union		28	13	18	5	3	1	68
Police & bureaucrats					1	1	1	3
General Public	12	149	48	82	38	19	8	356
Total	12	186	62	110	44	23	11	448

While analysing the attitude of the respondents regarding the major interest groups behind the 'I' faction, it is seen that 229 (33.83%) out of 677 did not answer this question. Among those who responded 15.18 per cent believes that trade unions constitute the major interest group behind the 'I' faction. Only 2.9 per cent believe that planters and agriculturists constitute the major interest group behind it. However the majority consisting of 79.46 per cent (356) of the respondents believes that the general public constitutes the largest group behind the 'I' faction.

TABLE NO. 26
THE INTEREST GROUPS BEHIND THE ANTONY FACTION

Interest group	*Qualification*							
	Below SSLC	*SSLC*	*Under Graduate*	*Graduate*	*Post Graduate*	*Professional (Diploma)*	*Professional (Degree)*	*Total*
Abkaris/ Contractors		3		5				8
Businessmen & Industrialists		4	1	1		1		7
Plantors/ Agriculturists		18	11	18	3	3		53
Trade Unions		8	2	4	1		1	16
Police & bureaucracy							1	1
General Public	8	148	48	81	38	18	9	350
Total	8	181	62	109	42	22	11	435

As per the above table, the general public is indicated as the largest interest group behind the 'A' faction. At the same time 53 (12.18%) out of 435 respondents consider planters and agriculturists as the major interest group behind the 'A' faction. Here also 242 (35.75%) out of 677 did not answer this question. The percentage of persons refusing to answer this question in the two tables is very high. The other two groups are insignificant since they are numerically very weak. Other than the general public, businessmen and industrialists are shown as the main interest groups behind the third group. Abkaris and contractors occupy the second place after the general public as far as the fourth group is concerned.

The feedback also reveals that there is no regional nor linguistic basis for the existence of groups in the Congress party. This is evident from the following table.

TABLE NO. 27
WHETHER THE CONGRESS FACTIONS HAVE A REGIONAL OR LINGUISTIC BASIS

Qualification	*Yes*	*No*	*Total*
Below SSLC	3	15	18
S.S.L.C	33	230	263
UG	11	87	98
Graduate	16	137	153
PG	2	56	55
Professional (Diploma)	5	32	37
Professional (Graduate)	5	10	15
Total	75	564	639

38 out of 677 did not answer this question. Only 11.74 per cent of the respondents assign a place to regionalism and linguism in the politics of Congress factionalism.

III. Economic Status and Factional Orientation

A leveling process has already taken place in the Kerala society when compared with other Indian states. As such in Kerala, the connection between economic status and factional orientation do not matter much.

The following table brings out the factional orientation of different income groups. The dominance of Karunakaran group among all income categories is clearly discernable in the table below.

TABLE NO. 28
THE GROUP ORIENTATION OF DIFFERENT INCOME GROUPS

Monthly income	*Name the group you belong*				
	AK	*KK*	*GK*	*VR*	*Total*
Below 1000	48	67			115
1000-5000	112	161	12	9	294
5000-8000	21	30		1	52
8000-10000	11	23	2		36
Above 10000	14	32	1	2	49
Total	206	313	15	12	546

A total of 131 out of 677 were unwilling to clearly reveal their income. Most of the career politicians declare that they have no stable income of their own.

Nearly 49.16 per cent of the respondents coming from all income groups denied the existence of any caste-communal basis for factionalism. All income categories agreed to this. The following table reveals this.

TABLE NO. 29
THE CASTE-COMMUNAL BASIS OF CONGRESS FACTIONALISM (INCOME WISE CATEGORISATION)

Income	*Caste/communal basis*		
	Yes	*No*	*Total*
Below 1000	65	69	134
1000-5000	100	262	362
5000-8000	23	35	58
8000-10000	15	25	40
Above 10000	33	26	59
Total	236	417	653

But it is seen that 48.51 per cent of those below the Rs. 1,000/- level believes in a caste-communal basis of Congress factionalism. This is more, i.e. 55.93 per cent in the above Rs. 10,000/- category. It shows that the higher income groups are more concerned with their caste-communal status.

IV. Leadership Role in the Organisation and the Factional Dynamics

Leadership is a way of thinking about institutional heirs, a way of thinking about the stewardship as confronted with ownership. Leaders are responsible for effectiveness (Max Dec Pree 1994:19). The leader is a symbol of the group. He is the person who gives direction and controls the activities of the group. Leadership is a process of mutual stimulation, while domination is a process of control in which by assumption of superiority a person or a group regulates the activities of others (Sprott 1956:73). A leader has direct dynamic relationship with followers. He possesses little coercive power, his power being a product of his own ability to persuade his followers (Carl J. Frederick 1967:125). The search for values of security and equality has led to changes in the character of politics. If one were to delineate this new pattern of politics by leadership, it would include a shift in the centre of conflict resolution and initiative (Dipti Kumar Biswas 1978:100). Traditionalist leadership can be as strong as charismatic leadership (Gwendolen M Carter & John H. Herz 1967:143).

The leader must feel the trend of events or the under currents in the social and political spheres of the society and also be able to assess their potentialities and magnitude. The leader should have personal contact with different varieties of people in the society. Robert Mitchels suggests qualities like strength of conviction, relatively wide knowledge and forceful will for efficient leadership (Robert Mitchels 1915 :64).

The respondents were classified into nine categories based on their leadership roles. Even ordinary activists play a leadership role, though at the bottom level and as such that role is also counted. The respondents at different leadership levels confirm the presence of groupism in the party as is seen in the following table.

TABLE NO. 30

TABLE SHOWING WHETHER GROUPS EXISTS IN CONGRESS

Position held	*Yes*	*No*	*Total*
DCC President	14		14
DCC Secretary	38	1	39
DCC Member	30	1	31
Bloc President	34		34
Bloc Secretary	25	1	26
Mandalam President	36	2	38
Mandalam Secretary	31	2	33
Activists	299	9	308
Others *	99	24	123
Total	606 (93.81%)	40 (6.19%)	646

Note*: Others include respondents from the feeder organisations of the party.

Even those who play the top most leadership roles accept openly that groups exist in the party. As nominees of their respective groups this is expected of them. It is not only the top party functionaries who consider factionalism in the party as a concrete reality, but also the activists at the lower leadership levels. This is an indication that factionalism in the party is not the result of personality clash alone. Its roots go deeper. The divide is so deep that party men place more importance to factions than the party. Naturally, a party member not aligned to any of the factions finds it extremely difficult to get the patronage of the party leadership. The unceremonial removal of Thennala Balakrishna Pillai as the KPCC President in May 2001, inspite of his choice as the consensus candidate, is a pointer in this regard.

Similarly 516 (81.9%) out of 630 respondents in the table below, makes it known that groups are not inevitable. This seems contradictory to the earlier revelation that groups do exist in the party. Here one can notice the difference between theory and practice. Being a nominee of groups to different leadership positions they practice groupism and at the same time openly deny its inevitability.

TABLE NO. 31
TABLE SHOWING WHETHER GROUPS ARE INEVITABLE

Position held	*Yes*	*No*	*Total*
DCC President	2	10	12
DCC Secretary	8	22	30
DCC Member	5	21	26
Bloc President	4	30	34
Bloc Secretary	6	20	26
Mandalam President	10	28	38
Mandalam Secretary	15	18	33
Activists	40	268	308
Others	24	99	123
Total	114 (18.1%)	516 (81.9%)	630

In the above table 114 (18.1%) out of 630 says that groups are inevitable to the party. This hard core can be considered as the ultimate beneficiaries of the factional feud. It is this eighteen percent who calls the shots in the party.

The leadership position wise responses reveals that most of the top party posts are filled by Karunakaran loyalists. Among the 14 DCC Presidents, his group has seven followed by Antony group with five. Based on the respondents leadership position in the party, their factional orientation is examined below.

TABLE NO. 32
THE RESPONDENTS GROUP ORIENTATION BASED ON THEIR LEADERSHIP POSITION IN THE PARTY

Leadership position	*Name of the group you belong*				
	AK	*KK*	*GK*	*VR*	*Total*
DCC President	5	7	1	1	14
DCC Secretary	13	18	2	2	35
DCC Member	10	16	1	1	28
Bloc President	7	21	2	2	32
Bloc Secretary	11	13	1	1	26
Mandalam President	10	16	1	1	28
Mandalam Secretary	10	16	1	1	28
Activist	112	181	6	3	302
Others *	28	25			53
Total	206 (37.73%)	313 (57.33%)	15 (2.74%)	12 (2.2%)	546

Note: *Others include respondents from the feeder organisations of the party.

As is evident in the table above Karunakaran group has a clear lead of 19.6 per cent than the Antony faction. This is also evident from many other tables placed elsewhere. The other two groups together command only 4.95 per cent of support.

It would be worthwhile here to examine whether the practice of nomination by the high command in accordance with the existing formula of apportioning offices among different factions correspond to their actual strength. The following table examines this.

TABLE NO. 33
THE PRESENT PERCENTAGE WISE REPRESENTATION OF THE FOUR FACTIONS IN DIFFERENT LEADERSHIP POSITIONS IN THE DISTRICTS

Leadership position	*Name of the faction*			
	AK	*KK*	*GK & VR*	*Percentage wise combined representation of AK, GK & VR factions*
DCC President	35.71	50	14.29	50.0
DCC Secretary	37.14	51.43	11.43	48.57
DCC Member	35.72	57.14	7.14	42.86
Bloc President	21.88	65.63	12.50	34.38
Bloc Secretary	42.31	50.0	7.69	50.0
Mandalam President	35.71	57.14	7.14	42.85
Mandalam Secretary	35.71	57.14	7.14	42.85

The table above indicates that the Karunakaran group which ought to get 57.33 per cent (Table No. 32) representation at different leadership levels almost touches that level and goes beyond that in four categories. At the DCC President, DCC Secretary and Block Secretary levels it is well below. The Antony faction which ought to have had 37.73 per cent representation as per table No.32, nearly touches that figure and goes beyond that level in six out of the seven categories shown in the table above. The other two groups have almost double the representation in all categories than it actually deserves i.e 4.95 per cent. There is truth in the 'I' group's accusation that the present representation does not correspond to its actual strength. It is a known fact that the second, third and fourth factions have a common enemy in Karunakaran and all of them together has managed to secure more representation in leadership positions than their actual strength except at the Block President level. As per the responses in Table No.32 together they are eligible to have only 42.67 per cent representation. But they have managed to secure more than their due through the politics of factionalism.

The following table indicating the opinion of the respondents about the predominant group in the party shows that the Karunakaran group dominates the Congress party at all levels in Kerala. Statistical analysis too supports that the Congress respondents accept the predominance of the Karuṇakaran faction, as the calculated value of chi-square 26.51 is less than the table value 36.42 at 5 per cent level of significance and 24 degrees of freedom (See Appendix XII).

TABLE NO. 34
THE LEADERSHIP ROLE OF THE RESPONDENTS AND THEIR CHOICE INDICATING THE PREDOMINANT GROUP IN THE PARTY

Party	*Predominant group(x)*				
position	*AK*	*KK*	*GK*	*VR*	*Total*
DCC President	5	7			12
DCC Secretary	11	22			33
DCC Member	10	20	1		31
Bloc President	7	27			34
Bloc Secretary	10	16			26
Mandalam President	12	26			38
Mandalam Secretary	9	24			33
Activist	70	230	4	4	308
Others	26	89			115
Total	160	461	5	4	630

(x): This does not mean that a respondent belonging to a faction should invariably indicate his group as the predominant one. He may indicate another group as the predominant one based on his own assessment.

In the last Assembly elections (2001) the Congress party returned to power with a thumping majority. One of the reasons for this is considered to be the consolidation of caste-communal groups behind the Congress and the UDF. It is in this context that the possibility of a Christian consolidation in favour of A.K. Antony due to his projection as the next chief minister has to be examined. The feedback confirms this. See the table below for details.

TABLE NO. 35
TABLE EXAMINING WHETHER THERE WAS A CONSOLIDATION OF CHRISTIAN VOTES IN THE LAST ASSEMBLY ELECTIONS (2001)

Party position	*Consolidation of Christian votes*		
	Yes	*No*	*Total*
DCC President	6	8	14
DCC Secretary	32	7	39
DCC Member	21	10	31
Bloc President	25	9	34
Bloc Secretary	19	7	26
Mandalam President	24	14	38
Mandalam Secretary	13	18	31
Activist	205	103	308
Others	73	34	107
Total	418 (66.56%)	210 (33.44%)	628

An overwhelming majority of Congress party members positioned at different leadership levels and engaged in different leadership roles in the party believed that a consolidation of Christian votes in favour of A.K. Antony as the next chief minister helped the Congress party and the UDF in the last elections to gain a convincing victory. Congress party respondents at two leadership levels disagreed with this. Among the District Congress Committee Presidents (DCC), still six out of fourteen agreed that a consolidation as indicated above has taken place. As the top most functionaries of the party in the district, the other eight DCC Presidents might have felt it wise to project the victory as a political victory. Again out of the thirty one Mandalam Secretaries who responded, eighteen disagreed with the suggestion of a Christian consolidation in favour of A.K. Antony as the next chief minister.

The opinion of the grassroot level workers assumes significance in this context since it is they who are in constant touch with the voters and the general public. As such they know the ground realities better and are quite frank enough to admit this. Their responses too indicate a Christian consolidation in favour of the Congress and the UDF in the 2001 Assembly elections.

Similarly the possibility of a reassembling Hindu votes in the 2001 Assembly elections in favour of K. Karunakaran against the Antony-Sonia dominance in the party as a balance against the Christian consolidation was tested and verified as per the details of the following table.

TABLE NO. 36
TABLE EXAMINING THE POSSIBILITY OF A REASSEMBLING OF HINDU VOTES IN THE LAST ASSEMBLY ELECTIONS IN FAVOUR OF KARUNAKARAN

Party position	*Reassembling Hindu votes*		
	Yes	*No*	*Total*
DCC President	8	6	14
DCC Secretary	27	12	39
DCC Member	24	7	31
Bloc President	16	18	34
Bloc Secretary	18	8	26
Mandalam President	23	15	38
Mandalam Secretary	18	15	33
Activist	190	118	308
Others	58	40	98
Total	382 (61.51%)	239 (38.49%)	621

A look at the figures in the above two tables suggest that Congress respondents generally feel that there has been a Christian consolidation behind Antony as well as a reassembling of Hindu votes in favour of K. Karunakaran in the last (2001) Assembly elections. It is seen that 66.56 per cent of Congress respondents believed in a Christian consolidation behind Antony and 61.51 per cent believed in the possibility of a counter reassembling of Hindu votes in favour of K. Karunakaran, thus indirectly helping both the Congress and the UDF to stage an impressive victory.

The Hindu voters felt that the LDF was more accommodative to Christian and Muslim political and religious outfits this time than ever before whose secular credentials were always suspect. In the dislodging of the LDF government, the Karunakaran factor which resulted in the reassembling of a considerable portion of Hindu votes belonging to both the BJP and the CPI(M) also played a key role.

A section of the traditionally anti-congress, Hindu voters of the CPI(M) who detested the party's hobnobbing with the Muslim fundamentalist outfit, Indian National League (INL) and those sections of the Hindus who wanted to try BJP as an alternative to Congress, but disgusted with its continuing inability to emerge so, identified their interests this time with Karunakaran who invoked a veiled Hindu communal card by challenging the Sonia-Antony combination. His revolt and the yielding of the Congress high command to his demands send the message that he is the only person capable of safeguarding Hindu interests in a Muslim and Christian dominated UDF governmental setup which was supposed to replace the five years of LDF rule (Suresh Kumar 2001: 193-94).

This does not mean that Karunakaran's support base in the Congress is increasingly becoming Hindu based. Infact the available feedback indicates that Karunakaran group has more Christian and Muslim supporters among Congressmen than the other factions. Table No. 22 of Chapter V indicates that 54.29 percent of the Congress respondents belonging to the Christian community and 50.82 percent of the respondents belonging to the Muslim community are with Karunakaran; while it is 61.62 percent in the case of the Hindus. For the Antony faction the corresponding figures are 40 percent, 44.26 percent and 33.8 per cent respectively. No wonder Antony faction is skillfully trying to gate crash into the Hindu base of Karunakaran.

An overwhelming majority of Congressmen at all levels of leadership consider Karunakaran as the right choice to ward off the CPI(M) and LDF challenge as is seen in the following table.

TABLE NO:37
THE CHOICE OF THE RESPONDENTS (LEADERSHIP ROLE WISE) AS TO WHO IN THEIR OPINION IS BEST SUITED TO TAKE UP THE CPI (M) AND LDF CHALLENGES AMONG THE FOUR FACTION LEADERS

Party position	*To face the CPI(M) & LDF*				
	AK	*KK*	*GK*	*VR*	*Total*
DCC President	5	7		1	13
DCC Secretary	10	22	2	2	36
DCC Member	10	20	1		31
Bloc President	9	25			34
Bloc Secretary	11	15			26
Mandalam President	12	20	1	1	34
Mandalam Secretary	7	22	2	2	33
Activist	100	177	4	2	283
Others	30	76	5	2	113
Total	194 (32.17)	384 (63.68)	15 (2.49)	10 (1.66)	603

Out of the 14 DCC Presidents nominated in 2001, five are in favour of Antony, seven in favour of Karunakaran and one in favour of Vayalar Ravi. One DCC President who was nominated to that post purely on the basis of factional loyalty reserves his comments. While analysing the opinion of the middle level leaders who were in this leadership position since 1992 on the basis of party election, it is seen that among the Block Presidents, nine out of thirty four were in favour of Antony and twentyfive out of thirtyfour were with Karunakaran. In the case of elected Mandalam

Presidents 12 (35.39%) out 34 were with Antony and 20 (58.82%) out of 34 favours Karunakaran. The activists who constitute the real base of the party overwhelmingly support Karunakaran. Seventyfour (10.93%) out of the six hundred and seventy seven respondents remains silent. This is higher than that of the respondents favouring the third and fourth groups. This highlights the irrelevance of these two splinter groups.

The anatomy of the political and economic context of the factional dynamics reveals the following.

(1) There is a relationship between age and group orientation in the sense that the elder Congressmen are more favourably inclined to the 'I' faction. This is clearly evident in the case of those in the 50-65 age group and above.

(2) Those in the younger age group overwhelmingly support Karunakaran's style of functioning as is evident from Tables 10, 12,14,16,17 and 18.

(3) The analysis reveals that Karunakaran will continue to play a dominant role in the Congress and the UDF. Among all age groups Karunakaran is rated high, far ahead of others as the chief minister, as the opposition leader, as the leader of UDF and in meeting the CPI(M) and BJP challenge.

(4) There is no relationship between age and opinion about ideological orientation of factionalism.

(5) There is no relationship between age and opinion about personality clash as a root cause of factionalism.

(6) There is no relationship between educational status and group orientation.

(7) There is no relationship between income level and group orientation.

(8) There is no direct relationship between leadership role and group orientation. This may be due to the practice of nomination to the higher leadership positions.

(9) Unless the present imbalance in leadership positions between the 'I' group and the others is rectified, factional feud will take an ugly turn in the near future.

References

Brubacher John S (1962): *Modern Philosophy of Education*, New York, Mc Graw Hill Company INC,

Carter M.Gwendolen & John H. Herz (1967): *Government and Politics in the Twentieth Century*, New Delhi Wile of Easter Pvt. Ltd.

Diptikumar Biswas (1978): *Political Sociology: An Introduction*, Calcutta, Firma KLM,

Frederick J.Carl (1967): *An Introduction to Political Theory* , New York, Harper & Row,

Hollins T.H.B (1964): (ed) *Aims in Education: The philosophic approach* , Manchester: Military Press,

Robert Mitchels (1915):*Political Parties*, New York, Hearst International Library Comp,

Lipset S.M (1960): *The Political Man*, London Heinemann.

Mathew E.T (1999): "Educated Unemployment in Kerala: Incidence, causes and policy implications", in B.A Praksh (ed) *Kerala's Economic Development: Issues and Problems*, New Delhi, Sage,

Panigrahi P.K (1998): *Political Elite in Tribal Society*, New Delhi, Commonwealth Publications.

Pree Max Dec (1994): *Leadership is an Art* , London, Arrow Random House,

Sajal Basu, (1990): *Factions ideology and politics: Coalition politics in West Bengal*, Calcutta, Minerva Associates.

Sheth D.L (1975): 'Social Bases of Party support' in D.L Sheth's (ed) *Citizens and Parties: Aspects of Competitive Politics in India*, New Delhi, Allied Publishers.

Sprout W.J.W (1956), *Social Psychology*, London Methnn & Com Ltd.

Stacey Barrie (1978), *Political Socialisation in Western Society: An analysis from Life span perspective*, New Delhi, Arnold Heinemann.

Suresh Kumar (2001): 'Ideological Chimera, Peoples Mandate and the Left Debacle: Kerala Assembly Elections 2001", *The Indian Journal of Political Science*, Vol. 62, No. 2.

Seven

Findings and Conclusions

A 'faction' is a group of persons forming a cohesive, usually contentious, minority within a larger group. Factionalism refers to internal dissensions or conflict within an organisation. A 'group' is a number of individuals coming together because of certain similarities. When these similarities are asserted, it amounts to groupism. The term 'factionalism' in the context of this study is understood as 'power politics' in which different ideological positions, personal interests, group interests and different styles of leadership play a key role. These factors promote dissention and discord in all political parties the only difference being one of factional assertion. This study uses the term groupism to denote power politics in the Congress party. In short, these terms are used in the study to refer to the "inharmonious combination" existing in the Congress party in Kerala.

Faction leaders aim at absolute power for themselves. They attempt to manage and control the party by bringing into existence factions by articulating differences. These differences may be real or fake. This is true of the Congress party in Kerala which is highly faction-ridden. Personality clashes, differences in the style of functioning, group rivalries, ideological differences, generation gap and squabbling for personal gains by even invoking caste-communal sentiments provide momentum to the dynamics of factionalism in the Congress party in Kerala. The various interests that emerged in the party over a long period of time gradually overshadowed the ideological and organisational potential of the Congress party. Kerala is a state where the Congress party has successfully implemented the policy of governance through coalitions inspite of the acute factionalism prevailing in the party. However, in Kerala the emergence of factionalism and its penetration to all levels of the party gave rise to a new kind of factionalism since 1982.

The analysis of the factional dynamics in the Congress party in the pre 1982 period reveals that the Kerala Pradesh Congress Committee (KPCC) was not different from the other Pradesh Congress Committees as far as factionalism was concerned. In the pre-independence period regionalism, linguism and casteism had a role in the emergence of different groups in the Congress party. The aftermath of independence saw the emergence of factions based on regionalism, communalism and casteism. The late 1950's, 60's and 70's witnessed the emergence of 'youth power' in the Congress party in Kerala. This became the basis for subsequent factional fights in the party, which erupted at different intervals in different forms. The tussle between the younger generation and the older generation, clash between the legislative wing and the organisation wing and the authoritarian style of functioning vs the democratic style were the issues through which factionalism manifested itself during that period. Though the concept of faction during the 1960's and 1970's centered on age, it was not exclusively generational differences that alone caused the formation of factions at that time. Other factors like lust for power, personal rivalry, differences in style of functioning and ideological orientation also characterised this phase of Congress factionalism.

Consequent to the split in the Congress party at the national level in 1978, Antony and his group deserted the Cong(I) and aligned with its arch-rival the CPI(M); to contest the 1980 Assembly election. Prior to that Antony, who had occupied the chair of the chief minister as the Cong(I) leader after Karunakaran's resignation, resigned as chief minister in protest against the party's decision to support Indira Gandhi, his former mentor in a Loksabha by-election. He handed over the chief ministership to the CPI leader P.K.Vasudevan Nair. This U turn in his political career turned out to be a mis-adventure which could be corrected only in 1982 with his return to the Cong(I) party led by Indira Gandhi after ditching the Left Democratic Front (LDF).

Politics took a full circle in Kerala, with the 'A' group's, return to the camp led by Karunakaran. Soon the re-union of the two Congress factions took place in 1982. Despite this, the two groups continued to exist resulting in the emergence of a new type of factionalism. Factions soon became bigger than the party and persons bigger than factions. An objective assessment of the post-merger scenario suggests that, it was to keep the Congress juggernaut rolling in the run up to the Lok Sabha election of 1984 that the 'A' group was accommodated in 1982 by the Congress high command. But the reluctance of the state unit of the Cong(I) to give space to the other group either in the party or in the government drew the factional faultlines for the coming decades with the result that it is now back to the drawing board again. The present position is that the Congress high command will have to get off its high horse and come to terms with the realities of factional politics if it wants to retain its position in Kerala. Congress factionalism in the state has not demolished the Congress ideology or structure; but it has shaken the moral foundations of its national leadership consisting of persons who have no ground support to bank on.

The following six hypotheses have been selected for empirical validation:- that factions actually constitute the basic unit of the Congress party in Kerala; though groupism is permanent, group loyalty is fluctuating; in spirit, groupism is bi-factional; different sections and classes are adequately represented in all factions; congress factionalism is not ideological, caste-communal based or issue oriented, it tends to be a product of the desire for personal power and prestige; and that Congressmen are not favourably disposed to the practice of nominations.

Factionalism starts from the top and percolates down to the bottom. Factionalism at the grassroot level is neither logical nor rational. Though the vast majority have no idea of the politics of factionalism, they have specific needs and wants, either individually or collectively. The Congress party's support base depends on how well these needs are articulated through faction leaders. Through this the different factions have widened the social base of the party. In due course, Congressmen identify themselves with the top faction leaders. They identify their interests with a factional dispensation that could deliver them the goods. Naturally different factions compete with one another to enlist supporters. As such, factions function as the basic unit of the party that provides momentum to Congress politics in the state. The competition to enlist supporters permeates in to the feeder organisations like the KSU, Youth Congress, INTUC, Employees Associations, Karshaka Congress, Mahila Congress, Dalit Congress and the Sevadal. The lack of agreement among members belonging to these organisations leads to dissensions. The prominent cadres of the factions act as a nucleus in these organisations to enlarge their group's support base. They try to elevate their loyalists to the leadership positions of these organisations. The selection of candidates to the parliamentary bodies, appointment of party office bearers, and distribution of government offices on factional lines also proves that factions actually constitute the basic unit of the Congress party in Kerala.

The study also confirms that eventhough group loyalty is fluctuating; groupism is permanent in the party. Inspite of the ceasefire announced in 1982 between the two major factions, factionalism is on the increase as is evident from the responses. The contention is upheld by 98.93 per cent of the Congress respondents. Similarly 93.81 per cent of the respondents openly confirmed that groupism is a reality in the party. These factional leaders find it difficult to placate their loyalists all the time. This results in the loyalists being wooed by the opposite faction resulting in a change of allegiance by the so called loyalists. But the Congressmen despise this tendency. This is evident from the insignificance of the third and fourth groups in the politics of Congress factionalism.

The third hypothesis stating that Congress factionalism is bi-factional even today inspite of the presence of four groups, also stands endorsed. An examination of the support bases of the four factions in the Congress party corroborates this. The study reveals that the 'I' faction enjoys the support of 57.33per cent of Congress men while the 'A' faction has a support base of 37.73 per cent. Even though 37.73 per cent support the 'A' group, its hardcore consists of only 25.40 per cent. The other two groups remain small enclaves of a few detractors. Together they carry with them a covey of 4.94 per cent of Congressmen. These groups are stop gap arrangements as they can be allured by other groups.

An analysis of the social base and the political and economic context of fationalism support the fourth hypothesis that different sections and classes are adequately represented in all factions. The sample data collected for the study reveals this. Out of the 677 respondents, 215 belonging to various factions were occupying different leadership positions in the party. They belonged to different castes and communities. Out of the Christians in leadership positions 58.82 per cent belonged to the 'I' group, 37.25 per cent to the A' group and 1.96 per cent each to the third and fourth groups. Among the Nairs in leadership positions 52.73 per cent belonged to the 'I' group, 30.91 per cent to the 'A' group, 10.91 per cent to the third group and 5.45 per cent to the fourth group. In the case of the Ezhava community the corresponding figures were 51.92 per cent, 30.77 per cent, 3.85 per cent and 9.62 per cent. Among the SC/ST's in leadership positions, 66.67 per cent belonged to the 'I' group and 33.33 per cent to the 'A' group. In the case of the Most Backward Caste's it was 75 per cent and 25 per cent respectively for the 'I' group and the 'A' group. Among the Muslim respondents in leadership positions, 59.09 per cent belonged to the 'I' group and 40.51 per cent to the 'A' group. Tables 9(a),(b),(c),(d) and Table 10 (a) & (b) of the fourth chapter substantiate this.

While analysing the attitude of the respondents regarding the major interest groups behind the Congress factions we cannot ignore the opinion of the 21.4 per cent of the respondents who firmly believe that there is a link between economic interest groups and Congress factionalism. Among the respondents 15.18 per cent believe that trade unions constitute the major interest group behind the 'I' faction. At the same time 12.18 per cent of the respondents consider planters and agriculturists as the major interest group behind the 'A' faction. Businessmen and industrialists are shown as the major interst groups behind the third group. Akbaris and contractors are the interest groups behind the fourth group.

Surprisingly, the fifth hypothesis that factionalism in the party does not have an ideological base stands negated, while the irrelevance of the caste-communal basis is confirmed. The analysis reveals that 50.84 per cent of the respondents confirmed the ideological orientation of factionalism. The statistical analysis too confirmed this. At the peripheral level, it may seem foolish to look for the ideological faultlines separating the factions in the Congress party, since personality clash is projected as the root cause of factionalism. Ofcourse personality clash is one of the many reasons for factionalism. The authoritatian style of functioning of Karunakaran also strengthened this view. The ideological orientation of factionalism is linked to the emergence of a socially, economically and politically assertive group centering on a section of the Christian community. The emergence of coalition governments in the state resulted in the crystallisation of such a group. This section was longing for political power to further their economic, educational and religious interests. This group is championing the cause of the neo-liberal agenda of the Antony government. The historic necessity of realising their economic, educational and religious interests fuels their ambition to capture the leadership of the United Democratic Front (UDF) and the government. Their aspirations are rooted through the 'A' faction of the Congress. It is natural that such a move is resisted by others. As such the faction rivalry in the party, in part, is a psychological response to the threats of insecurity prevailing among other sections of the party. An element of ideological disharmony is thus discernible in the factional feuds.

The sixth hypothesis that majority of Congressmen are against the practice of nomination to party posts also stands confirmed. The respondents have confessed that this practice has not helped to maintain the caste-comunal equations in the party. More than 77 per cent of the respondents did not favour nominations by the high command to party posts.

Thus the study confirms all the hypotheses except the one which suggests the Congress factionalism has no ideological roots and that it is a product of the desire for personal power and prestige.

Apart from the empirical testing of the hypotheses, the study also sheds light on other aspects of factionalism. The study reveals that there is no relationship between caste and factional orientation in the politics of congress factionalism. It denies the existence of a caste support base for Karunakaran. However, there is a slight Christian consolidation behind the 'A' faction. But the study points out to such a consolidation mainly outside the party. Though the

'I' group at present enjoy a majority among the Hindu, Christian and Muslim communities, there are indications pointing to the possibility of a growing preference of the Muslim community for the 'A' faction.

Among the 'I' group supporters; the Other Backward Communities (OBC's) top the list, closely followed by the SC/ST communities. The Forward Castes top in the Antony faction followed by the OBC's. In the case of the Most Backward Castes (MBC's) also, the 'I' group has overwhelming support than the 'A' faction.

The study reveals that elder congressmen are in favour of the 'I' group and that the younger age group overwhelmingly supports Karunakaran's style of functioning. This indicates the personality of Karunakaran playing a dominant role in Kerala politics in the years ahead. But whether the age factor will permit him is anybody's guess.

Congressmen consider Karunakaran to be the most effective leader to counter the challenges of the CPI(M) and BJP. He is also rated far ahead of Antony in providing leadership to the congress party, united democratic front and the government.

In fact no political leader in Kerala has the reputation that Karunakaran has as the protector of partymen. It is the consistency of positions that made him the most respected leader of the Congress party in Kerala. This shows that consistency of positions, to a large extent decides the strength, relevance and longetivity of a faction and the faction leader. The 'I' faction and its leader K Karunakaran is way ahead of others in this. It is only natural that the vast majority of Congressmen irrespective of group affiliations consider the 'I' group as the predominant one representing the Congress ethos.

As is evident from the responses of the respondents, the 'I' group ought to have had 57.33 per cent representation at different leadership levels. The Antony group which deserved 37.73 per cent goes beyond that level in different leadership positions. The other two groups have almost double the representation in all the categories than its actual strength. Hence there is truth in the 'I' group's accusation that the present faction wise representation in the party leadership does not correspond to its actual strength. It is a known fact that the second, third and fourth groups have a common enemy in Karunakaran and all of them together have managed to secure more representation in leadership positions.

The last three decades of Kerala politics centered on two personalities; EMS Namboodiripad, the CPI(M) leader and K. Karunakaran the Cong(I) leader. In another sense the decades witnessed the clash between a practical theoretician and a political pragmatist. Karunakaran's significance in Kerala politics lies in the fact that he has transformed the Congress party with only nine MLAs in the Assembly in 1967 to the position of the major party in the Assembly having 62 MLAs in 2001.

The CPI(M) has established an impressive support base in Kerala through radical politics. This support base was challenged by Karunakaran in the 1970's by a coalition of competitive and contradictory parties having caste-communal and regional basis. It was his pragmatic approach that laid the base for the Congress party's return to power, as the leader of the United Democratic Front (UDF).

As the architect of the United Democratic Front (UDF) he was instrumental in widening the social and political base of the party since 1982. It was his efforts in this direction that checked the Marxist infiltration into the traditional vote banks of the democratic forces. As a master manipulator and tactician he even turned the tide against his opponents. The taming of the leaderships of the Nair Service Society (NSS), Sree Narayana Dharma Paripalana Yogam (SNDP) and the Muslim and Christian communities prevented the left's designs to woe these sections. His contributions in loosening the grip of the caste-communal leaders over their followers as is evident from his role in the internal politics of these organisations, helped the Congress party to reach out to these sections directly. The fact that many of his ardent CPI(M) critics of yesteryears became his fellow travellers in the later decades is a testimonial to his pragmatic politics.

The study discloses that the ultimate beneficiaries of the factional feud in the party are 18.1 per cent. It is this hardcore who calls the shots in the party. The study also divulges the fact that only 21.32 per cent of the congressmen belonging to the 18-35 age group see in Antony the potential to effectively lead the party and the UDF. This naturally cast aspersions on his faction's ability to play the role of the leader of the UDF in the coming years.

In the ultimate analysis, there are five major determinants of Congress factionalism. Each of these determinants produce a variety of causes that adds fuel to the ongoing factional feud. Firstly, the very nature of the party itself mainly centering around issues like organizational election, system of nomination and candidates selection promotes factional tendencies in the party. Secondly, the nature of the UDF coalition and the leadership role of the Congress party in it is potent with chances of outreak of factional infighting due to the pressures of the communal-regional parties and the consequent divergence of approach among Congress factions in dealing with it. Personal factors constitute the third determinant and it acquires complex dimensions because of two factors viz; the generation gap and differences in the style of functioning. Indiscipline and public statements by responsible leaders as the fourth determinant of Congress factionalism arises mainly out of frustration and because of the fact that it often goes unpunished. The fifth major determinant of factionalism i.e. the weakening of the high command has contributed to three major developments around the faction leaders. They are (i) open hobnobbing with other parties (ii) hobnobbing with caste-communal forces more openly and (iii) import of the dynastic culture. These developments have taken the Congress factionalism to new heights.

The above determinants and causes have worked together; some more prominently than others at different points of time, and all aided by the course of political events and factional tendencies inherent in the social milieu of Kerala pushed the factional conflict in the Congress party to new heights. The Congress party in Kerala has lived through factionalism right from the beginning by its ability for survival.

Appendix - I

The list of member of the KPCC Executive Committee during 1982, 1983-1987, 1992, 1998 and 2001

The members of the KPCC Executive committee with A.L Jacob as President in 1982

1. A.L Jacob
2. K. Karunakran
3. A.K Antony
4. Oommen Chandy
5. K.G Adiyodi
6. K. Kunjambu
7. T.H Musthaffa
8. Thachady Prabhakaran
9. M.M Jacob
10. P.P George
11. P. Balan
12. V.M Sudheran
13. Thennala Balakrishna Pillai
14. Aryadan Mohammed
15. V.S Vijayaraghavan
16. M.I Shanavaz
17. Thiruvanchiyoor Radhakrishnan

List of the KPCC Executive with C V Padmarajan as President in 1983

1. C. V Padmarajan
2. K. Karunakran
3. A. K Antony
4. Oommen Chandy
5. K.G Adiyodi
6. K. Kunjambu
7. T.H Musthaffa
8. Thachady Prabhakaran
9. M .M Jacob
10. P.P George
11. P. Balan
12. V.M Sudheeran
13. Thennala Balakrishna Pillai
14. Aryadan Mohammed
15. V.S Vijayaraghavan
16. M.I Shanavaz
17. N P Moideen
18. N. Ramakrishnan
19. K. Raghavan Master
20. U K Bhasi
21. K. P Gangadhara Menon
22. K.S Vasudeva Sarma
23. Saraswathy Kunjukrishnan
24. T.K Gopalakrishnan
25. P A Antony
26. P P Thankachan
27. M T Thomas
28. Kurien joy
29. M C Cherian
30. Thalekunnil Basheer
31. Thiruvanchiyoor Radhakrishnan

List of KPCC Executive with A.K Antony as President in 1987

1. A.K Antony
2. K. Karunakran
3. Oommen Chandy
4. C.V Padmarajan
5. K. Vasudeva Panicker
6. K. Kunjambu
7. T.H Musthaffa
8. V.S Vijayaraghavan
9. Thachady Prabhakaran
10. M.M Jacob
11. P.P George
12. P. Balan
13. Thennala Balakrishna Pillai
14. Aryadan Mohammed
15. P. Sureswaran Master
16. M.I Shanavaz
17. K.K Ramachandran Master
18. Thoppil Ravi
19. Mullappally Ramachandran
20. G. Karthikeyan
21. Damodaran Kalassery
22. P.C Chacko
23. K.R Narayanan
24. S. Krishnankumar
25. P.J Kurien
26. A.G Adiyodi
27. Vakkom Purushothaman
28. A. Charles
29. K.V Thomas
30. T.K.C Vaduthala
31. I. Rama Rai
32. N. Ramakrishnan
33. K. Raghavan Master
34. N.P Moideen
35. U.K Bhasi
36. K.P Gangadhara Menon
37. P.A Antony
38. P.P Thankachan
39. Kurien Joy
40. M.T Thomas
41. M C Cherian
42. K.S Vadudeva Sarma
43. M. Shamsudeen
44. Thalekkunnil Basheer
45. Vayalar Ravi
46. K.K Sreenivasan
47. M.M Hassan
48. Pandalam Sudhakaran
49. K.P Noorudeen
50. K. Sankaranarayanan
51. M.P Thami
52. V.M Sudheeran
53. P. Bhaskaran
54. K.P Viswanathan
55. K.Mohammedali
56. M.T Padma
57. Rosamma Chacko
58. V. Dinakaran
59. K.A Chandran
60. K.C Joseph
61. N.Manoharan Mastrer
62. M.A Kuttappan
63. P.T Mohanakrishnan
64. K.P Kunhikannan
65. K.S Narayanan Namboodiri
66. K.K Thomas
67. Ramesh Chennithala
68. Punalur Madhu
69. Leela Damodara Menon
70. V.P. Marakkar
71. M. Aliyar
72. P.K Gopalakrishnan
73. V.K Kurien
74. N. Mohan Kumar

75. M V G Namboothiri
76. M A John
77. T.G Padmanabhan Nair
78. Prof. G.K Sasidharan
79. C.V Vijayan
80. C. Arjunan
81. M. Kamalam
82. A L Jacob
83. N. Sundaran Nadar
84. P.K Velayudhan
85. A A Rahim
86. C Haridas
87. N.K Balakrishnan
88. P R Francis
89. A Nafeesath Beevi
90. Saramma Jacob
91. Saraswathy Kunjukrishnan
92. Jameela Ibrahim
93. P.K Gopalan
94. T. Hariharan
95. Palai K M Mathew
96. Paul P Mani
97. N K Kunjukrishnan
98. M P Govindan Nair
99. M V Rajan Master
100. M Gilbert
101. S S Harihara Iyer
102. A C Chacko
103. K P Madhavan
104. K. Sadiri Koya
105. P S John
106. M K Hemachandran
107. Thundathil K. Pillai
108. Xavier Arackal
109. N Azhakesan
110. Manimangalathu Kuttiali
111. Raghavan Pozhekkadavil
112. Sidharthan Kattungal
113. A C Jose
114. Jose Kuttiani
115. P A Aboobaker
116. T K Varkey
117. N K Sreenivasan Nair
118. M B K Alavil
119. K V K Panicker
120. Prem Nazir
121. P Vijayadas
122. K.K Balakrishnan
123. M. Kunjukrishna Pillai
124. Raichel Sunny Panavelil
125. T S Purushothaman
126. M O Samnel
127. D Sugathan
128. K J John
129. Prof. Abraham Kalayil
130. P A Madhavan
131. V Govinda Menon
132. K Sukumaran
133. P V Showkath Ali
134. M K Mohammed
135. C P Varghese
136. P Ramakrishnan
137. Kottara Vasudev
138. Thomas Kallan
139. Saktan Nadar
140. R M Parameswaran
141. M D Jose
142. K Sudhakaran
143. M K Raghavan
144. C G Janardhanan
145. K Gopinathan
146. G.ukundan Pillai
147. K Ahammed Haji
148. Karimbil Krishnan
149. Thiruvanchiyoor Radhakrishnan

List of KPCC Executive with Vayalar Ravi as President in 1992

1. Vayalar Ravi
2. K. Karunakaran
3. A.K Antony
4. C V Padmarajan
5. G Karthikeyan
6. K A Chandran
7. K V Thomas
8. A Sujanapal
9. K Muraleedharan
10. K. K Balakrishnan
11. Smt. Rosamma Chacko
12. George J Mathew
13. M M Hassan
14. Hidur Mohammed
15. N Venugopal
16. Benny Behanan
17. T. Sarat Cahndra Prasad
18. Oommen Cahndy
19. K. Sankara Narayanan
20. P P George
21. T H Musthaffa
22. N Ravi Krishnan
23. M R Raghuchandra Pal
24. Thennala B. Pillai
25. Ramesh Chennithala
26. M I Shanavas
27. K C Venugopal
28. P C Chacko
29. P A Joseph
30. A V Gopinath
31. K K Ramachandran Master
32. Thachady Prabhakaran
33. P T Mohana Krishnan
34. Aryadan Mohammed
35. P Balan
36. N P Moideen
37. K S Vasudeva Sarma
38. M A Kuttappan
39. V P Marackar
40. RajaMoham Unnithan
41. Leela Damodara Menon
42. J Joseph
43. Kodumon Gopinathan Nair
44. M. Aliyar
45. V. Dinakaran
46. G.K Pillai
47. M A John
48. Jose kuttiani
49. G. Balachandra
50. A A Samad
51. Kadavoor Sivadasan
52. Prof. A D Musthaffa
53. K SadiriKoya
54. Sidharthan Kattingal
55. K P Kunhikannan
56. Thalekunnil Basheer
57. Palode Ravi
58. P T Thomas
59. M C Cherian
60. K M I Methes
61. Karunalil SUkumaran
62. P J Kurian
63. M M Jacob
64. M P Gangadharan
65. I Rama Rai
66. U K Bhasi
67. E M Augusty
68. Kaviyad D. Panicker
69. Kurian Joy
70. Thiruvanchiyoor R.

List of KPCC Executive with Thennala Balakrishna Pillai as President in 1998

1. Thennala BalakrishnaPillai
2. K. Muraleedharan
3. K. Karunakaran
4. A.K Antony
5. Vayalar Ravi
6. C V PAdmarajan
7. K. Muraleedharan
8. A. Sujanapal
9. P.P George
10. M M Hassan
11. Kadavoor Sivadasan
12. Thiruvanchiyoor R.
13. K.P Kunhikannan
14. M.I Shanavas
15. Pandalam Sudhakaran
16. Rosamma Chacko
17. A. Hidur Mohammed
18. M. Kamalam
19. Mercy Ravi
20. Benny Behanan
21. Sobhana George
22. K. M Raghavan
23. Varkala Kahar
24. K. C Aboo
25. K P Thomas
26. K.P Dhanapalan
27. Adoor Prakash
28. Anto Antony
29. Joseph Vazhakkan
30. N. Venugopal
31. Ajay Tharayil
32. Kodikkunnil Suresh
33. K.K VijayaLakshmi
34. T.H Musthaffa
35. Oommen Chandy
36. G. Karthikeyan
37. Ramesh Chennithala
38. P.P Thankachan
39. P C Chacko
40. Sarath Chandra Prasad
41. M P Gangadharan
42. A Charles
43. A A Samad
44. Alphonsa John
45. K C Rosakutty Teacher
46. Jameela Ibrahim
47. M T Padma
48. Mullappally R.
49. P J Kurian
50. Vakkom Purushothaman
51. K. Sankara Narayanan
52. V M Sudheeran
53. K P Unnikrishnan
54. Aryadan Muhammed
55. Thalekunnil Basheer
56. P Balan
57. A V Gopinath
58. Malethu Sarala Devi
59. T P Hassan

List of KPCC Executive with K. Muraleedharan as President in 2001

1. K. Muraleedharan
2. P P Thankachan
3. M I Shanavas
4. C N Balakrishnan
5. Benny Behanan
6. Thalekunnil Basheer
7. K P Kunhikannan
8. Raja Mohan Unnithan
9. U K Bhasi
10. T. Sarat Chandra Prasad

11. N. Venugopal
12. K. C Rosakutty Teacher
13. K K Vijayalakshmi
14. M K Raghavan
15. Ajay Tharayil
16. P K Velayudhan
17. K C Aboo
18. Joseph Vazhakkan
19. K C Kadambooran
20. J Joseph
21. Satheesan Pacheni
22. N K Abdul RAhman
23. T G Viswanathan
24. V V Prakash
25. Josy Sebastian
26. Mannar Abdul Latheef
27. Pandalam Pratapan
28. Kunnathoor Balan
29. Alphonsa John
30. Punalur Madhu
31. Ajeeb M Sahib
32. V P Sajeendran
33. A. K Abdul Majeed
34. P S John
35. Visalakshi A
36. N. Peethambara Kurup
37. Sooranadu Rajasekharan
38. K. Sivadasan Nair
39. C R Jaya Prakash
40. Anto Antony
41. Joy Thomas
42. K P Dhanapalan
43. M P Bhaskaran Nair
44. V S Vijayaraghavan
45. E. Mohammed Kunhi
46. M. Veeran Kutty
47. K.P Thomas
48. Sunny Joseph
49. Kodoth Govindan Nair
50. K. Karunakaran
51. A.K Antony
52. P.C Chacko
53. P. Balan
54. K.P Noorudheen
55. K.S Vasudeva Sharma
56. Rosamma Chacko
57. M. Kamalam
58. Varkala Kahar
59. N.P Moideen
60. Kurian Joy
61. A A Samad
62. Mullapppally R.
63. A. V Gopinath
64. Peeliphose Thomas
65. M. T Padma
66. A Charles
67. Haji Abdul Gafoor
68. K. P Unnikrishnan
69. Bharatheepuram Sasi
70. I Rama Rai
71. A. K Hafees
72. Malethu Sarala Devi
73. Jameela Ibrahim
74. V.S Sivakumar
75. E. M Augusty
76. N D Appachan
77. K M Ummer
78. Palode Ravi
79. Sathya Seelan
80. Ramakrishnan
81. Padmaja Venugopal
82. Babu Prasad
83. A. Balaram
84. N. Sakthan Nadar
85. K. N Viswanathan
86. P.M Niyas
87. Pandalam Sudhakaran
88. K.V Padmanabhan
89. C Mohana chandran
90. A K Mani

Appendix - II

The Names of Congress Candidates who Contested the Assembly Elections since 1982 and their Factional Orientation

1982 Congress (I) Candidates

N. Ramakrishnan
T V Bharathan
K Raghaan Master
Manimangalathu Kuttiali
K K Ramachandran Master
M P Gangadharan
P. K Gopalakrishnan
Mullappally Ramachandran
T K C Vaduthala
P P George
K Karunakaran
P P THankachan
Jose Kuttiani
K K Sreenivasan
Thennala Balakrishna Pillai
C V Padmarajan
K. Karunakran
N Sundaran Nadar
T. kumaran aster
M Janardhanan
M T Padma
P. Suresan Master
Pandalam Sudhakaran
K K Balakrishnan
K. Sankara Narayanan
M P Thami
K.S Narayanan Namboodiri
Raghavan Pozhekkadavil
A L Jacob
T H Musthaffa
Ramesh Chennithala
P J Thomas
Suresh Babu
G Karthikeyan
M R Raghuchandra Pal

1982 Congress (A) Candidates

K. C Joseph
K P Noorudeen
N P Moideen
Cyriac John
P Balan
Jose Thannickal
P. Narayanan
P K Gopalan
A Balaraman
Aryadan Muhammed
K A Chandran
V M Sudheeran

Sidharthan Kattungal
A C Jose
K. Mohammedali
K K Thomas
Vayalar Ravi
Thannirmukkom Padmanabhan
Thoppil Ravi
S. Varadarajan Nair
K.P Viswanathan
P.K Velayudhan
Benny Behanan
Oommen Chandy
Thachadi Prabhakaran
M C Cherian
Vakkom Purushothaman
M M Hassan

1987 Congress (I) Candidates

K.P Kunhikannan
K. Kunjukrishnan Nair
A P Jayaseelan
P Ramakrishnan
A Sujanapal
Vijaya D Nair
P P George
Pandalam Sudhakaran
M P Thami
K. Sankara Narayanan
K P Gangadhara Menon
Narayan Namboodiri
Raghavan Puzhekkadavil
M I Shanavas
M K Raghavan
T H Mushtaffa
V Dinakaran
K K Sreenivasan
Thennala Balakrishanan
K Suresh Babu
Kaviyad Divakara Panicker
G Karthikeyan
Sundaran Nadar
N Manoharan Master
P. Bhaskaran
K Sudhakaran
K Raghavan Master
M T Padma
M. Kamalam
K K Ramachandran Master
P T Mohan Krishnan
Leela Damodara Menon
A Thankappan
M Aiyappan Master
A Balaram
K. Karunanakran
A L Jacob
P P Thankachan
Rosamma Chacko
Ramesh Chennithala
Damodaran Kalassery
K C Rajan
C V Padmarajan
N Peethambara Kurup
Sakthan Nadar

1987 Congress (A) Candidates

K C Joseph
K P Noorudeen
Aryadan
M K Raghavan
N P Moideen
P Balan

K A Chandran
M C Paul
Sidharthan Kattungal
A C Jose
K. Mohammed Ali
Oommen Chancy
Vayalar Ravi
Thoppil Ravi
P Vijayadas
M M Hassan
Thiruvanchiyoor Radhakrishnan
K K Thomas
K P Viswananthan
V M Sudheeran
K P Dhanapalan
Malippuram Bhaskaran
Benny Behanan
P K Gopi
K. Gopinathan
K P Madhavan
Palode RAvi
K C Thankaraj
M A Kuttappan
P J Francis

1991 Congress (I) Candidates

K P Kunhikannan
C K Sreedharan
K Sudhakaran
K K Ramachandran Master
K C RTosakkuty Teacher
A Sujanapal
P Sankaran
Pandalam Sudhkaran
K Sakaranarayanan
M Aiyappan Master
P P George
Raghavan Pozhekkadavil
K S N Namboodiri
K. Karunakarn
George Eden
P P Thankachan
P J Joy
E M Augusty
K K Balakrishnan
V DInakaran
Sobhana George
V. Sasidharan
Hidur Muhammed
C V Padmarajan
Kottara Vasudev
N Remakrishnan
A D Musthaffa
K Raghavan Master
A Balram
M T Padma
P T Mohan Krishnan
Leela Damodaran menon
A Ramaswamy
AV Gopinath
Rosamma Chacko
T. Chandramohanan
M P Thami
Therambil Ramakrishnan
T H Musthaffa
M I Shanavas
V J Paulose
George J Mathew
D Sugathan
K K Sreenivasan
Jameela Ibrahim
Punalur Madhu
Alphonse John
Kadavoor Sivadasan

Varkala Kahaar
R M Parameswaran
B Vijayakumar
Sarat Chandra Prasad
G. Karthikeyan
M R Raghuchandra Pal.

1991 Congress (A) Candidates

M P Murali
K C Joseph
K P Noorudeen
K C Aboo
P Balan
M K Shamsudeen
K P Viswanathan
Dominic Preseantion
K Babu
K Moni
Cherian Philip
Thiruvanchiyoor Radhakrishnan
P J Francis
Thachadi Prabhakaran
M A Kuttappan
Ezhukon
Palode Ravi
George Marcus
M K Raghavan
P Ramakrishnan
Kadameri Balakrishnan
Aryadan Mohammed
K A Chandran
V M Sudheeran
K. Mohammed Ali
K Kunjambu
P T Thomas
K K Thomas
Oommen Chandy
M C Cherian
Vayalar Ravi
M Murali
Thankappan
A Thankappan
M M Hassan
Thambanoor Ravi

1996 Congress (I) Candidates

K P Kunhikannan
K N Kannoth
A D Musthaffa
M P Krishnan Nair
P Sankaran
A Sujana Pal
K C Rosakutty Teacher
P T Mohana Krishnan
C M Sundaram
T A Radhakrishnan
T V Chandramohanan
P P george
Mercy Ravi
C P Krishnan
K Sudhakaran
K C Kadambooran
RadhaRaghavan
R K Ravi Varma
K K Ramachandran Master
Pandalam Sudhakaran
A P Anil Kumar
Chellamma Teacher
V Balaram
Therambil Ramakrishnan
Savithri Lakshmanan
Rosamma Chacko

P J Joy
George Eden
T H Musthaffa
E M Augusty
Mohan Sanker
N Moham Kumar
K K Nair
Visalakshy
Alphonsa John
Sarat Chandra Prasad
M R Raghuchandra Pal
V P Marakkar
P P Thankachan
V J Paulose
George J Mathew
K K Balakrishnan
Sobhana George
Adoor Prakash
Karunakara Pillai
Kadavoor
K Mohanakumar

1996 Congress (A) Candidates

Sony Sebastian
Satheesan Pacheni
C Valsalan
Aryadan Mohammed
K V Prabhakaran Nambiar
M Guruswamy
K A Chandran
M K Abdul Salam
K K Rahulan
Dominic Presentation
K. Mohammed Ali
A K Moni
A K Antony
J Joseph
M Murali
Prayar Gopalakrishnan
Thiruvanchiyoor Radhakrishnan
G Priyadarsan
Manvila Radhakrishnan
M M Hassan
George Mascreen
K C Joseph
K P Noorudeen
K C Aboo
M I Shanavas
P Balan
K Achuthan
M V Suresh
K P Viswanathan
M A Kuttappan
K Babu
P T Thomas
Oommen Chandy
P J Francis
Thachady Prabhakaran
Peelipose Thomas
Ezhukone Narayanan
C V Padmarajan
Vakkom Purushothaman
Palode Ravi
B Vijayakumar
Thampanoor Ravi

1996 Congress (Reformists)

V D Satheesan
Punalur Madhu
K C Venugopal
G Karthikeyan

2001 Congress (I) Candidates

C. K Sreedharan	N. Ramakrtishnan
A D Musthaffa	Radha Raghavan
N D Appachan	P Sankaran
A Sujanapal	A P Anil Kumar
M P Gangadharan	C P Mohammed
R Chellamma	V Balram
T V Mohanachandran	Therambil Ramakrishnan
P P George	Savithri Lakshmanna
I U Radhakrishnan	P J Joy
M A Chandra Sekharn	K V Thomas
P P Thankachan	C V Balachandran
V J Paulose	E M Augusty
George Mathew	D Sugathan
Sobhana George	Maleth Sarala Devi
Bijili Panaveli	K K Nair
Adoor Prakash	Pandalam Sudhakaran
Kadavoor Sivadasan	Varkala Kahar
K Mohama Kumar	Alphonsa John
Sakthan Nadar	

2001 Congress (A) Candidates

C J Krishnan	K C Joseph
Karimbil Krishnan	K K Ramachandran Master
K P Rajan	Balakrishna Kidav
Aryadan Mohammed	P Balan
T.H Musthaffa	Satheesan Pacheni
K Sankara Narayanan	K Achuthan
K A Chandran	K A Thulaso
K P Viswanathan	M K Paulson
M A Kuttappan	Domenic Presentation
K Babu	K Mohammed Ali
P T Thomas	A K Moni
Oommen Chandy	Prathapan T N
A K Antony	P J Francis
M M Hassan	M Murali
Thiruvanchiyoor Radhakrishnan	Prayar Gopalakrishnan
Ezhukone Narayanan	Prathapa Varma Thampan

Vakkom Purushothaman	Palode Ravi
B Vijayakumar	Thampanoor Ravi
Sundaran Nadar	

2001 Congress (III group) Candidates

M. Narayanan Kutty	Sajeev Maroli
K Balanarayan	C Prakash
V S Vijayaraghavan	V D Satheeshan
K C Venugopal	Hidur Mohammed
G Karthikeyan	

2001 Congress (IV group) Candidates

K Sudhakaran	K Surendran
K Prabhakaran	K V Padmanabhan
Mercy Ravi	

Appendix - III

The Names of Congress Candidates who Contested in the Lok Sabha Elections of 1984, 1989, 1991 1996, 1998 and 1999 and their Factional Orientation

Congress Candidates to Loksabha 1984

Congress (A) group	Congress (I) group
Ram Rai	Mullappally Ramachandran
P A Antony	K.G Adiyodi
P J Kurian	V S Viajyaraghavan
Vakkom Purushothaman	K V Thomas
K Kunhambu	S Krishna Kumar
Thalekkunnil Basheer	A.Charles

K R Narayanan (with out group)

1989

Congress (A)	Congress (I)
I Rama Rai	Mullappally Ramachandran
P A Antony	Sujanapal A
Pala K M Mathew	K Muraleedharan
Vakkom Purushothaman	V S Vijayaraghavan
P J Kurian	Savithri Lakshmanan
Kodikkunnil Suresh	K V Thomas
Thalekkunnil Basheer	Ramesh Chennithala
	S Krishnakumar
	A Charles

K R Narayanan (without group)

1991

Congress (A)	Congress (I)
Mullappally Ramachandran	K C Venugopal
Palai K M Mathew	Ratna Singh

Vakkom B Purushothaman
P J Kurian
Kodikkunnil Suresh
Thalekkunnil Basheer

K Muraleedharan
V S Vijayaraghavan
P C Chacko
Savithri Lakshman
K V Thomas
Ramesh Chennithala
A Charles
S Krishna Kumar

K R Narayanan (without group)

1996

Congress (A)
I Rama Rai
A C Jose
V M Sudheeran
P J Kurian
Kodikkunnil Suresh
Thalekkunnil Basheer
Mullappally Ramachandran

Congress (I)
K Muraleedharan
V S Vijayaraghavan
K K Vijayalekshmi
K Karunakaran
K V Thomas
P C Chacko
S Krishna Kumar
A Charles

Congress (III) group
Ramesh Chennithala

K P Unnikrishnan (Without group)

Source: Lok Sabha Election Reportage 1996, '98,'99, Department of Public Relations, Government of Kerala.

1998

Congress (A)
Khader Mangad
A C Jose
V M Sudheeran
M M Hassan
P J Kurian
Kodikkunnul Suresh
Mullappally Ramachandran

Congress (I)
P M Suresh Babu
P Sankaran
V S Vijayaraghavan
K K Vijayalakshmi
K Muraleedharan
George Eden
P C Chacko
K C Rajan
K Karunakaran

Congress (III) group
Ramesh Chennithala

P M Suresh Babu (Without group)

Source: Lok Sabha Election Reportage '96,'98,'99, Department of Public Relations, Government of Kerala.

1999

Congress (A)
Khader Mangad
A C Jose
V M Sudheeran
Kodikkunnil Suresh
M I Shanavas
P J Kurian
Mullappally Ramchandran

Congress (III)
Ramesh Chennithala
M T Padma

P M Suresh Babu (Without group)

Congress (I)
P M Suresh Babu
K MUraleedharan
Pandalam Sudhakaran
K Karunakaran
George Eden
P C Chacko
M P Gangadharan
V S Sivakumar

Appendix - IV

Chapter V, Table 12: Chi-square Result of the Caste-wise Table Showing the Predominant Group in the Congress Party

O	*E*	*(O-E)*	*(O-E)²*	$\frac{(O-E)^2}{E}$
73	66.54	6.46	41.7316	0.6272
75	82.54	–7.54	56.8516	0.6888
1	1.02	–0.02	0.0004	0.0004
11	9.90	1.1	1.21	0.1222
186	191.72	–5.72	32.7184	0.1707
245	237.82	7.18	51.5524	0.2168
3	2.93	0.07	0.0049	0.0017
27	28.52	–1.52	2.3104	0.0810
2	2.08	–0.08	0.0064	0.0031
0	0.03	0.03	0.0009	0.0300
1	0.31	0.69	0.4761	1.5358
1	1.66	–0.66	0.4356	0.2624
1	2.06	–1.06	1.1236	0.5454
0	0.02	–0.02	0.0004	0.0200
0	0.25	–0.25	0.0625	0.2500
				4.55

Degree of freedom (r – 1) (c – 1) = (4 – 1) (4 – 1) = 9d.f

Table value of chi-square for 9 d.f and 5% level of significance = 16.92.

Appendix - V

Chapter V, Table 14: Chi-square result of the table examining Nair community support to (I) group

O	E	(O-E)	$(O-E)^2$	$\frac{(O-E)^2}{E}$
25	28.55	–3.55	12.6025	0.4414
38	34.39	3.61	13.0321	0.3790
1	0.42	0.58	0.3364	0.8010
4	3.86	0.14	0.0196	0.0051
249	245.45	–3.61	13.0321	0.0531
292	295.61	–3.61	13.0321	0.0441
3	3.58	–0.58	0.3364	0.0940
32	33.14	–1.14	1.2996	0.0392
				1.86

Degree of freedom (r – 1) (c – 1) = (4 – 1) (2 – 1) = 3 × 1 = 3d.f

Table value of chi-square for 3d.f and 1% level of significance = 11.34

Appendix - VI

Chapter V, Table 15: Chi-square Result of the table Examining Christian Support to the 'A' group

O	*E*	*(O-E)*	$(O-E)^2$	$\frac{(O-E)^2}{E}$
46	34.76	11.24	126.3376	3.6346
31	43.68	–12.68	160.7824	3.6809
1	0.52	0.48	0.2304	0.4431
6	5.04	0.96	0.9216	0.1829
223	234.24	–11.24	126.3376	0.5394
307	294.32	12.68	160.7829	0.5463
3	3.48	–0.48	0.2304	0.0662
33	33.96	–0.96	0.9216	0.0271
				9.12

Degree of freedom (r – 1) (c – 1) = (4 – 1) (2 – 1) = 3 × 1 = 3d.f

Table value of chi-square for 3d.f at 5% level of significance = 7.82

Appendix - VII

Chapter V - Table 24: Chi-square Result of the Table Examining whether Congress Factionalism has Ideological Roots

O	E	(O-E)	$(O-E)^2$	$\frac{(O-E)^2}{E}$
181	181.5	-0.5	0.25	0.001
98	79.31	18.69	349.32	4.40
54	72.2	-18.2	331.24	4.59
176	175.6	0.4	0.16	0.0009
58	76.7	-18.7	349.69	4.56
88	69.81	18.19	330.88	4.74
				18.29

Degree of freedom (r – 1) (c – 1) = (3 – 1) (2 – 1) = 2 × 1 = 2d.f

Table value of chi-square for 2d.f at 1% level of significance = 9.21

Appendix - VIII

Chapter V, Table 26: Chi-square Result of the Caste-communal Orientation to Congress Factionalism.

O	*E*	*(O-E)*	*(O-E)²*	$\frac{(O-E)^2}{E}$
136	129.02	6.98	48.72	0.38
66	56.74	9.26	85.75	1.50
34	50.24	–16.24	263.74	5.25
221	227.98	–6.98	48.72	0.21
91	100.26	–9.26	85.75	0.86
105	88.8	16.2	262.44	2.96
				11.17

Degree of freedom (r – 1) (c – 1) = (3 – 1) (2 – 1) = 2 × 1 = 2d.f

Table value pf chi-square for 2d.f and 1%level of significance = 9.21

Appendix - IX

Chapter V - Table 28: Chi-square Result of the Table Examining whether Christian Community Constitute the Major Support base of the Antony Group

O	E	$(O-E)$	$(O-E)^2$	$\frac{(O-E)^2}{E}$
54	46.01	7.99	63.84	1.39
22	19.90	2.1	4.41	0.22
8	18.09	–10.09	101.81	5.63
302	309.99	7.99	63.84	0.21
132	134.09	–2.09	4.37	0.03
132	121.91	10.09	101.81	0.84
				8.32

Degree of freedom (r – 1) (c – 1) = (3 – 1) (2 – 1) = 2 × 1 = 2d.f

Table value of chi-square for 2d.f and 5% level of significance = 5.99.

Appendix - X

Chapter VI, Table 4: Chi-square Result of the Different Age Groups Regarding the Caste-communal Roots of Congress Factionalism

O	E	(O-E)	$(O-E)^2$	$\frac{(O-E)^2}{E}$
63	54.93	8.07	65.1249	1.1856
107	111.31	4.31	18.5761	0.1669
50	57.46	-7.46	55.6516	0.9685
16	12.29	3.71	13.7641	1.1199
89	97.07	-8.07	65.1249	0.6709
201	196.69	4.31	18.5761	0.0944
109	101.54	7.46	55.6516	0.5481
18	21.17	-3.17	10.0489	0.4747
				5.23

Degree of freedom (r – 1) (c – 1) = (4 – 1) (2 – 1) = 3 × 1 = 3d.f

Table value of chi-square for 3d.f and 5% level of significance = 7.82

Appendix - XI

Chapter VI, Table 5: Chi-square Result whether Congress Factionalism is Ideology Oriented

O	E	$(O-E)$	$(O-E)^2$	$\frac{(O-E)^2}{E}$
52	77.28	4.72	22.2784	0.2883
149	157.60	–8.6	73.96	0.4693
80	81.85	–1.85	3.4225	0.0418
22	16.27	5.73	32.8329	2.0180
70	74.72	–4.72	22.2784	0.2982
161	152.40	8.6	73.96	0.4853
81	79.15	1.85	3.4225	0.0432
10	15.73	–5.73	32.8329	2.0873
				5.73

Degree of freedom (r – 1) (c – 1) = (4 – 1) (2 – 1) = 3 × 1 = 3d.f

Table value of chi-square for 3d.f and 5% level of significance = 7.82

Appendix - XII

Chapter VI, Table 34: Chi-square Result of the Leadership Role of the Respondents and their choice Indicating the Predominant Group

O	E	(O-E)	$(O-E)^2$	$\frac{(O-E)^2}{E}$
5	3.05	1.95	3.8025	1.25
11	3.38	2.62	6.8644	0.82
10	7.87	2.13	4.5369	0.58
7	8.63	-1.63	-2.6569	0.31
10	6.6	3.4	11.56	1.75
12	9.65	2.35	5.5225	0.57
9	9.65	-0.65	0.4225	0.04
70	78.2	-8.2	67.24	0.86
26	29.21	-3.21	10.3041	0.35
7	8.78	-1.78	3.1684	0.36
22	24.15	-2.15	4.6225	6.11
20	22.68	-2.68	7.1824	0.19
27	24.9	2.1	4.41	0.18
16	19.03	-3.03	9.1809	0.48
26	27.81	-1.81	3.2761	0.17
24	27.81	-3.81	14.5161	0.52
230	225.38	4.62	21.3444	0.28
89	84.15	4.85	23.5225	0.28
0	0.08	-0.08	0.0064	0.08
0	0.21	-0.21	0.0441	0.21
1	0.24	-0.76	0.5776	0.2
0	0.22	-0.22	0.0484	0.22
0	0.17	-0.17	0.0289	0.17
0	0.29	0.29	0.0481	0.29
0	0.29	0.29	0.0481	0.24
4	10	-6	-36	3.6
0	0.73	0.73	0.5329	0.73
0	0.1	-0.1	0.1	0.1
0	0.26	0.26	0.0676	0.26
0	0.20	0.02	0.04	2.25
0	0.27	-0.27	0.0729	0.27
0	0.21	-0.21	0.0441	0.21
0	0.3	-0.3	0.09	0.3
0	0.3	-0.3	0.09	0.3
4	2.4	1.6	2.56	1.07
0	0.91	-0.91	0.8291	0.91
				26.51

Degree of freedom (r – 1) (C – 1) = (9 – 1) (4 – 1) = 8 × 3 = 24d.f
Table value of Chi-square for 24 d.f and 5% level of significance = 36.42

Appendix - XIII

Politics of Congress Factionalism in Kerala Since 1982

Questionnaire administered to party cadres and activists

A
Socio-Economic Background

1. Name :
2. Sex : Male/ Female
3. Age : 1. 18/35 2. 35/50 3. 50/65 4. Above 65
4. Religion : 1. Hindu 2. Christian 3. Muslim 4. Others
5. Caste : 1. FC 2. OBC 3. MBC 4. SC/ST please specify
6. Education : 1. S.S.L.C., 2. Under Graduate 3. Graduate
   4. Post Graduate 5. Professionals (Diploma Holders etc)
   6. Professionals (Graduates and above)
7. Occupation and Income:

Sl.	*1. Source*	*2. Amount*
1.	Respondentent's monthly salary income.	1. 1000-5000 2. 5000-8000 3. 8000-10000 4. 10000 and above
2.	Respondentent's spouse's monthly salary	1. 1000-5000 2. 5000-8000 3. 8000-10000 4. 10000 and above
3.	Other source of income (investment, business, etc)	
4.	Any Other	

8. Current Position in the party
9. State Previous positions held

B

1. Do you believe that different groups exists in the Congress in Kerala?

   1. Yes 2. No

2. Do you think that groups are inevitable for the Congress party in Kerala?

   1. Yes 2. No

3. If yes what are the reasons for it?
4. Name the Congress group to which you belong?
5. Point out the reasons for your support to this group
6. Nature of difference of group conflict before 1969 and after 1969:
   I. No difference
      1. Yes 2. No
   II. Before 1969 it was policy oriented
      1. Yes 2. No
   III. It was both policy oriented and personal differences.
      1. Yes 2. No
   IV. After 1969 it was only personality oriented
      1. Yes 2. No
   V. After 1969 it was basically policy oriented.
      1. Yes 2. No
   VI. After 1969 it was policy oriented and personality oriented.
      1. Yes 2. No
   VII. It was more personality oriented and less ideological oriented.
      1. Yes 2. No
7. Which group in your opinion is currently the predominant group in intra party politics?
   1. A.K. Antony
   2. K. Karunakaran
   3. G. Karthikeyan
   4. Vayalar Ravi
8. Do you believe that the ideological/policy issues constitute the major reason for Congress factionalism today?
   1. Yes 2. No
9. Do you believe that the personality clashes form the root cause of Congress factionalism?
   1. Yes 2. No
10. Do you believe that the Congress groupism has a caste or communal basis?
    1. Yes 2. No
11. Is there any link between vested economic interest groups and Congress groupism? If yes please explain?
    1. Yes 2. No
12. How loyalists are recruited in each faction of the Congress party?
13. What are the scope and relevance of loyalists in the factional conflict of the party?
14. Comment on the importance of Youth Congress as a factor in factional politics of the party?

15. Do you think that the relevance of Youth Congress has declined considerably due to factionalism?

    1. Yes 2. No

16. How do you account for the relevance of K.S.U. in the factional politics of the congress party?
17. Do you think that strength of the K.S.U. has declined during the last two decades consequent to party factionalism?

    1. Yes 2. No

18. How do you assess the nature of Congress factionalism since the merger of the various groups in 1982?

    A. Resulted in intense factionalism
    B. Lead to a temporary decline in factionalism
    C. Helped the unity of the Congress party for future

19. What are the major economic interest group behind K.Karunakaran? (Identify the priorities as 1,2,3,4,5,6)

    A. Abkaris, Contractors, Mafia A
    B. Businessmen/Industrialists B
    C. Planters/Agriculturists C
    D. Trade Unions D
    E. Police and Bureaucracy E
    F. Others if any specify F

20. What are the major economic interest groups behind A.K.Antony? (Identify the priorities as 1,2,3,4,5,6)

    A. Abkaris, Contractors, Mafia A
    B. Businessmen/Industrialists B
    C. Planters/Agriculturists C
    D. Trade Unions D
    E. Police and Bureaucracy E
    F. Others if any specify F

21. What are the major economic interest groups behind G. Karthikeyan? (Identify the priorities as 1,2,3,4,5,6)

    A. Abkaris, Contractors, Mafia A
    B. Businessmen/Industrialists B
    C. Planters/Agriculturists C
    D. Trade Unions D
    E. Police and Bureaucracy E
    F. Others if any specify F

22. What are the major economic interest groups behind Vayalar Ravi? (Identify the priorities as 1,2,3,4,5,6)

    A. Abkaris, Contractors, Mafia A
    B. Businessmen/Industrialists B
    C. Planters/Agriculturists C

D. Trade Unions D
E. Police and Bureaucracy E
F. Others if any specify F

23. Is there any regional basis for the existence of various groups? If yes please explain.
    1. Yes 2. No
24. Is there any minority linguistic pressure groups behind Congress factionalism?
    1. Yes 2. No
25. Has there been a consolidation of Christian votes in favour of the Congress during the last Assembly election? If yes please explain the reasons.
    1. Yes 2. No
26. Do you think that there has been a reassembling of Hindu votes of Congress in the last Assembly election due to the adamant stand by K. Karunakaran against Antony - Sonia dominance in the selection of candidates?
    1. Yes 2. No
27. Do you believe that the support of Karunakaran group comes mainly from the Nair Community?
    1. Yes 2. No
28. If not which are the prominent caste and communities that support Karunakaran Group?
29. Do you believe that the support of Antony group is mainly from the Christian Community?
    1. Yes 2. No
30. If not which are prominent caste and communities that support Antony Group?
31. Do you believe that the Vayalar Ravi Group derives its support mainly from the Ezhava Community?
    1. Yes 2. No
32. If not which are the prominent caste and communities that support Vayalar Ravi group?
33. Would you please Indicate the Communal support base of the Reformist group led by Karthikeyan?
    1. Nair 2. Ezhava 3. X'ian 4. Muslim 5. O.B.C/ 6. All
34. In your opinion which group in the congress is best suited to address the following challenges
    1. The CPI (M) and LDF
    2. The B.J.P.
    3. The regional parties
    4. In giving effective leadership to the U.D.F.

35. Although there is an erosion of youth and student community from the Congress, which group in the party can still claim the support base of the youth and students?

    None   Don't know

36. How would you assess Mr. K. Karunakaran in the following aspects.
    1. Very good 2. Good 3. Average 4. Bad 5. Very bad
    I. As opposition leader
    II. As Chief Minister
    III. As leader of U.D.F
    IV. As protector of party members
    V. Ability to establish a working relationship with caste and communal forces

37. How would you assess Mr. A.K. Antony according to the following aspects.
    1. Very good 2. Good 3. Average 4. Bad 5. Very bad
    I. As opposition leader
    II. As Chief Minister
    III. As leader of U.D.F
    IV. As protector of party members
    V. Ability to establish a working relationship with caste and communal forces

38. Do you agree to the practice of nomination of the party's office bearers and committees by the High Command?

    1. Yes   2. No

39. If yes don't you think that this practice goes against the principle of inner party democracy?

    1. Yes   2. No

40. Do you forsee the possibility of group rivalry within the Karunakaran group? If yes please specify?
41. What are the prospects of Congress party in Kerala in the midst of intense factionalism?
42. Are you aware of any basic principle or technique through which group's share among themselves privileges like seat sharing, cabinet posts, party posts, Heads of public offices etc.

    1. Yes   2. No

43. If yes, specify the details.
44. Do you think that the nomination by the High-Command will help to maintain caste and communal balances or group balances in the party? If yes can this method be considered as a health tendency?

    1. Yes   2. No

45. Have you ever changed the group loyalty? If yes give two or three reasons.

46. Are you in favour of the unification of the various groups in the Congress?

    1. Yes 2. No

47. Do you think that it is impossible to unify the various groups of the Congress party in Kerala?

    1. Yes 2. No

48. Is there a logic in defending group politics in Congress party?

    1. Yes 2. No

49. Given the kind of factionalism, do you believe that the party is more a coalition than a solid organization.
50. What are the prospects of the Congress party at the national level in the coming decades?

Appendix - XIV

Politics of Congress Factionalism in Kerala Since 1982

Interview Schedule administered to Senior Party Leaders

1. How do you understand and interpret the politics of factionalism in the Congress in Kerala?
2. Do you think that groupism in the party has strengthened the Congress in Kerala? If yes how?
3. Is there a caste/communal basis behind Congress factionalism?
4. What is your view regarding frequent shifts in group loyalties?
   Does it reveal the identification of a member within a particular group to protect his own self interest?
5. What do you think of the future prospects of the Congress party in Kerala in the midst of the ongoing intense group rivalry?
6. What are the important factors that aggravated the group rivalry in the party during the last two decades?
7. In your opinion what are the sources of strength of the Congress Party which ensure a continued mass base?
8. Do you agree to the practice of nomination of the party office bearers? Don't you think it is undemocratic?
9. Do you think that election in the party can be held in the near future?
10. Are you personally in favour of leading a government with the support of communal or regional parties?

Bibliography

Primary Sources

(A) Government Publications

Government of India (1993): *Census of India 1991 (Series 12) Paper 3 of 1991*, Final Populations Totals, The Manager, Government of India Press.

Government of India (2001): *Census of 2001 services 33 Kerala*, Sheela Thomas, Thiruvananthapuram, Department of Census.

Government of Kerala (undated): *Assembly Elections Since 1951*, Thiruvananthapuram, Department of Public Relations.

Government of Kerala (1991): *Backgrounder to Lok Sabha/Assembly Elections*, Thiruvananthapuram, Department of Public Relations.

Government of Kerala (1991): *Report on the Election to Kerala Legislative Assembly and Lok Sabha*, Thiruvananthapuram, Department of Public Relations.

Government of Kerala (1999): *Lok Sabha Elections Reportage 1996, 98, 99*. Thiruvananthapuram, Department of Public Relations.

Government of Kerala (2001): *Assembly Election Reportage 1996*, Thiruvananthapuram, Department of Public Relations.

(B) Party Publications

Indian National Congress (1962): *Constitution of Indian National Congress*, New Delhi, AICC.

Indian National Congress (1999): *Constitution of Indian National Congress & Rules*, New Delhi, AICC.

(C) Party Records

Kerala Pradesh Congress Committee (1983): *Minutes of the meetings of the KPCC Executive Committee* 27.3.1980 to 29.4.1983, Trivandrum, KPCC office.

KPCC (1984): *Minutes of the meetings of the KPCC office bearers & Ministers held at Thrissur on 15 January 1983 to July 1984*, Trivandrum, KPCC Office.

KPCC (1986): *KPCC Executive Meetings Attendance Register from 6th January 1984 to 7th September 1986*, Trivandrum KPCC Office.

KPCC (1986): *Minutes of the meetings of the KPCC office bearers, Congress Ministers and DCC Presidents from 31 August 1984 to 11 February 1986*, Trivandrum, KPCC Office.

KPCC (1986): *Register of office bearers from June 1986 to 1988*, Trivandrum, KPCC.

KPCC (1987): *Minutes of the meetings of the KPCC Executive, Congress parliamentary party, functional organisations Presidents, DCC Presidents, MPs , Congress candidates and special invitees on 5th May 1987*, Trivandrum KPCC.

KPCC (1988): *Minutes of the meetings of the KPCC Executive 1988*, Trivandrum, KPCC Office.

KPCC (1989): *Minutes of the meetings of the KPCC from 30.1.1988 to 11 March 1989*, Trivandrum KPCC office.

KPCC (1990): *Minutes of the meetings of the KPCC from 1.4.89 to 10.1.90*, Trivandrum KPCC Office.

KPCC (1990): *Minutes of the meetings from 25.1.90 to 29.10.90*, Trivandrum, KPCC Office.

KPCC (1991): *Minutes of the meetings of the KPCC office bearers and DCC Presidents from November '90 to November 1991*, Trivandrum KPCC office.

KPCC (1992): *Minutes of the meetings of the KPCC Office bearers from 3rd February 1992 to 21st November 1993*, Trivandrum KPCC Office.

KPCC (1994): *Minutes of the KPCC meetings Book No.1*, Trivandrum KPCC office.

KPCC (1995): *Minutes of the KPCC meetings Book No.2*, Trivandrum KPCC Office.

KPCC (1998): *Minutes of the meetings of the KPCC Office bearers from 1995 to 1998*, Trivandrum, KPCC Office.

KPCC (2000): *Minutes of the meetings of the KPCC from 1998 to 2000 Trivandrum* KPCC Office.

KPCC (Undated): *Register for Hotline messages from the AICC*, Trivandrum KPCC office.

KPCC (Undated): *Register for Disciplinary Action Committee*, Trivandrum, KPCC Office.

(D) Election Guides

Kalakaumudi (1979): *Lok Sabha, Election Guide (I) 1980*, (M), Thiruvananthapuram, Laisa Publications.

Kalakaumudi (1980): *Kerala NiyamaSabha, Election Guide (II) 1980*, (M), Thiruvananthapuram, Laisa publications.

Malayala Manorama (1982): *Malayala Manorama Election Guide, 1982* (M)Kottayam, Manorama publication.

Malayala Manorama (1984): *Malayala Manorama Election Guide 1984* (M), Kottayam, Manorama publication.

Malayala Manorama (1987): *Malayala Manorama Election Guide 1987* (M), Kottayam, Manorama publication.

Malayala Manorama (1989): *Malayala Manorama Election Guide 1989* (M), Kottayam, Manorama publication.

Malayala Manorama (1991): *Malayala Manorama Election guide 1991* (M), Kottayam, Manorama publication.

Malayala Manorama (1996): *Malayala Manorama Election Guide 1996* (M), Kottayam, Manorama publication.

Malayala Manorama (1998): *Malayala Manorama Election Guide 1998* (M), Kottayam, Manorama publication.

Malayala Manorama (1999): *Malayala Manorama Election Guide 1999* (M), Kottayam, Manorama publication.

Malayala Manorama (2001): *Malayala Manorama Election Guide 2001* (M), Kottayam, Manorama publication.

Secondary Sources

(A) Books

Abdul Azeez (1992): *Rise of Muslims in Kerala Politics*, Thiruvananthapuram, CBH.

Abdur Rahiman K.K (1964): *Kerala Congress Directory*, Ernakulam, Crescent Publication.

Abott W. David & Edward t. Rogowsky (1978): *Political Parties*, USA, Rand McNally.

Acharya Kripalani J B (1948): *The Future of the Congress*, Bombay, Hind Kitabs Ltd.

Alexander P.C (1991): *My Days With Indira Gandhi*, New Delhi, Vision Books.

Alexander P.C (1995): *The Perils of Democracy*, Bombay, Somaiyya Publication.

Alford R. Robert (1964): *Party and Society: The Anglo American Societies*, USA, Rand McNally &Com

Anil Bhatt (1997): "Caste, Class and Politics – An empirical profile of social stratification in India" in Verinder Grover (Ed) *Foundations of Political System and Sociological Aspects*, New Delhi, Deep & Deep.

Anoop C. (1997): *EMS Anubhavam:Yojichum, Viyojichum* (M), Thiruvananthapuram, New Indian Books.

Arie De Ruijter (1998): *The Purse and the Power: Aspects of Centre State Relations in India*, New Delhi, B.R Publishing Corporation.

Arjun Sharma (1993): *Caste, Class and Politics in Rural India*, New Delhi, Khanna Publications.

Asghar Ali Engineer (1995): *Kerala Muslims*, New Delhi, Ajanta Publication.

Asok Mehta (1979): *A Decade of Indian Politics 1966-77*, New Delhi, S. Chand & com.

Attarchand(1991): *Prime Minister P V Narasimha Rao: The Scholar and Statesman* , New Delhi, Gyan publishing house.

Bailey F.G (1963): *Politics and Social Change: Orissa in 1959*, Berkley, University of California Press.

Bakshi S.R (1985): *Nehru and Congress: The Emergence of New Ideology*, New Delhi, Criterion.

Bakshi S.R (1994): *EMS Namboothiripad*, New Delhi, Anmol publishers.

Bakshi S R, S R Sharma, S. Gajrani (1993): *Contemporary Political Leadership in India: Sonia Gandhi*, New Delhi, APH Publishing Corporation.

Balakrishnan E (1998): *History of the Communist Movement in Kerala*, Ernakulam, Kurukshetra Prakasan.

Balakrishnan Nair A (1994): *The Government and Politics of Kerala*, Thiruvananthapuram: Indira Publication.

Balakrishnan Nair. A (1996): *Landmarks in the Administration of Kerala*, Thiruvananthapuram: IIPA Regional Branch.

Barnett Marguerite Ross and others (1975): *Electoral Politics in the Indian States: Party Systems and Cleavages*, New Delhi, Manohar Book Service.

Basant Chatterjee (Undated): *The Congress Splits*, New Delhi, S. Chand & Co.

Beals Alan (1960): "Leadership in a Mysore Village" in Richard L Park and Irene Tinker (ed) *Leadership and Political Institutions in India*, Princeton, Princeton University Press.

Beteille Andre (1996): "Caste in Contemporary India", Fuller C J (Ed), *Caste Today*, New Delhi, Oxford.

Bidyut Chakraborty (1993): *Whither India's Democracy*, Calcutta, K.P Bagchi & Com.

Bipan Chandra, Auditya Mukherjee & Mridula Mukherjee, (ed) (1999): *India since Independence* , New Delhi, Viking.

Bhabani Sengupta (1989): *Rajiv Gandhi: A Political Study*, New Delhi, Konark Publishers.

Bhagat K.P (1962): *The Kerala Mid Term Election of 1960*, Bombay, Popular Book Depot.

Bhambhri C P (1999): *Indian Politics Since Independence* Vol.II, New Delhi, Shipra Publishers.

Bhat Nagar S. & Pradeep Kumar (1988): *Regional Political Parties in India*, New Delhi, Ess Ess Publications.

Biju M R (1999): *Parliamentary Democracy and Political Change in India*, New Delhi Kanishka.

Brass R. Paul (1965): *Factional Politics In An Indian State*, London: Cambridge University Press.

Brass R. Paul (1975): *Language, Religion and Politics in North India*, New Delhi, Vikas.

Brass R. Paul (1984): *Caste, Faction and Party in Indian Politics* Vol.I, Faction and Party, New Delhi, Chanakya.

Brass R. Paul (1994): *Politics of India Since Independence*, Cambridge, Cambridge University Press.

Brecher Michael (1966): *Succession in India: A study in Decision Making*, London, Oxford.

Brubacher John S (1962): *Modern Philosophy of Education*, New York, Mc Graw Hill Company INC,

Carter T. Anthony (1975): *Elite Politics in Rural India: Political Stratification and Political Alliances in Western Maharashtra*, New Delhi, Vikas.

Carter M.Gwendolen & John H. Herz (1967): *Government and Politics in the Twentieth Century*, New Delhi, Wile of Easter Pvt. Ltd.

Chopra P N Ramgopal, M L Bhargava (1986): *A Century of Indian National Congress*, New Delhi, Agam Prakasam.

Corbridge Stuart and John Harriss (2000): *Reinventing India: Liberalisation Hindu Nationalism and Popular Democracy*, New Delhi, OUP.

Craig Baxter Yogendra K Malik Charles H Kennedy and Robert C Oberst (1993): *Government and Politics in South Asia*, USA, West View Press.

Day J Alan & Henry W Degen Hardt (1984): *Political Parties of the World*, London, Longman.

Dhar P.N (2000): *Indira Gandhi, The Emergency and Indian Democracy*, New Delhi, Oxford.

Dhillon H S (1955): *Leadership and Groups in a Ssouth Indian Village*, New Delhi, Planning Commission Programme, Evaluation Organisation.

Diptikumar Biswas (1978): *Political Sociology: An Introduction*, Calcutta, Firma KLM.

Dolobran Lord Lloyd (1939): *Leadership in Democracy*, London, University of Oxford..

Douglas Tom (1979): *Group Processes in Social Work: A Theoretical Analysis*, U.K, John Wiley & Sons.

Drucker H M (1979): *Multi Party Britain*, London, Macmillan.

Dua B D (1985): *Presidential Rule in India: 1950-1984: A study in Crisis Politics*, New Delhi, rev. ed. S.Chand.

Duverger Maurice (1954): *Political Parties*, London, Methuen & Co.

Editor (1999): *Perspectives on Kerala History*: The Second Millennium Vol.II, Part II, Thiruvananthapuram, Kerala Gazetteers Department.

Eldersveld J Samuel (1971): *Political Parties; A Behavioural Analysis*, Bombay, K.K Vora

Eldersveld J Samuel (1978): *Citizens and Politics: Mass Political Behaviour in India*, USA, University of Chicago.

Epstein D Leon (1967): *Political Parties in Western Democracies*, New York, Prager.

Fic M Victor (1970): *Kerala: Yenan of India, Rise of Communist Power 1937-1969*, Bombay, Nachiketa Publications.

Franda Marcus M (1971): *Political Development and Political Decay in West Bengal*, Culcutta, Firma KLM.

Franda Marcus M(1979): *Small is politics: Organisational Alternatives in India's Rural Development*, New Delhi, Wiley Eastern.

Frederick J Carl (1967): *An Introduction to Political Theory*, New York, Harper & Row.

Fukunaga Masaaki (1993): *Society Caste and Factional Politics: Conflict and continuity in Rural India*, New Delhi, Manohar.

Gajarani. S (1998): *Sonia Gandhi: President of AICC*, New Delhi, APH.

Gandhi M.K (1999): *Congress and Its Future*, Ahmedabad, Navajeevan Trust.

Gehlot N S (1998): *Current Trends in Indian Politics*, New Delhi, Deep & Deep.

Girija K.Mookerjee (1974), *History of Indian National Congress*, Meerut, Meenakshi Prakasam.

Girija Sankar (1995): *A History of the Congress Socialist Party*, Jodhpur, Twenty First Century Publishers.

Gopakumar. G (1984): *The Congress party and State Politics: Emergence of New Style Politics,New Delhi, Deep & Deep*

Gopakumar G (1986): *Regional Political Parties and State Politics*, New Delhi, Deep & Deep.

Gopal Krishna (1981): *Political Dynamics* Vol.III, New Delhi, ICSSR.

Govindan Kutty K (1994): *K Karunakaran*, New Delhi, Har Anand

Hague Rod, Martin Harrop and Shaun Breslin (1992): *Comparative Government and Politics: An Introduction*, London, Macmillan.

Hardgrave L. Robert (1975): *India: Government and Politics in a Developing Nation*, Princeton, Princeton University Press.

Hardgrave L Robert (1993): *Political Sociology of South India*, New Delhi, Manohar.

Hari Jaisingh (1989): *India After Indira; The Turbulent Years* (1984-85), New Delhi, Allied.

Haridwar Rai & Jawaharlal Pandey (1997): "Intra Party Democracy: The Experience of the Indian National Congress" In Verinder Grover (Ed) *Political Parties and Party System*, New Delhi, Deep & Deep.

Hausen Thomas Blom and Christophe Jalfrelot (1998): (Ed), *The BJP and the Compulsions of Politics in India*, New Delhi, Oxford University Press.

Hemachandran M.K (1997), *Ente Kazhinja Kaalam* (M), Kottayam, DCB.

Hill L. John (1991): (ed) *The Congress and Indian Nationalism*, London, Curzon Press.

Hollins T H B (1964): (Ed): *Aims in Education; The Philosophic Approach*, Manchester, Mulley Press.York, Oxford.

Janak Rai Jai & Rajiv Jai,(1999): *Revival of Two Party System in India: Ruling Vs Combined Opposition*, New Delhi, Regency.

Janardan Thakur (1999): *Prime Ministers: Nehru to Vajpayee*, Mumbai, Eeswar.

Jayachandran T.N (2000): *Kerala 2000*, Thiruvananthapuram, State Institute of Languages

Jayaram N & Satish Sabewal (Ed) (1996): *Social Conflict*, New Delhi, Oxford.

Jean Blondel & Maurizio Cotta (1999): *Party and Government*, London, Macmillan.

Jitendra Singh (1959): *Communist Rule in Kerala*, New Delhi.

Johari J.C (1997): "Young Turks and Radicalisation of Politics" In Verinder Grover (ed) *Political Parties and Party Systems*, New Delhi, Deep & Deep.

John K.C (1975): *Melting Pot: Kerala 1950's-1970's*, Trivandrum, Prasanthi Printers.

John K C(1999): *Kerala Rashtreeyam Oru Asmbanhda Natakam* (M), Aluva, Pen Books.

John KC (2001): *Beyond The Dead line*, Thiruvananthapuram, Kesari Memorial Trust.

John Baker, Christopher (1976): *The Politics of South India*, New Delhi, Vikas.

John P. John (1983): *Coalition Governments in Kerala*, Trivandrum Institute for the Study of Public Policy and Management.

Jose Chander N (1986): *Dynamics of State Politics*, New Delhi, Sterling Publishers.

Jose Chander N (1997): "Coalition Politics; Kerala Model" in Subhash C Kashyap (ed), *Coalition Governments and Politics in India*, New Delhi, Uppal Publishing House.

Joseph Vadakkan Fr. (1974): *Ente Kuthippum Kithappum* (M) Autobiography, Kottayam, New man Publishers.

Kaimal P K V (1994): *Revolt of the Oppressed; Punnapra Vayalar 1946*, New Delhi, Konark Publishers.

Kalim Bahadur & M.C Paul (2000): *Contemporary India*, New Delhi, Netaji Institute of Sub continental Studies.

Kamal K L, Ralph C Meyer (1977): *Democratic Politics in India*, New Delhi, Vikas.

Kate Nash (2000): *Contemporary Political Sociology: Globalisation, Politics and Power*, UK Oxford, Blackwell Publishers.

Kaushik P D (1986): *The Congress Ideology and Programme 1920-1985*, New Delhi, Gitanjali Publishers.

Kaviraj Sudipta (Ed) (1997): *Politics in India*, New Delhi, Oxford.

Keraleeyan V. S (1969): *Keralathinte Veera Puthran* (M), Kozhikode.

Key V O (Jr) (1956): *Politics, Parties and Pressure Groups*, New York, Crowell CO.

Khanna S K (1998): *Crisis in Indian Democracy*, New Delhi, Commonwealth.

Khanna S K (1999): *Contemporary Indian Politics*, New Delhi, Discovery Publishing House.

Kochanek A Stanley (1968): *The Congress Party in India: Dynamics Of One party Dominance*, Princeton: Princeton University Press.

Kochanek A Stanley (2002): "Mrs. Gandhi's Pyramid: The New Congress" in Zoya Hasan (Ed), *Parties and Party system in India*, New Delhi, Oxford University Press.

Kovoor E.M (1965): *T.M Varghese* (M), Kottayam NBS

Krishna Chakraborty, Swapan Kumar Bhattacharya (1993): *Leadership, Factions and Panchayat Raj*, New Delhi, Rawat.

Kumar K N (1990): *Political Parties in India: Their Ideology and Organisation*, New Delhi, Mittal.

Kundu C L & D N Tutoo (1988): *Educational Psychology*, New Delhi, Sterling.

Kundra T N (1996): *Glimpses of Indian National Congress: From Inception to Attainment of Freedom (1885-1947)*, New Delhi, Regency.

Lane E Robert. (1972): *Political Man*, New York, The Free Press.

La Palambora Joseph & Myron Weiner (1969): *Political Parties and Political Development*, New Jersey, Princeton University Press.

Laswell D Harold and Abraham Kaplan (1957): *Power and Society: A framework for political enquiry*, USA, University of Yale.

Lees D John & Richard Kimbler (1972): *Political Parties in Modern Britain*, London, Routledge & Kegal paul.

Lipset S.M (1960): *The Political Man*, London Heinemann.

Lowie H Robert. (1950): *Social Organisation*, London. The Free Press.

Madhavan Kutty V. K (1998): *The Southern Discomfort*, New Delhi, Har Anand.

Madhava Menon T (2000): *A Handbook of Kerala*, Thiruvananthapuram, International School of Dravidian Languages.

Mahendra P.Singh (1975): *Cohesion in a Predominant Party: The Pradesh Congress and Party Politics in Bihar*, New Delhi, S. Chand.

Mahendra Prasad Singh (1981): *Split in a Predominant Party, The Indian National Congress in 1969*, New Delhi, Abhinav.

Mahendra Prasad Singh, Rekha Saxena (1996): *India's Political Agenda: Perspectives on the Party System*, New Delhi, Kalinga Publication.

Mahendru K.C (1984): *Gandhi and the Congress Socialist Party 1934-38: An Analysis of their Interaction*, Jalandhur: ABS Publication.

Mammen P M (1997): "The Multi-party System in Kerala" in Verinder Grover (Ed) *Political Parties and Party System*, New Delhi, Deep & Deep.

Mani Sankar Aiyar (1993): *In Rajiv's Foot Prints: A Year in Parliament*, New Delhi, Konark.

Mankekar D.R (1964): *Red Riddle in Kerala*, Bombay, Manakthala and Son.

Manor James (1997): "Parties and Party System", In Partha Chatterjee (ed) *State and Politics in India*, New Delhi, Oxford.

Marshall M Bouton (Ed) (1987): *India Briefing 1987*, New Delhi, Oxford University Press.

Mary Carras (1972): *The Dynamics of Indian Political Factions: A Study of District Councils in the State of Maharashtra*, Cambridge, Cambridge University Press.

Mathew E T (1999): "Educated Unemployement in Kerala: Incidence causes and Policy implications", B A Prakash (Ed) *Kerala's Economic Development Issues and Problems*, New Delhi, Sage.

Mayer P.B(1987): "Development and Demise", in Jim Masselos (ed) *Struggling and Ruling: The Indian National Congress 1885-1985*, New Delhi, Sterling.

Meenakshi Jain (1991): *The Congress Party (1967-77): Role of Caste in Indian Politics*, New Delhi, Vikas.

Mehrotra N.C (1980): *Political Crisis and Polls in India*, New Delhi, Deep & Deep.

Mekhala Kulapati (1999): *Political Disputes and Controversies*, New Delhi, Kanishka.

Merchant Minhaz (1991): *Rajiv Gandhi*, New Delhi, Penguin Books.

Merriam Edward Charles and Harold Foote Gosnell (1949): *The American Party System: An Introduction to the Study of Political Parties in the US*, USA, Macmillan.

Mitchell Robert (1915): *Political Parties*, New York, Hearst International Library Co.

Mookerjee H C (1945): *Congress and the Masses*, Calcutta, The Book House.

Nageswar Prasad (1980): *Ideology and Organisation in Indian Politics: A Study of Political Parties at the Grassroots*, New Delhi, Allied Publishers.

Nagendra Reddy, M Venkal Tao & P. Venkareswara Rao (Ed) (1990): *P.V Narasimha Rao: Years of Power*, New Delhi, Har Anand Publication.

Nagla B.K (1984): *Factionalism, Politics and Social Structure*, Jaipur, Rawat.

Nagla B.K (1999): *Political Sociology*, New Delhi: Rawat.

Nair K.S (1984): *Congress Party and Kerala Politics*, Trivandrum, College Book House.

Namboodiripad E M S(1968): *Kerala- Yesterday, Today and Tomorrow*, Calcutta, National Book Agency.

Namboodiripad E M S (1984): *Kerala Society and Politics: An Historical Survey*, New Delhi, National Book Agency .

Namboodiripad E M S (1994): *The Communist party in Kerala: Six Decades of Struggle and Advance*, New Delhi, National Book Centre.

Narang A.S (1985): *Indian Government and Politics*, New Delhi, Gitanjali Publishing House.

Narasimha Rao P V(1998): *The Insider*, New Delhi, Viking.

Narayana Pillai. C (1972): *Thiruvithamkoorile Swathanthiya Samara Charitram*, (M), Trivandrum, Harward Publications

Narayana Pillai. C(1976): *Pattom Muthal Panampally Vare* (M),Kottayam, DCB.

Nayanar E.K (1982): *My Struggles: An Autobiography*, New Delhi, Vikas Publishing House.

Nayantara Sahgal (1978): *Indira Gandhi's Emergence and Style*, New Delhi, Vikas.

Neuman Sigmund (1956): *Modern Political Parties*, USA, University of Chicago Press.

Nihal S Singh (1993): *The Rocky Road of Indian Democracy: Nehru to Narasimha Rao*, New Delhi, Sterling Publishers.

Nossiter T.J (1982): *Communism in Kerala: A Study in Political Adaptation*, Oxford, London.

Om P Gautam (1985): *The Indian National Congress; An Analytical Bibliography*, New Delhi, B.R Publishing Corporation.

Padma Charan Misra and K.S Padhy (2000): *Factional Politics in Rural India*, New Delhi, Discovery Publishing.

Pande B.N (1985): *The Concise History of Indian National Congress (1885-1947)*, New Delhi, Congress Centenary Committee.

Pande B.N (1989): *Indira Gandhi*, New Delhi, Government of India Publication Division.

Panigrahi P K (1998): *Political Elite in Tribal Society*, New Delhi, Commonwealth Publications.

Park L Richard and Irene Tinker (1960), (Eds): *Leadership and Political Institutions in India*, Princeton, Princeton University Press.

Partha Chatterjee (ed) (1993): *State Politics in India*, New Delhi, Oxford.

Pattabhi Sitaramayya (1935): *The History of Indian National Congress*, Vol.I (1885-1935), Bombay, Padma Publications.

Pattabhi Sitaramayya (1947): *The History of Indian National Congress*, Vol.II (1935-1947), Bombay, Padma Publications.

Pattom G. Ramachandran Nair (2000): *Pattom Muthal Nayanar Vare* (M), Sindhu, Palkulangara, Trivandrum.

Perunna K.N Nair (1967): *Keralathile Congress Prasthanam* (M), Thrissur, Current Books.

Peter Donald De Souza (2000): "Caste Secularisation Process in India", DL Sheth (Ed) *Contemporary India*, New Delhi.

Pillai A K (1986): *Congressum Keralavum* (M), Thiruvananthapuram, Prabhath Book House.

Plamentz John (1970): *Ideology*, London, Pall Mall.

Pradeep K Chhibber (1999): *Democracy without Associations: Transformations of the Party System and Social Cleavages in India*, New Delhi, Vistar.

Pradeep Mandav (2000): *Communalism in India: A Paradigm Shift to Indian Politics*, New Delhi, Authors Press.

Prasannan R. (2000): *Adiyandhravasthayude Alayolikal: Niyama Sabhayil Nisabdanayi* Part II (M), Thrissur, Current Books.

Pree Max Dec (1994): *Leadership is an Art*, London, Arrow Random House.

Pulinkunnu Antony (1997): *P.T Chacko* (M), Kottayam, Current.

Pushpa Asthana (1988): *Party System in India: Development and Decay*, New Delhi, Criterion Publications.

Puthuppally Raghavan (1996): *Viplava Smaranakal* (M), Vol.5, Kottayam, DC Books.

Rajan Mahan (1999): *Women in Indian National Congress*, New Delhi, Rawat Publishers.

Rajendran G (1974): *Ezhava Community and Kerala Politics*, Trivandrum, Kerala Academy of Political Science.

Rahman M.M (1970): *The Congress Crisis*, New Delhi, Associated Publishing House.

Rajni Kothari, Gopalakrishna, Ramstray Roy, Ghanshyam Shah (1967): *Party System and Election Studies*, New Delhi, Allied.

Rajni Kothari (1989): *Politics and the People: In Search of Humane India* Vol.I & II, New Delhi, Ajanta Publication.

Ralhan O P (1996): *Encyclopedia of Political Parties*, New Delhi, Anmol.

Ram Gopal (1986): *India under Indira*, New Delhi, Criterion Publication.

Ramachandran S. (2000): *P. Balan: Thalaratha Porali*,(Mal), Kottayam, Current Books.

Ramakrishnan Nair. R (1964): "Government and Politics in Kerala" In V.K Sukumaran Nayar (Ed) *Kerala Society and Politics*, Trivandrum: Department of Politics, University of Kerala.

Ramakrishnan Nair. R (1965): *How the Communist Came to Power in Kerala*, Trivandrum, Kerala Academy of Political Science.

Raman Pillai K. (1998): "Moonnu Desakangal Pinnitta Rashtreeya Keralam", In N. Vijayan (ed) *Keralathinte Moonnu Desakangal* (M), Thiruvananthapuram, State Institute of Languages.

Ramesh Kumar (1994): *Congress and Congressism in Indian Politics*, New Delhi, Deep &Deep.

Ranajit Guha (1982): *Subaltern Studies: Writings on South Indian History and Society*, New York, Oxford.

Rao R P (1971): *The Congress Splits*, Bombay, Lalvin Publishing.

Rastogi P N (1973): *The Nature and Dynamics of Factional Conflict*, Meerut, The Macmillan Company of India.

Reba Som (1995): *Differences with in Consensus: The Left and Right in the Congress 1929-1939*, Delhi, Orient.

R.K.G (2000): *India A Nation in Turmoil*, New Delhi , UBSPD.

Roberts K Geoffrey (1970): *Political Parties and Pressure Groups*, London, Weiden FFeld and Nicolson.

Rose Richard (1974): *The Problem of party government*, London, Macmillan.

Rudolph L Lloyed and Susanne H Rudolph (1990): "Organisational Adaptation of the Congress under Rajiv Gandhi's Leadership" in Richard Sission and Ramshray Roy (Ed) *Diversity and Dominance in Indian Politics: Changing Bases of Congress Support*, New Delhi, Sage.

Sadasivan S. N (1977): *Party and Democracy in India*, New Delhi, Tata Mc Graw Hill.

Sajal Basu (1990): *Factions, Ideology and Politics: Coalition Politics in West Bengal*, Calcutta: Minerva Associates.

Sanal P Thomas (2000): *Leader: Autobiography of K. Karunakaran*, Kottayam, Current.

Sankara Pillai T.P (1969): *Democracy in Kerala and Pattom A. Thanu Pillai*, Trivandrum, Mahatma Printing, Thycaud.

Sankaran Kutty Nair T P (1998): *Society and State Politics: Issues and Perspectives*, Trivandrum, Indian Institute of Political Studies.

Sanker Ghose (1975): *Indian National Congress: Its History and Heritage*, New Delhi, AICC.

Sarat Chandra Mallick (1986): *Humanism, The Congress Philosophy*, Bhuvaneswar, Nehru Study Centre.

Sartori Giovanni (1976): *Parties and Party system: A Frame work for Analysis*, Vol.I, Cambridge, Cambridge University Press.

Saloma S John (1973): *Parties: The Real Opportunity for Effective Citizens Politics*, New York, Vintage Books.

Scalapino A. Robert & Junnosuke Masumi (1971): *Parties and Politics in Contemporary Japan*, USA, University of California Press.

Seldon Antony & Stuart Ball (1994): *Conservative Century*, London, Oxford University Press.

Sher Singh Dagar (1996): *Indian National Congress: Hume to Sonia Gandhi*, New Delhi, Gyan Sagar.

Sheshadri K (1999): *Stagnancy and Change in Indian Society and Politis*, Jaipur, Aalekh Publishers.

Sethi J.D (1975): *India in Crisis*, New Delhi, Vikas Publishing House.

Shefter Martin (1996): *Political Parties and the State: The American Historical Experience*, USA, Princeton University Press.

Sheth D L (1975): *Citizens and Politics: Aspects of Competitive Politics in India*, New Delhi, Allied Publishers.

Singh S D (1999): *Fragmental Party System: A Study of the Viability of Political Parties*, Ranchi, Catholic Press.

Singh M P (1990): "The Congress System in the 1980's and Beyond: Patterns of Recruitment Strategies of Mobilisation and Inter Party Mobilisation" in Richard Sission and Ramshray Roy (Ed) *Diversity and Dominance in Indian Politics: Changing Bases of Congress Support Vol.I*, New Delhi, Sage.

Singh V B (1993): *Political Fragmentation and Electoral Process: 1991 Elections in Uttar Pradesh*, New Delhi, Ajantha Publishers.

Sirsikar V.M (1994): *Politics of Modern Maharashtra*, Bombay, Orient Longman.

Sisson Richard 91970): "Caste and Political Factions in Rajasthan", in Rajni Kothari (Ed), *Caste in Indian Politics*, New Delhi, Orient Longman.

Sisson Richard (1972): *The Congress Party in Rajasthan: Political Integration and Nation Building in an Indian State*, London University of California.

Sisson Richard and Ramshray Roy (1990) (Ed): *Diversity and Dominance in Indian Politics Vol.I: Changing Bases of Congress Support*, New Delhi, Sage.

Somarajan C N (1988): *Pressure Groups and Democratic Politics*, New Delhi, Deep & Deep.

Sood P (1981): *Re emergence of Indira Gandhi*, New Delhi, S. Chand & Comp.

Sprout W.J.W (1956), *Social Psychology*, London, Methun & Com Ltd.

Sreedhara Menon A (1987): *A Concise History of Modern Kerala (1885-1957)*, Madras, S. Viswanadhan Publishing Company.

Srinivas M.N (1976): *The Remembered Village* , New Delhi Oxford University Press.

Srinivas M.N (1994): *The Dominant Caste*, New Delhi, Oxford University Press.

Stacey Barrie (1978), *Political Socialisation in Western Society: An analysis from Life Span Perspective*, New Delhi, Arnold Heinemann.

Subhash C Subhash (1971): *Indian Political Parties: Programmes, Promises and Performance*, New Delhi, Research Publication in Social Sciences.

Subhash C Kashyap (Ed) (1972): *Indian Parties and Politics*, New Delhi, Research Publications in social Science.

Subhash C Kashyap (Ed) (1997): *Coalition Government and Politics in India*, New Delhi, Uppal Publishing House.

Subrata Mukherjee (2000): "Crisis of the Congress: From Mass Consensual Origins to Restrictive Politics" in S R Chakravarty and others (Ed) *Contemporary India*, New Delhi, Netaji Institute of Sub Continental Studies.

Sudha Pai (2000): *State Politics: New Dimensions*, New Delhi, Shipra.

Suresh K Tameri (1971): *The Wonder Elections 1971: Indira vs the Right*, New Delhi, Vivek Publishing House.

Surya Narayana Misra (1989): *Party Politics and Electoral Choice in an Indian State*, New Delhi, Ajanta Publications.

Sydney Verba, Norman H. Nie & Joe - on Kim (1978): *Participation and Political Equality: A Seven-Nation Comparison*, Cambridge: Cambridge University Press.

Thomas E.J (1985): *Coalition Game Politics in Kerala*, New Delhi, Intellectual Publishing House.

Thomas Pantham (1976): *Political Parties and Democratic Consensus*, New Delhi, Macmillan.

Tope T K (1986): *Bombay and Congress Movement*, Bombay; Maharashtra State Board of Literature and Culture.

Varghese T.C (1970): *Agrarian Change and Economic Consequences: Land Tenures in Kerala 1850-1960*, New Delhi, Allied.

Varghese Kulangara V J (1993): *K M Mani: Jubilee Smaranakal* (M), Ernakulam, Labour India Publishers.

Verinder Grover (1997): *Political Parties and Party System*, New Delhi, Deep & Deep.

Verinder Grover and Ranjana Arora, *India: Fifty Years of Independence*, New Delhi, Deep & Deep.

Vijayan N (Ed) (1998): *Kerlathinte Moonnu Desakangal* (M), Thiruvananthapuram, State Institute of Languages.

Vrindavan G Venugopalan (1992): *K. Karunakaran*, Aluva, Islamiya Book Stall.

Walch James (1976): *Faction and Front: Party Systems in South India*, New Delhi, Young Asia Publications.

Webb Paul (2000): *The Modern British Party System*, New Delhi, Sage.

Weiner Myron (1967): *Party Building in a New Nation: The Indian National Congress*, Chicago, University of Chicago.

Weiner Myron (1989): *The Indian Paradox: Essays in Indian Politics*, New Delhi, Sage.

Weiner Myron, & Ashuthosh Varshney (1989): *Indian Paradox: Essays in Indian Politics*, New Delhi, Sage.

Wood Cock George (1967): *Kerala : A Portrait of Malabar*, London, Faber & Faber.

Wood R. John (1984): *State Politics in Contemporary India*, USA, West View Press.

Wood Santhosh (1984): Trade Union Leadership in India, New Delhi, Deep & Deep.

Yogendra K Malik & Asok Kapur (1998): *India: Fifty years of Democracy and Development*, New Delhi, APH.

Yogesh Atul (2000): *Mandate for Political Transition: Re-emergence of Vajpayee*, New Delhi, Rawat.

Zaidi A.M (1984): *Aloud and Straight: Frank Talks at Party Meetings*, New Delhi, Indian Institute of Applied Political Research.

Zenab Banu (1999): *Decline and fall of Indian Politics*, New Delhi, Kanishka.

Zoya Hasan (Ed)(2000): *Politics and State in India*, New Delhi, Sage.

Zoya Hasan (2002): *Parties and Party politics in India*, New Delhi: Oxford University Press.

(B) Unpublished PhD Dissertations

Bhaskaran N K (1983): *Democratic Movements in Travancore*, Thiruvananthapuram, University of Kerala, Department of Politics.

Gopakumar G (1980): *The Congress Party in Kerala since 1967*, Thiruvananthapuram, University of Kerala, Department of Politics.

Jayadevan N (1999): *Student Movement and Kerala Politics from 1956-80*, Thiruvananthapuram, University of Kerala, Department of Politics.

Jayaraj D (1977): *Democratic Government in Kerala 1957-80*, Thiruvananthapuram, University of Kerala, Department of Politics

Krishnakumari S (1994): *Coalition Politics in Kerala 1970-85*, Trivandrum, University of Kerala.

Prabha Prasanna Kumar (1998): *Inter party Relations in the coalition governments in Kerala in the 1980s*, Thiruvananthapuram, University of Kerala, Department of Politics.

Sadasivan Nair K (1970): *The Congress Party in Kerala 1947-63*, Thiruvananthapuram,University of Kerala,Department of Politics.

Sebastian A A (1994): *Role of Chief Minister in coalition governments: A Case Study of Kerala*, Thiruvananthapuram, University of Kerala, Department of Politics.

Varghese T (1982): *The Kerala Congress : A Case Study*, Thiruvananthapuram, University of Kerala, Department of Politics.

Yamuna Devi S (1998): *The Nair Service Society and Kerala Politics since 1970 – A Study*, Thiruvananthapuram University of Kerala, Department of Politics.

(C) Select Articles

Achutha Menon C (1991): "Keralathile Thiranjeduppu Phalam", *Kalakaumudi*. 14 July

Anoop C (1999):"Close Up: Thiruvananthapuram", *Kalakaumudi*, Vol.1253, 12 September.

Anosh Malekar (2002): 'Gujarat Matrix'. *The Week*, Vol.21, No.2, 15 December.

Aravindakashan P (1991): "Hit with Poll Axe", *The Week*. 10 February.

Firth Raymond (1957): "Introduction to Faction in Indian and Overseas Indian societies", *British Journal of Sociology*, Vol.8.

Frontline (1987): "Kerala at the Polls", *Front Line*, Vol.4, No.8, April 18-May 1.

Gopakumar G (2001): 'Congress Partiyum Kerala Rashteeyavum', *Malayalam*, 16 February.

Gouridasan Nair C(1992): "Nebulous in Kerala", Front Line, September 11.

Harinder Rai and Jawaharlal Pandey (1971): "Intra Party Democracy: The Experience of the Indian national Congress", *Journal of Constitutional and Parliamentary Studies*, Vol.5, October-December.

Jacob George (2000): "Murivetta Simham", India Today (M), 18 April.

Kalakumudi (1982): 'Chaaram Moodiya Kanalkattakal (M)', Kalakaumudi, Vol.349, 9 May

Kalakaumudi (1982): "Eeni Vijayathinte Parajayam" (M), *Kalakaumudi*, vol.353, 6-June.

Kalakaumudi (1982): "Bharanakakshi Managerude Chiri" (M), *Kalakaumudi*, vol.357, 4-July.

Kalakaumudi (1998): "Edathottu Kanneriyunna Sonia",(M) *Kalakaumudi*, vol.1202, September 20.

Kalakaumudi (1984): "Joseph Groupinte Uriyadi", (M) *Kalakaumudi*, vol.433, 1 January.

Kalakaumudi (1985): "Karthikeyante Poovedi" (M), *Kalakaumudi*, vol.501, 21 April.

Kalakaumudi (1986): "Delhiyil Mani Nirathiya Fayalukal", *Kalakaumudi*,(M), vol.547, 9-March.

Kalakaumudi (1986): "Karunakarante Puthiya Kallakkali", (M), *Kalakaumudi*, vol.551, 6 Apirl.

Kalakaumudi (1986): "Sreenivasante Vyangyam" (M), *Kalakaumudi*, vol.561, 15 June.

Kalakaumudi (1986): "Ee Yudham Eniyum Neelum", (M), *Kalakaumudi*, vol.573, 7 September.

Kalakaumudi (1987): "A Tale of Two Parties", *Kalakaumudi*, (M) vol.594, 1- February.

Krishna Kumar R (1998): "Adhoc Arrangement", *Front Line* Vol.15, No.15, July 18-31.

Krishna Kumar R (2001): 'Evenly Poised', Front Line, Vol.18, No.10, 12-25 May.

Krishna Kumar R (2001): "A Record of Sorts", *Front Line*, Vol.18, No.11, May 25-June 8.

Lekshmy Iyer (2000): 'The Fading Charm of Sonia', *India Today*, Vol.XXV, No.16, 17 April.

Miller D F (1962): "Factions in Indian Village politics", *Pacific Affairs*, Spring.

Mohanan B (1999): "Verdict of Kerala Elections 1998", *ISDA Journal*, 9(2).

Muraleedharan Nair V (1996): "Nair Service Society and 1996 Kerala Elections", *ISDA Journal*, 7(4).

Nair K.P (1985): "Kerala's Unholy Coalition Politics", *Front Line* 15-28 June.

Nair K P (1987): "Kerala- A Water Shed", *Front line*, Vol.4, No.7, April 14-27.

Nair K P (1989): "Kerala: Fight of the Fronts", *Front Line*, 11-24 November.

Nair K P (1992): "Kerala Politics in the Cauldron", *The Hindu*, 29 February.

Nair K.P (1992): "Cong (I) Charade: In Kerala Karunakaran under siege", *Front Line*, Oct 23.

Narendran (1998): "Jayikkunna Antonyum Thakarunna Antony Groupum" , *Malayalam*, Vol.1, No.38, 30 January.

Nicholas Ralph W (1965): "Village Factions and Political Parties in Rural West Bengal", *Journal of Commonwealth Political Studies*, II November.

Norr, Katleen Fordham (1976): "Factions and Kinship: The case of a south Indian village", *Asian Survey*, Vol.16, No.12, December.

Palash Kumar (2000): 'Last of the Rebels', *The Week*, vol.18, No.48, 12 November.

Parameswaran R (1985): "Big Blow for the left", *Caravan*, No.783, 2 January.

Parvathy Menon (2001): 'Walking upto Realities', *Front Line*, Vol18, No.7, Marhc 31-April.13.

Sajeevan A (2000): "Leaguea, Leaguea Koodevide", *Kalakaumudi*, (M) Vol.1300, 6 August.

Sankar M (2001): Antoniyum Oommen Chandyum Yuvakkale Kuruthikoduthu", *Malayalam*, Vol.4, No.41, 13 April.

Sarat Lal K S (2001): "Karunakarante Thriptiyum Poorna Thriptiyum" (M), *Kalakaumudi*, Vol.1343, 27 May.

Sasikumar V. (1983): "Antony Muthal Antulay Vare" (M), *Kalakaumudi*, vol. 425, 6 November.

Sreedharan E V (1999): 'Nehruvinte Veettil Ninulla Dathedukkal', Kalakumudi, (M)1238, 30 May.

Sreedhar Pillai (1983): "Surprise Move", *India Today*, vol.8, No.17, September.

Sreedhar Pillai (1984): "Patching Up", *India Today*, VÒl.9, No.15, August 15.

Sreedhar Pillai (1986): "Truce Time", *India Today*, Vol.11, No.1, 15 January.

Sreedhar Pillai (1986): "Compromise Formula", *India Today*, Vol. V, No.11, 15 June.

Sujathan P (1997): 'Onnam Kattil Eru Munnanikkum Patharal', *Kalakaumudi* (M), No.1162, 21 December.

Sujathan P (2000): "Pankuvaippukar Nanichu: Congressil Thiranjeduppu"(M), *Kalakaumudi*, VOl.1272, 23 January.

Sujathan P (2001): 'Congrassinte Grahappizhakal', *Kalakaumudi* (M), Vol.1336, 8 April.

Sujathan P (2001): 'Cherthalayude Dharmasangadam;, *Kalakaumudi*,(M) Vol.1339, 29 April.

Sujathan P (2001): "Kerala Congressile Kolilakkom", *Kalakaumudi*, (M) VOl.1345, 10 June.

Sukumar Muralidharan (1999): "A Kargil Election", *Front Line*, Vol.16, No.19, 11-24 September.

Sumit Mitra (1997): 'Can the Congress Survive Sitaram Kesari', *India Today*, Vol.XXII, No.38, 9-15 December.

Suresh Kumar R.K (2001): "Ideological Chimera, Peoples verdict and the Left Debacle: The Kerala Assembly Elections 2001", *The Indian Journal of Political Science*, Vol.2, No.2, June 2001.

Shubratha Bhattachaya (1985): "Kerala Fragile Coalition", *The Sunday*, 6-12 October.

Swapan Dasgupta (2001); "Two winners and a Photo Finish", *India Today*, Vol.35, No.20, 8-14 May.

Thomas Isaac T M & S. Mohana Kumar (1991): 'Kerala Elections, 1991: Lessons and Non-lessons', *Economic And Political Weekly*, 23 November.

Venu Menon (1985): "For God's Sake", *Illustrated Weekly of India*, 15 July.

Venkitesh Ramakrishnan (1999): "A Strategy against Communalism", *Front Line*, vol.16, No.19, 11-24 September.

Viju V Nair (1997): "Congrassinte Vilakkath BJP kku Athazham", *Kalakaumudi*, (M) No.1162, 21 December.

Vinu Abraham (2001): 'Foul Start', *The Week*, Vol.19, No.19, 22 April.

Vinu Abraham (2001): 'Left, right, Left.....next?', *The Week*, Vol.19, No.21, 6 May.

Vinu Abraham (2001): "Left with Bloody Nose", *The Week*, Vol19, No.24, 27 May.

Zafar Agha (1996): 'Under Assault', *India Today*, 31 July.

(D) Newspapers

Chandrika (M)

Deepika (M)

Deshabhimani (M)

Hindustan Times

Indian Express

Kerala Kaumudi (M)

Madhyamom (M)

Malayala Manorama (M)

Mathrubhumi (M)

The Hindu

The Times of India

Index